THE LAWGIVERS' STRUGGLE

HOW CONGRESS WIELDS POWER IN NATIONAL SECURITY DECISION MAKING

DAVID J. TRACHTENBERG

Published by
National Institute Press®
9302 Lee Highway, Suite 750
Fairfax, Virginia 22031

Library of Congress Cataloging-in-Publication Data

Names: Trachtenberg, David J., author.
Title: The lawgivers' struggle : how Congress wields power in national security
    decision making / David J. Trachtenberg.
Description: Fairfax, Virginia : National Institute Press, [2020] | Includes
    bibliographical references and index. |
Summary: "The Lawgivers' Struggle explains how the U.S. Congress exercises its
    constitutional authorities to formulate and shape American national
    security policy, sometimes in support of administration priorities and
    sometimes in opposition to them. Drawing on the author's experiences as a
    congressional staffer working for the House Armed Services Committee, it
    describes the processes that Congress uses and the tools it has as its disposal
    to wield influence in national security decisions. The book illuminates the
    legislative process, explaining the "how" and "why" of congressional
    decision making. It describes the dynamic that characterizes the relationship
    between the executive and legislative branches of government and the
    historical origins of the power struggle between the branches that continues
    to this day. The book serves as a valuable resource for students, government
    professionals, and everyday American citizens who wish to better
    understand how their government works"-- Provided by publisher.

Identifiers: LCCN 2020026808 | ISBN 9780985555337 (paperback)
Subjects: LCSH: National security--United States--Decision making. | National
    security--Law and legislation--United States. | United States. Congress-
    Decision making. | Legislative bodies--United States.
Classification: LCC KF4850 .T73 2020 | DDC 328.73/0746--dc23
LC record available at https://lccn.loc.gov/2020026808

For my sister Anita, wife Stephanie, and children Kara and Ryan, whose unconditional love and support inspire me daily.

And for my parents, Doris and Sam, who taught me that what matters in life is not who you are or what status you achieve, but what you leave behind and how you affect the lives of others.

ACKNOWLEDGEMENTS

To those like me, for whom writing a book does not come easily or naturally, a project like this is both daunting and exhilarating. Daunting, because the process of organizing thoughts, researching facts, and expressing concepts concisely is incredibly challenging. Exhilarating, because as the process progressed it became increasingly exciting to see how this work was taking shape in a way that captured what I truly wanted to express. Yet, I am a firm believer in the axiom that no one accomplishes anything of significance by himself, and this project is no exception.

This book would not have been possible without the love and support of family and friends (some of whom stood behind me while others pushed me forward!), all of whom provided extraordinary encouragement throughout this journey. To all of them, I am eternally grateful.

To my family, I owe the greatest thanks. They suffered the most through my expressions of angst over whether I would ever finish this project and whether it would actually amount to anything. At a minimum, they have each earned a thank-you dinner at their restaurant of choice and an autographed copy.

Importantly, I owe tremendous thanks to the National Institute for Public Policy (NIPP), not only for its willingness to publish this manuscript but for allowing me the flexibility to take the time required to research, compile the data, and draft this book. In particular, I owe an immense debt of gratitude to Dr. Keith B. Payne, NIPP's President and Chief Executive Officer, for initially encouraging me to undertake this effort.

Beyond running the institute, where I now serve as Vice President, Keith has been a good friend and colleague since my days as a college student at the University of Southern California (USC) in the 1970s. We have worked collaboratively throughout the years in various capacities – together at the Pentagon under two administrations; during my time as an independent consultant in national security affairs; as a member of the Nuclear Strategy Forum, which Keith ran; and in various other endeavors. Throughout the years, he has been one of my greatest supporters.

I also owe thanks to Amy Joseph, NIPP's Chief Operating Officer, whose assistance throughout this extended process has helped keep me sane and on track. Amy has been an indispensable resource and a truly gracious colleague, who has always put up with my odd idiosyncrasies with a smile and a kind word. Most importantly, she was kind enough not to chastise me for single-handedly contributing to the global deforestation crisis by expending multiple reams of paper in the process of continuously editing and updating this work.

Along with Keith, who painstakingly read through each chapter and provided valuable edits, I am indebted to my colleagues, Ambassador Robert G. Joseph, Mr. Christopher Williams, and Mr. Brian Green, who agreed to review earlier drafts of this manuscript. Bob, Chris, and Brian all provided helpful comments and suggestions that vastly improved the substance and readability of this book. Any errors of fact or cognition contained in these pages, however, are mine alone.

Sincere thanks are also due to many other long-time friends and colleagues. Though too numerous to mention here, one stands out in particular as meriting special recognition. Dr. Charles M. Kupperman has been a mentor, friend, and strong advocate on my behalf since I was an undergraduate student at USC. Throughout my more than four-decade career in the national security field, Charlie has gone to bat for me on multiple occasions. He, more than anyone, is responsible for whatever successes I have achieved in my professional life, and for that I will be eternally grateful.

By now, the reader may have surmised that some of my closest relationships were forged during my days at USC. Indeed, my interest in pursuing a career in national security was fostered under the tutelage of the late Dr. William R. Van Cleave at USC. He was in every way an outstanding professor and public servant, who created the Defense and Strategic Studies (DSS) program in California, transitioned it to his Midwest home in Springfield, Missouri at Southwest Missouri State University (now part of the Missouri State University [MSU] system), and which is now headquartered and run in the national capital region. I am privileged to be teaching again in the MSU DSS program, including teaching a course that is the subject of this book. To the students who have labored and, hopefully, learned something in my class, and to those who will follow in their classroom footsteps, this book is also dedicated.

Finally, I must gratefully acknowledge the support of the Sarah Scaife Foundation, whose generosity has allowed me to complete this project. Its expression of confidence in the value of such a work is sincerely appreciated.

TABLE OF CONTENTS

PREFACE

At the time of this writing, the nation is in the throes of a global pandemic that is threatening the health, safety, and livelihood of all Americans. The spread of the coronavirus (COVID-19) has severely disrupted daily life and economic activity worldwide, including in the United States. In response, President Donald J. Trump has declared a national emergency and unprecedented measures are being taken to combat this unseen but deadly threat. As a result, the president and the Congress are being challenged to put partisan differences aside and to work together for the good of the country. However, in the highly charged political atmosphere of 2020, and in the midst of a tumultuous presidential election campaign, rallying together to defeat a common and lethal threat has proven to be easier said than done. Disagreements between Democrats and Republicans in Congress and between some Congressional leaders and the White House over the best courses of action to take in response to this national emergency have again raised concerns over whether the executive and legislative branches of government can work together for the common good.

This current crisis follows on the heels of a divisive impeachment battle that saw the U.S. Senate acquit President Trump, voting not to remove him from office after the House of Representatives impeached him for allegedly engaging in what the Constitution refers to as "Treason, Bribery, or other high Crimes and Misdemeanors." This is only the third time in American history that a U.S. president has been impeached, and the highly partisan nature of this activity divided the nation and heightened concern over whether the Congress is playing a productive or destructive role in focusing its attention on this issue, as opposed to other issues that may matter more to Americans or that may be of greater significance to U.S. national security and global stability.

Perhaps in part as a consequence of this activity,[1] the Congress in 2019 again failed to pass a budget on time to fund the operation of the federal government. Under the U.S. Constitution, Congress has the responsibility to appropriate funds so that the government can conduct its business. Until year's end, however, when an omnibus budget resolution was finally passed by the Congress and signed into law by the president, the government was operating under what is termed a "Continuing Resolution" or "CR," that allows the government to remain open until such time that a budget can be approved and enacted. In recent years, the lack of a budget has led to personnel furloughs, government shutdowns, and significant hardship for much of the federal workforce. Failure to pass a budget on time also leads to significant disruption in spending plans that affect important programs. In the area of defense and national security, this can have devastating consequences. As Secretary of Defense Mark Esper has stated: "Every day that we have a Continuing Resolution means it's a day in which our training, our maintenance, our modernization and everything is impaired…."[2]

Most Americans are unfamiliar with the way Congress conducts its business, the authorities it enjoys under the

---

[1] Senate Majority Leader Mitch McConnell (R-KY) stated, "There are things we have to do that we are not making any progress on because of the impeachment obsession over in the House." Cited in "Impeachment hearings live updates," *The Washington Post*, 19 November 2019, available at https://www.washingtonpost.com/politics/impeachment-hearings-live-updates/2019/11/19/c5ea3bba-0a54-11ea-bd9d-c628fd48b3a0_story.html.

[2] Secretary of Defense Mark T. Esper, "Transcript of Press Briefing in Norfolk, Virginia," 25 September 2019, available at https://www.defense.gov/Newsroom/Transcripts/Transcript/Article/1971526/secretary-of-defense-esper-press-briefing-in-norfolk-virginia/.

Constitution, the tools it has as its disposal to shape U.S. policy in both the foreign and domestic spheres, and the impact its decisions have on the future security of the country. Indeed, most Americans may not care. Public opinion surveys repeatedly indicate a vast majority of Americans see Congress as dysfunctional, overly partisan, responsible for gridlock, and generally unwilling or incapable of adequately addressing the country's needs. Yet, the Congress can have a huge impact on U.S. national security — sometimes greater than that of the president — so understanding what Congress does, how it does it, and why is critically important.

This book is intended to strip away the mythology that often colors the discussion regarding Congress' true role in national security decision making. It draws on literature by constitutional scholars and others, as well as information gleaned from my personal experiences working both on Capitol Hill as a Professional Staff Member on the House Armed Services Committee, and at the Pentagon in senior policy positions under two administrations. It is intended not only to inform and educate, but to clarify many of the seemingly arcane and indecipherable practices that Congress uses to enact its priorities, especially in the area of national security.

Former Princeton University professor Edwin S. Corwin described the Constitution as "an invitation to struggle for the privilege of directing American foreign policy."[3] That struggle continues to this day, with the executive and legislative branches of government often at odds over the

---

[3] Cited in James M. Lindsay, "Invitation to Struggle: Congress, the President, and U.S. Foreign Policy," in Daniel S. Hamilton and Teija Tiilikainen, Editors, *Domestic Determinants of Foreign Policy in the European Union and the United States*, (Center for Transatlantic Relations, The Paul H. Nitze School of Advanced International Studies, and the Finnish Institute of International Affairs, Washington, D.C., 2018), p. 145, available at https://archive.transatlanticrelations.org/wp-content/uploads/2018/01/ch07_Lindsay.pdf.

proper authorities and responsibilities of each, including in the national security realm. On occasion, Congress has been deferential to executive branch desires and actions – some would say too deferential. However, examples abound where Congress has not only been assertive but has successfully driven the national security policy agenda in ways that conflict with the preferred outcomes, policies, and priorities of the administration in power.

This book begins by exploring the foundational sources of congressional authority, to include the U.S. Constitution and *The Federalist Papers*. It then reviews the organization and operation of both the legislative and executive branches of government in order to provide a framework for understanding the interaction between the two. Motivations for, and influences on, congressional behavior are also examined. Special emphasis is placed on Congress' role in shaping national security policy regarding weapons of mass destruction (WMD), and various case studies are reviewed to provide insight into congressional thinking on these critical issues. In addressing this, the book takes the reader through the process of developing the annual National Defense Authorization Act, which authorizes funding for the Department of Defense and a variety of WMD and counter-WMD initiatives.

It is my hope that through a review of historical documents as well as contemporary instances of congressional activity related to defense and national security issues, combined with relevant examples drawn from personal experiences, this book will remove much of the confusion over congressional prerogatives and activities and provide concrete illustrations of the "how" and "why" of congressional actions. The book provides practical, not just theoretical, examples of congressional influence on U.S. defense policy, covering both Republican and Democratic administrations, as well as periods of time when both houses of Congress were controlled either by one political party or when party control was split between the House of Representatives and the Senate. These examples help explain and illustrate the dynamic between both chambers, the role of congressional staffers, and how Congress can wield its power in multiple ways to shape the contours of U.S. national security policy.

The struggle for dominance in national security policy making will continue — as the Founding Fathers intended — over serious and complex issues of war and peace that will help determine the ultimate longevity of the "American experiment." I firmly believe, however, that armed with better knowledge of congressional policies and procedures, government employees and future policy practitioners in the area of national security will be better positioned to understand and effectuate policies that are critical to the defense of the nation — and to do so more effectively through a more robust understanding of congressional motivations, influencers, tools, and timelines for action.

CHAPTER ONE

INTRODUCTION TO THE ROLE OF CONGRESS IN NATIONAL SECURITY ISSUES

National security policy practitioners today often lack an understanding of how the legislative branch of government affects U.S. foreign and defense policy. This lack of understanding of the congressional role in setting the nation's foreign and defense policy agenda is due to a variety of factors, including the arcane and seemingly byzantine rules under which Congress operates; the scarcity of higher-level education courses that explain the authorities and responsibilities of the legislative branch; the low regard in which the general public holds Congress as an institution; a prevalent belief that national security policy issues fall almost exclusively within the purview of the executive branch of government; and a corollary view that Congress is an impediment to, rather than a facilitator of, sound policy.

Congress is viewed with disdain by many Americans, who see it as increasingly partisan and either unwilling or incapable of successfully tackling the nation's critical security imperatives (indeed, a public opinion survey in 2013 ranked Congress' approval rating lower than root canals, cockroaches, and used car salesmen);[4] hence, interest in Congress and its workings is low.

---

[4] Tom Jensen, "Congress Less Popular Than Cockroaches, Traffic Jams," Public Policy Polling, January 8, 2013, available at
https://www.publicpolicypolling.com/polls/congress-less-popular-than-cockroaches-traffic-jams/.

Moreover, there is no academic curriculum at the nation's colleges and universities – including U.S. military academies – that teaches the role of the legislative branch and its interactions with the executive (the last engagement most students have with the topic is in elementary or high school, which generally provides an incomplete and misleading exposition of the workings of Congress).

Unfortunately, most students or professionals seeking careers in the federal government focus exclusively on the executive branch, i.e., the Departments of State, Defense, and the intelligence agencies. Few, if any, consider working on Capitol Hill, even though the experience can provide significant policy experience and serve as a major steppingstone to other government positions and agencies.

This lack of understanding risks complicating and making more inefficient the workings of government at a time when threats to the nation require greater collaboration and "whole-of-government" solutions. For those interested in public service in support of the nation's defense, an understanding of the role the legislative branch of government plays in critical national security issues is essential.

Policy must be implemented for it to be successful. And the successful implementation of policy requires resources. Without the necessary fiscal/budgetary resources to take the required actions, no policy will succeed. The role of the Congress is to provide the necessary monetary resources and to ensure they are used prudently. The role of the executive branch is to "execute" policy, which necessitates a strong partnership with Congress—made more difficult when congressional processes and drivers are not well understood and when Congress is viewed in an adversarial role.

Knowledge of the processes by which Congress establishes and shapes U.S. foreign and defense policy, and the means by which it appropriates funding for critical national security activities, is essential to understanding the impact of congressional actions on an agency's workforce, policies, programs, and budgets. Understanding how the majority and minority parties use congressional rules and tools to advance their own legislative agendas will not only lead to a greater appreciation of the Congress' important role but can help agencies plan and execute strategies for successfully implementing their own agendas.

Public Perceptions of Congress

Congress is held in generally low esteem by the public, which sees lawmakers as overly partisan and more focused on winning re-election than solving the nation's problems. Opinion polls occasionally show Congress' approval rating dipping into single digits. A recent Gallup Poll shows Congress' approval at less than 20 percent.[5] Trend analysis indicates that Congress has not seen approval ratings above 30 percent in more than a decade — the longest such stretch since polling on the matter started.[6] One organization even created a "legislative futility index" to track the lack of useful congressional action over the years, looking at indicators such as time in session, bills passed, and votes taken. According to its analysis, "Congress set a record for legislative futility by accomplishing less in 2011 than any other year in history."[7] Another more recent analysis

---

[5] See Gallup Poll data, Congress and the Public, available at https://news.gallup.com/poll/1600/congress-public.aspx.

[6] Harry Enten, "Congress' Approval Rating Hasn't Hit 30% in 10 Years. That's a Record," CNN, 1 June 2019, available at https://www.cnn.com/2019/06/01/politics/poll-of-the-week-congress-approval-rating/index.html.

[7] Stephen Dinan, "Congress Logs Most Futile Legislative Year on Record," *The Washington Times*, 15 January 2012, available at https://www.washingtontimes.com/news/2012/jan/15/congress-logs-most-futile-legislative-year-on-reco/.

concluded that "2019 was a record-breaker for Senate futility."[8]

Typically, foreign and defense policy matters are not front and center in the public eye, and most members of Congress do not campaign or get elected on national security issues.[9] As former Speaker of the House Tip O'Neill famously said, "All politics is local." And local politics are generally focused on pocketbook issues like jobs and the economy. To quote James Carville, campaign strategist for former President Bill Clinton, "It's the economy, stupid." There are, of course, exceptions to every rule, such as after the September 11, 2001 terrorist attacks, but in general foreign policy concerns are not determinative in U.S. congressional elections.

The relationship between the executive and legislative branches of government is often seen as adversarial. This is especially, though not exclusively, true when the White House and Congress are controlled by different political parties. Political partisanship and acrimony are increasingly viewed as the norm by the electorate, and even by members of Congress themselves. The longest-serving member of Congress, Rep. John Dingell (D-MI), retired in 2014, saying, "I find serving in the House to be obnoxious."[10]

---

[8] Jonathan Miller, "Key Votes 2019: Amid partisan acrimony, legislative wins in Congress were hard to come by," *Roll Call*, 28 January 2020, available at https://www.rollcall.com/2020/01/28/key-votes-2019-amid-partisan-acrimony-legislative-wins-in-congress-were-hard-to-come-by/.

[9] For the purposes of this book, references to "members of Congress" include both members of the U.S. House of Representatives and the U.S. Senate.

[10] See Carl Hulse and Ashley Parker, "John Dingell to Retire After Nearly 60 Years in House," *The New York Times*, February 24, 2014, available at https://www.nytimes.com/2014/02/25/us/politics/dingell-to-retire-from-congress.html. Also see Sean Sullivan, "Longest-Serving Rep. John Dingell To Retire," *The Washington Post*, February 24, 2014,

Commentators frequently refer to a "do-nothing Congress," or opine that the rancor between political parties within Congress or between the executive and legislative branches is without precedent. As an article in *Politico* noted a few years ago, "Google 'worst Congress ever,' and you'll get nearly 5.4 million results — many of them scathing takes on two years of dysfunction, partisan warfare and all-around mayhem on Capitol Hill."[11] Yet, history demonstrates that the mechanics of legislating and policy making were not intended by the Founders to be easy. As Edwin S. Corwin, former president of the American Political Science Association famously noted, the Constitution "is an invitation to struggle for the privilege of directing American foreign policy."[12]

For all this, the public's dim view of Congress and Congress' reputation for inaction are not fully justified by the record. Numerous major defense and national security policy initiatives resulted from congressional actions. For example, the Department of Defense (DoD) Reorganization Act of 1986 (the "Goldwater-Nichols" Act, named for its congressional co-sponsors) ushered in the most extensive organizational and operational changes to DoD since the department's creation by the National Security Act of 1947. The Cooperative Threat Reduction (CTR) program ("Nunn-Lugar") was the instantiation of a strong, bipartisan congressional desire to tighten controls on WMD systems and materials in the former Soviet Union after the USSR's demise. And the National Missile Defense Act of 1999, passed overwhelmingly by both houses of Congress with

---

available at https://www.washingtonpost.com/news/post-politics/wp/2014/02/24/longest-serving-rep-john-dingell-to-retire/.

[11] Jonathan Topaz, "'Worst Congress Ever,' By the Numbers," *Politico*, December 17, 2014, available at
https://www.politico.com/story/2014/12/congress-numbers-113658.

[12] Cited in Lindsay, "Invitation to Struggle: Congress, the President, and U.S. Foreign Policy," op. cit.

veto-proof margins, established deployment of a national missile defense "as soon as is technologically possible" as a matter of U.S. policy.[13] These examples are discussed in more detail below.

The Push and Pull of Executive-Legislative Branch Tensions

From the early days of the Republic, the relationship between the president and the Congress has veered from cooperative and conciliatory to combative and confrontational. In some instances, the disagreements became so sharp that the relatively straightforward process of passing a budget became an uphill struggle. In the area of national security, failure to pass a budget on time can have disastrous consequences.

Many policy makers lack basic knowledge of the various inputs that drive congressional actions and behavior. They also do not fully comprehend the importance of engaging Congress proactively in support of executive branch priorities. Often, executive branch officials respond to congressional actions rather than attempt to shape them in ways more favorable to their desired outcome. This is a mistake.

The Life of a Committee Professional Staff Member

My observations on the role of Congress in national security decision making are informed by nearly seven years as a Professional Staff Member (PSM) on the House Committee

---

[13] "National Missile Defense Act of 1999," Public Law 106-38, July 22, 1999, available at
https://www.congress.gov/106/plaws/publ38/PLAW-106publ38.pdf.

on Armed Services (commonly referred to as the House Armed Services Committee or HASC)—the main authorization committee in the House of Representatives with responsibility for defense policy and programs.[14] I always wondered why the term "Professional" was applied to committee staff members, as it suggested there were "unprofessional" staffers as well. However, the term is meant to distinguish those staffers who work for the committee from those who are on the personal staff of individual members of Congress.

As a HASC PSM, I learned quickly the importance of the committee and the influence of its members on U.S. defense and national security policy. I also learned that individual PSMs have a great deal of influence and authority when it comes to dealing with the executive branch of government, as they are perceived as representing their bosses. Consequently, a PSM is often treated as the civilian equivalent of a three-star general officer.

This relationship was driven home early to me when soon after my hiring I was asked a question by one of the committee members about missile defense that I could not answer. I promised I would get back to him with the answer soonest; but at a time when the internet was still nascent and "Google" searching nonexistent, I felt overwhelmed and unprepared for the job I had just assumed. Before being hired by the Committee Chairman, Rep. Floyd D. Spence (R-SC), I provided contractor support to what was then the Ballistic Missile Defense Organization (BMDO).[15] As a contractor, I dealt with an Army major who served as the

---

[14] At the time I was hired in 1995, the Committee had officially changed its name to the House Committee on National Security, in order to better reflect the broad nature of its responsibilities. This change only lasted until 1998 when the committee reverted to its more commonly recognized name of House Armed Services Committee.

[15] The BMDO was a successor to the Strategic Defense Initiative Organization (SDIO) and later became the Missile Defense Agency (MDA).

liaison between my company and the BMDO front office. So, I did the only thing I could think of at the time, which was to place a call to the officer in the hope that he could provide me with the answer to my question.

Unfortunately, the officer wasn't available, so I left a voicemail message on his answering machine telling him I had just started at the HASC and asking him to call me back. When I hung up the phone, I was despondent, thinking that my tenure on the committee might be the shortest in history. But a short time later, my phone rang. "Hello, Dave? This is Mal O'Neill." It was Lieutenant General (LTG) Malcolm O'Neill, the Army three-star Director of BMDO on the line. "I hear you have a missile defense question," he said. "Do you need me to come up there and brief you or the chairman? I can be there in less than 30 minutes." I was surprised that the Director of the agency himself had returned my call, even more so when he said "If you ever have a question, don't hesitate to call me directly. If I don't know the answer right away, I'll get it for you soonest."

This was my first introduction to the influence that committee staffers have as representatives of their bosses. Of course, it didn't hurt that the BMDO budget was authorized by the HASC. This was a clear example of the relationship between the executive branch of government responsible for executing national security programs and the legislative branch of government responsible for oversight of those programs. It also illustrated how some officials of the executive branch do recognize the importance of interaction with Capitol Hill. In addition, it demonstrated that congressional staffers—especially committee staffers—generally have more and better access to information than nearly anyone else. Other congressional offices, government agencies and departments, industry officials, "think tanks," and lobbyists—not to mention just about anyone seeking government funding for a project or program — are eager to provide staffers with information.

The work of a committee PSM can be arduous, but highly rewarding. Aside from being treated with a level of gravitas usually reserved for senior officials or military officers, there are numerous opportunities for travel — including overseas — either with fellow staffers (referred to as staff delegations or "STAFFDELs") or with congressional members ("CODELs"). Before taking my first trip abroad as a PSM, I was asked by the HASC administrative personnel if I had a passport. I indicated I did, and produced my blue "tourist" passport, whereby I was promptly told that it was insufficient for foreign travel. I needed a red "official" passport because I would be traveling on official U.S. government business. At the time, the Congress was controlled by Republicans while the executive branch was controlled by Democrats, and both branches were often at odds with each other. So, I didn't process the fact that I would be representing the U.S. government abroad, albeit the legislative branch.

In my nearly seven years as a HASC PSM, I had the opportunity to travel to some exotic places and meet with presidents, premiers, and defense ministers. I visited China, Russia, and India, as well as lesser-frequented garden spots like Bosnia and Saudi Arabia. My visit to Saudi Arabia occurred as part of the HASC's investigation (then the House National Security Committee) of the June 25, 1996 terrorist bombing of the Khobar Towers complex in Dharan, which killed 19 American service personnel.[16] I traveled back to the Middle East as part of the committee's investigation into the bombing of the *U.S.S. Cole* in Aden harbor, Yemen on October 12, 2000.[17]

---

[16] The 14 August 1996 staff report on "The Khobar Towers Bombing Incident" is available at https://fas.org/irp/threat/saudi.pdf.

[17] The May 2001 HASC staff report on "The Investigation into the Attack on the *U.S.S. Cole*" is available at

On one STAFFDEL in 1997, I visited the only nuclear reactor at Chernobyl in Ukraine that remained operational after the 1986 explosion. On another trip, I visited a former Soviet biological weapons laboratory at Lyubuchany, outside Moscow, and met with a former Soviet biological weapons scientist whose work was now being redirected toward peaceful pursuits and funded through the DoD Cooperative Threat Reduction (CTR, or "Nunn-Lugar") program. This was part of an effort to prevent "brain drain"—whereby former Soviet scientists and WMD personnel would seek greener pastures by selling their skills and knowhow to potentially dangerous regimes and U.S. adversaries.

Committee PSMs have a real influence on U.S. national security policy. They advise committee members, who often defer to the staff for details on particular issues. They provide expertise in technology, policy, and budgetary matters; make recommendations for legislative initiatives; prepare reports and legislation; and assist members with oversight of executive branch activities and policy. PSMs also write the information memos for members prior to hearings that explain the background of an issue and offer proposed questions for the members to ask in an attempt to elicit relevant information from the witnesses. Perhaps most importantly, PSMs are responsible for working with the Office of Legislative Counsel to draft legislation that accomplishes the committee's objectives, and writing the committee report language that accompanies the annual National Defense Authorization Act (NDAA)—the main piece of substantive legislation passed by the HASC (and its Senate Armed Services Committee, or SASC, counterpart) each year.

As a HASC PSM, I contributed to the drafting of legislation that created the "Commission to Assess the

---

https://www.bits.de/public/documents/US_Terrorist_Attacks/HASC-colereport0501.pdf.

Ballistic Missile Threat to the United States" (the "Rumsfeld Commission"); the "National Missile Defense Act of 1999" that established as a matter of U.S. policy the requirement to deploy missile defenses to protect the United States "as soon as technologically possible"; and that prohibited DoD funding for construction of a chemical weapons destruction facility in the town of Shchuch'ye, Russia. Each of these actions had significant national security consequences and demonstrate how committee staffers can play a huge role in the formulation of national security policy (working in furtherance of committee priorities, of course).

As an example of the important role committee PSMs can play, I recall receiving a phone call from a colleague in the office of a member of Congress who was not on the HASC. He explained that his boss had received a letter from a constituent complaining about the role I personally had played in helping draft the aforementioned legislation cutting off DoD funding for the Russian chemical weapons destruction facility. Not knowing where his boss stood on the issue, I again had visions of an abbreviated tenure on the Hill. The letter stated in part:

> It has come to my attention that there is one member of the House Armed Services Committee staff, by the name of David Trachtenburg (sic.), who is particularly opposed to the funding of this chemical weapons destruction facility. I understand perfectly well that it is not his decision to make regarding funding. I also realize that staff members of various committees have quite a significant amount of influence on the process that Congress goes through regarding funding of any project. It disheartens me to think that one individual could potentially be

responsible for the discontinuance of funding for the facility.[18]

Fortunately, his boss agreed with our committee's chairman and the position we had adopted on the issue in the NDAA. Disaster averted.

Being a committee PSM is a superb way to develop and hone expertise on particular issues. It affords one the ability to gain useful skills that can be valuable to Congress or parlayed into future career opportunities. Not inconsequentially, a committee staffer can gain a unique perspective on how Congress actually works, an area that few citizens can appreciate. This is one reason why companies pay lobbyists to assist them with gaining congressional support for their programs.

Notwithstanding the above, the life of a committee staffer is not always tranquil and stress-free. The lack of job security is not an insignificant downside. PSMs are political appointees subject to the electoral fortunes of the members. This is different than being a civil servant or career employee. If you are hired by the majority party and the political landscape shifts and the majority becomes the new minority, you are at risk of losing your job. Moreover, your time is not your own and your life is not your own. You are a captive of Congress' schedule, which means that if Congress is in session late every night and on weekends considering an issue in your portfolio, so are you. The effort can be intense and the workload significant. A PSM must be an expert on everything in his or her portfolio and must know the answers to every member's questions on every topic within that portfolio. This can be quite stressful.

For example, once, during a HASC "mark-up" session of the NDAA ("mark-up" is described in Chapter Seven), the importance of knowing your subject matter backwards

---

[18] Constituent letter to Rep. Mark Green (R-WI) dated 10 February 2000.

and forwards became readily apparent. In a contentious and unusually partisan debate over whether the United States should take measures to accede to the "Ottawa Convention" banning the stockpiling and use of non-self-destructing anti-personnel landmines, members began arguing among themselves over the deployment of U.S. landmines in the Demilitarized Zone (DMZ) dividing North and South Korea. One member asked the question, "How wide is the DMZ?" This was not a question any of us on the staff were prepared for and we hesitated, which allowed the members to escalate the policy argument among themselves with a rare outburst of acerbity. Another member asked, "Isn't it just a line on a map?" At this point, it became obvious that not having command of the facts at one's fingertips could have disastrous consequences, as it is the staff's role to provide the facts so members don't wade into the turbulent waters of speculation and confusion.

My initial introduction to the NDAA process occurred during the fiscal year 1996 budget cycle. I was given responsibility for helping draft provisions in support of a national missile defense program, which the Clinton Administration opposed. As a consequence, President Clinton vetoed the NDAA, necessitating a renegotiation of the provisions and a time-consuming process that lasted for months. Each year's authorization and appropriation bills are supposed to be completed before the new fiscal year begins on October 1. In this case, the revised version of the NDAA was not signed into law by the president until February 10 — more than four months late.

Despite the stress and challenges of working on highly contentious and controversial policy issues, long hours, and the low esteem in which Congress is generally held, a survey of congressional staffers conducted in 2013 found that 80 percent had a high level of job satisfaction.[19] Perhaps

---

[19] Josh Hicks, "Hill staffers content with their work, but everything isn't perfect, survey shows," *The Washington Post*, 9 September 2013,

this is due to the fact that there are few other jobs in Washington where individuals can wield as significant an influence on the course of public policy.

Congressional National Security Initiatives

Examples abound of congressional initiatives with significant national security implications, and where members of Congress drove an issue that had major consequences for U.S. defense policy, with or without the support of the administration.

One of the most far-reaching changes to U.S. defense policy occurred with the passage of the "Department of Defense Reorganization Act of 1986." Though almost unknown by its official title, national security scholars and practitioners know the law by its more commonly recognized name, the "Goldwater-Nichols Act."

The Goldwater-Nichols legislation completely reworked the command structure of the U.S. military and is often said to be the most sweeping change to DoD since its creation by the National Security Act of 1947. The legislation was the result of a bipartisan push in Congress, led by its co-sponsors Sen. Barry Goldwater (R-AZ) and Rep. Bill Nichols (D-AL). It streamlined the military chain of command and was the genesis of what has come to be known as "jointness."[20]

---

available at https://www.washingtonpost.com/politics/ federal_government/hill-staffers-content-with-their-work-but- everything-isnt-perfect-survey-shows/2013/09/08/a5462ac6-1731- 11e3-a2ec-b47e45e6f8ef_story.html.

[20] The need for "jointness," where elements of each military service are effectively integrated into a joint fighting force, was popularized in the 1986 movie "Heartbreak Ridge," starring Clint Eastwood, a fictionalized account of "Operation Urgent Fury," the October 1983 U.S. invasion of Grenada. A scene in the movie shows a U.S. Marine in Grenada calling in an air strike by phoning Fort Bragg, which then routed the call to the appropriate Service. Though the account has achieved the status of

The concept of a "joint staff" and development of the "joint force" evolved from Goldwater-Nichols. The legislation is considered to have been so successful at integrating the various separate armed services into a unified joint service that it has spawned successor efforts, including a push for a "Goldwater-Nichols 2.0" that would make additional changes to the combatant command structure, military personnel system, and Joint Staff.[21]

Another major congressional initiative was the 1991 "Soviet Threat Reduction Act," which created the Cooperative Threat Reduction (CTR) Program, a DoD-funded effort to secure, dismantle, and eliminate former Soviet WMD in the wake of the dissolution of the Soviet Union and heightened concern over the potential for "loose nukes." This bipartisan legislation was co-sponsored by Senators Sam Nunn (D-GA), former Chairman of the Senate Armed Services Committee, and Richard Lugar (D-IN), former Chairman of the Senate Foreign Relations Committee, and came to be known as the "Nunn-Lugar" program.

Since its establishment, the Nunn-Lugar program has expanded in scope to include the control over and elimination of nuclear, chemical, and biological weapons outside the former Soviet states, including in Europe, Africa, Asia, and the Middle East. It has also expanded to include funding and programs by other federal entities, including the Departments of State and Energy.[22] Although

---

folklore legend, it is generally accepted that the inability of the Services to communicate directly with each other presented significant problems which Goldwater-Nichols sought to address.

[21] See, for example, Mark F. Cancian, "Goldwater-Nichols 2.0," Center for Strategic and International Studies, 4 March 2016, available at https://www.csis.org/analysis/goldwater-nichols-20.

[22] For background on the CTR program, see, for example, Justin Bresolin and Brenna Gautam, "Fact Sheet: The Nunn-Lugar Cooperative Threat Reduction Program," Center for Arms Control and Non-Proliferation, available at https://armscontrolcenter.org/fact-sheet-the-nunn-lugar-

the Nunn-Lugar program is generally considered a successful example of U.S. nonproliferation policy, it was extremely controversial in its early days, with concerns raised over its funding, timelines, and responsibility for specific projects. These concerns are addressed in more detail in Chapter Twelve.

One more example of congressional influence over U.S. national security policy is instructive—in this case, Congress and the administration were at loggerheads over the issue of missile defense. On March 23, 1983, President Ronald Reagan announced his Strategic Defense Initiative (SDI) program, which he hoped would make nuclear weapons "impotent and obsolete" by developing missile defenses that could protect the country against a Soviet nuclear attack.[23] At the time, however, the United States was constrained by the 1972 U.S.-Soviet Anti-Ballistic Missile (ABM) Treaty, which prohibited large-scale missile defenses to protect the homeland.

U.S. policy during the Cold War was based on the theory of a "balance of terror" that would leave both the United States and Soviet Union vulnerable to missile attack. It was thought this mutual vulnerability would be stabilizing by providing a disincentive for either side to strike the other first, the essence of deterrence.[24]

---

cooperative-threat-reduction-program/. Also see "The Evolution of Cooperative Threat Reduction: Issues for Congress," Congressional Research Service, 23 November 2015, available at https://www.everycrsreport.com/files/20151123_R43143_ea9728ba69f 622015c04aa39537330b196ec0da9.pdf.

[23] President Ronald Reagan, "Address to the Nation on Defense and National Security," 23 March 1983, available at https://www.reaganlibrary.gov/research/speeches/32383d.

[24] For an excellent description of Cold War deterrence theory and practice, see Keith B. Payne, *The Great American Gamble: Deterrence Theory and Practice From the Cold War to the Twenty-First Century*, National Institute Press, Fairfax, Virginia, 2008.

Reagan disliked the idea of leaving the United States vulnerable to nuclear attack but recognized the ABM Treaty stood in the way of developing a robust missile defense program to protect Americans. So, he initiated a legal review of the treaty, which determined that its provisions could actually allow certain advanced research and development on missile defense capabilities to proceed under a "broad interpretation" of the treaty's language. This led to a huge controversy over the next couple of years, with some in Congress taking the lead in challenging the Reagan Administration's interpretation. Sen. Nunn in particular led the opposition.

Nunn argued that the administration's "broad interpretation" of the ABM Treaty infringed on the Senate's constitutional "advice and consent" role regarding treaties.[25] In a series of powerful speeches on the Senate floor, he argued that when the Senate approved the ABM Treaty in 1972, it did so with the understanding that the treaty prohibited the kinds of research and development the Reagan Administration now argued were actually permissible, and that reinterpreting the treaty unilaterally by the executive branch without the consent of the legislative branch was unconstitutional.[26]

In the end, the Reagan Administration backed down and the justification for the SDI program was shifted; it was scaled back, Congress cut its budget, and the program was refocused to support much more modest objectives. Additional details regarding this example are discussed in Chapter Eleven.

---

[25] Michael R. Gordon, "Reagan Is Warned By Senator Nunn Over ABM Treaty," *The New York Times*, 7 February 1987, available at https://www.nytimes.com/1987/02/07/us/reagan-is-warned-by-senator-nunn-over-abm-treaty.html.

[26] "Nunn: Reagan Wrong on ABM, Senator Says Treaty Bans Star Wars Expansion," *The Washington Post*, 14 March 1987, available at https://www.orlandosentinel.com/news/os-xpm-1987-03-14-0110400069-story.html.

In sum, Congress' impact on defense and national security policy can be substantial, and the role of congressional staffers in helping members shape and mold that policy can likewise be significant. Because of this, a position on the Hill as a committee PSM can not only be immensely rewarding but a steppingstone to other positions in government or the private sector. Working on the Hill provides staffers with an opportunity to help craft national security policy. There are few similar opportunities elsewhere to influence the course of important decisions.

CHAPTER TWO

THE CONSTITUTIONAL AND HISTORICAL ORIGINS OF CONGRESSIONAL AND EXECUTIVE ROLES

The impact of Congress on U.S. national security is far-reaching and often rivals the influence of the executive branch. Nevertheless, its role and functions are poorly understood not only by Americans in general but by many government officials entrusted with developing policy solutions or executing the decisions of policy makers.

Armed with a better understanding of how Congress operates and the ways in which it impacts U.S. national security decisions, executive branch policy makers will be better equipped to work with Congress to negotiate solutions to the vexing problems facing the nation. Given the dynamic nature of today's international security environment, ensuring these two co-equal branches of government work collaboratively together has arguably never been more important.

Understanding the role and influence of Congress on national security policy requires a serious examination of the foundational documents created by the Founding Fathers, in particular, the U.S. Constitution and *The Federalist Papers*.

The Constitution establishes the authorities and responsibilities of the three branches of government. That the Founding Fathers devoted the first Article of the Constitution to the role of the legislative branch of government was not an accident. In fact, most of the authorities explicitly enunciated by the Constitution in the area of foreign and defense policy fall to the Congress.

These include the ability to regulate commerce with other countries, to "raise and support" the Army, and to "provide and maintain" a Navy. Perhaps the most significant power explicitly granted to the Congress is the power to declare war.

The Constitution has been both praised by some as a far-sighted document that has stood the test of time and provided a system of governance that is the envy of the world, and vilified by others as outdated, archaic, and the biggest impediment to true democratic government. For example, an opinion piece in *The New York Times* at the end of 2012 called the Constitution's provisions "archaic, idiosyncratic and downright evil."[27] An earlier *New York Times* article referred to the Constitution as "imbecilic."[28]

Regardless of how one feels about the wisdom of our Founding Fathers in crafting the U.S. Constitution, an understanding of the document and the powers it conveys is essential to understanding Congress and the role it plays in setting national policy.

In reality, there are few specific powers enumerated by the Constitution. It provides for a "Republic" (from the Latin *res publica*), a form of government where power derives from the people and the people's representatives rather than from a monarch.[29] Article IV, Section 4 of the

---

[27] Louis Michael Seidman, "Let's Give Up on the Constitution," *The New York Times*, 30 December 2012, available at https://www.nytimes.com/2012/12/31/opinion/lets-give-up-on-the-constitution.html.

[28] Sanford Levinson, "Our Imbecilic Constitution," *The New York Times*, 28 May 2012, available at https://campaignstops.blogs.nytimes.com/2012/05/28/our-imbecilic-constitution/.

[29] Benjamin Franklin is famously quoted as responding to a question about what type of government the Constitutional Convention of 1787 had agreed to by saying, "A republic, if you can keep it." See Richard R. Beeman, "Perspectives on the Constitution: A Republic, If You Can Keep It," National Constitution Center, (undated), available at https://constitutioncenter.org/learn/educational-resources/historical-

Constitution states, "The United States shall guarantee to every State in this Union a Republican Form of Government...." In this case, the term "Republican" refers to a representative democracy where the will of the people is exercised through the decisions of their elected representatives. James Madison, who later served as the fourth U.S. president, used the term in *Federalist 10* to argue against a pure democracy and for a representative one, explaining the difference between the two. Madison argued that the type of government agreed to by the delegates would diminish the opportunity for "factions" to dictate their will and control the government.[30]

Federalist 10 speaks of "the superior force of an interested and overbearing majority," which John Adams, the nation's second president, called the "tyranny of the majority."[31] He saw a bicameral legislature as the best way to avoid such a situation. Madison believed people will always disagree and that the causes of those disagreements cannot always be eliminated (e.g., the differences between property owners and non-property owners), but he believed the effects of those disagreements could be controlled through the governmental structure established by the Constitution. Madison also described in *Federalist 10* how the Constitution allows for the election of good representatives and not "unworthy candidates" who win by

---

documents/perspectives-on-the-constitution-a-republic-if-you-can-keep-it.

[30] James Madison, "The Union as a Safeguard Against Domestic Faction and Insurrection," *Federalist 10*, 23 November 1787, available at https://billofrightsinstitute.org/founding-documents/primary-source-documents/the-federalist-papers/federalist-papers-no-10/.

[31] John Adams, *The Works of John Adams, Vol. 6 (Defence of the Constitutions Vol. III cont'd, Davila, Essays on the Constitution)*, 1851 available at https://oll.libertyfund.org/titles/adams-the-works-of-john-adams-vol-6/simple#lf1431-06_label_005.

practicing "the vicious arts by which elections are too often carried."[32]

Despite the enduring relevance and reverence in which the Constitution is held by most scholars, the early framers of the document argued among themselves over its meaning even after it was written. For example, in 1793 President George Washington declared the United States to be neutral in the war between France and Great Britain. He did so without congressional consultation, which triggered a debate over whether a declaration of neutrality was an executive or legislative branch prerogative.[33] Alexander Hamilton and James Madison took different sides of the debate, with the former arguing for broad executive branch authorities in foreign policy and the latter contending that the legislative branch enjoyed broad latitude to make foreign policy decisions.[34] As described by American foreign policy scholar James M. Lindsay, "George Washington established that the president had the right to initiate the conduct of foreign policy," but "ultimately conceded that neutrality was a congressional prerogative."[35]

Clearly, disputes over which branch of government has authority and responsibility for foreign policy and national security decisions has been a point of contention since the early days of the Republic. Edwin Corwin's apt description, noted earlier, of the Constitution as "an invitation to struggle for the privilege of directing American foreign policy" is applicable even today, as the executive and legislative branches of government continue to spar over

---

[32] *Federalist 10,* op. cit.

[33] James M. Lindsay, *Congress and the Politics of U.S. Foreign Policy,* The Johns Hopkins University Press (Baltimore and London, 1994), pp. 13-14.

[34] Ibid.

[35] Ibid., pp. 14-15.

constitutional intent and various prerogatives. Yet, this is precisely what the Founders intended.

The struggle for primacy in national security decision making is not only ongoing but is a deliberate feature of the way our government was organized. The Founders did not want a government where governing was easy or consensus was commonplace; rather, it is through the conflict of ideas and the power of arguments that the best courses of action would rise to the top. I believe that our nation has achieved its greatness because of this, not in spite of it.

Powers of the Executive Branch

The Constitution gives the president relatively few specific powers related to national security policy; yet those powers are significant. For example, Article II, Section 2 designates the president as "Commander in Chief of the Army and Navy of the United States." However, how the president exercises this role and whether or not the concurrence of Congress is required in the exercise of this role have been sources of frequent disputes between the executive and legislative branches, including whether the president can unilaterally deploy the U.S. armed forces abroad in combat situations. In cases such as this, the Constitution does not provide specific guidance. In some instances, Congress has sought to legislate a role for itself;[36] in other instances, the courts have been asked to rule on how this constitutional authority is exercised.

Other powers granted to the president by the Constitution include the power to grant "reprieves and pardons" for crimes committed. This power was not

---

[36] The 1973 War Powers Resolution is a case in point and is discussed in more detail in Chapter Six.

universally supported by the Founders[37] and remains controversial to this day. In *Federalist Paper 74*, Alexander Hamilton argued in favor of "the benign prerogative of pardoning." More contemporary analysts have noted that the power to pardon is not absolute but is constrained by various constitutional and legal parameters established by Congress.[38]

There are numerous examples throughout history of presidents exercising the power of the pardon in ways that have proven controversial and divisive. For example, on Christmas Day in 1868, President Andrew Johnson pardoned "unconditionally, and without reservation" thousands of Confederate soldiers, an action intended to heal the nation's divisions after the Civil War, but which added to a list of grievances by Congress and ultimately led to his impeachment.[39]

Critics of the pardon have argued it has been used (or misused) for political reasons. These criticisms are generally bipartisan. Some have pointed to President Jimmy Carter's granting of amnesty to Vietnam War draft dodgers or President Gerald Ford's pardoning of Richard Nixon after the Watergate scandal as politically motivated and without justification. President George H.W. Bush pardoned six Reagan Administration officials involved in

---

[37] Patrick Henry, an "Anti-Federalist" who opposed ratification of the Constitution, argued that the power of the pardon would lead the United States toward the kind of monarchy in Britain that the original colonists rejected.

[38] For example, see the Fact Sheet on "Preventing and Deterring Unlawful Pardons" by the Protect Democracy Project, available at https://protectdemocracy.org/pardons/pardon-coalition-one-pager/.

[39] See Andrew Johnson Biography, available at https://www.biography.com/us-president/andrew-johnson. Also see Andrew Glass, "All Confederate soldiers gain presidential pardons, Dec. 25, 1868," *Politico*, 25 December 2018, available at https://www.politico.com/story/2018/12/25/this-day-in-politics-dec-25-1868-1074077.

the "Iran-Contra" scandal, including former Secretary of Defense Caspar Weinberger. President Bill Clinton pardoned 140 people on his last day in office, January 20, 2001 (an act referred to by *Time* magazine as "Pardongate"). And, in 2019, President Donald Trump pardoned a former business partner, Conrad Black. He also pardoned two U.S. Army officers convicted of murder while deployed in Afghanistan,[40] leading *The Washington Post* to declare it a "subversion of the justice and discipline that are so foundational to the nation's armed forces."[41] Clearly, the power of the pardon remains controversial more than 230 years after it was first enshrined in the Constitution.

Other powers granted to the Chief Executive in Article II include the power to make treaties (subject to the "advice and consent" of the Senate); to "appoint Ambassadors"; and to "receive Ambassadors and other public Ministers." Yet even these powers have been challenged by some in Congress. For example, although the president has the power to make a treaty, the Constitution is silent on whether the president has the exclusive authority to abrogate or withdraw from a treaty to which the Senate has given its advice and consent.[42] Other than these few examples, the Constitution is silent on the president's authorities in national security affairs.

---

[40] Of course, the presidential use of the pardon can also be for symbolic purposes, as multiple turkeys can attest during the Thanksgiving holiday, a symbolic gesture dating back to the Reagan Administration (though prior presidents ate, gifted, or simply released the birds).

[41] "Trump undercuts his military leadership — and dishonors troops who uphold our values," *The Washington Post*, 24 November 2019, available at https://www.washingtonpost.com/opinions/trump-undercuts-his-military-leadership--and-dishonors-troops-who-uphold-our-values/2019/11/24/67702788-0d66-11ea-8397-a955cd542d00_story.html.

[42] This issue is discussed in greater detail in Chapter Six.

Powers of the Legislative Branch

The Constitution gives more numerous, and arguably more substantial, powers to the Congress in the area of national security and foreign affairs. Most of these powers are enumerated in Article I, Section 8, which grants Congress the authority to "provide for the common Defence"; "to raise and support Armies"; "to provide and maintain a Navy"; "to make Rules for the Government and Regulation of the land and naval forces"; and "to provide for calling forth the Militia to execute the Laws of the Union, suppress Insurrections and repel Invasions." In general, Congress has the power "to make all laws which shall be necessary and proper for carrying into execution the foregoing powers...."

In the area of foreign policy, Congress also has the responsibility to "regulate Commerce with foreign nations"; to "define and punish Piracies and Felonies committed on the high Seas, and Offences against the Law of Nations"; and to "grant Letters of Marque and Reprisal." This latter power refers to the practice whereby the government would grant a license to an individual to capture enemy vessels at sea—considered a form of legalized piracy and a principled, respectable activity.

Perhaps the most consequential (and historically controversial) national security power granted to Congress under Article I, Section 8 is the power to "declare War."[43]

---

[43] Interestingly, a 2016 survey of college-age students showed that only 30 percent know that Congress has the exclusive authority to declare war. See Council on Foreign Relations and National Geographic, *What College-Aged Students Know About the World: A Survey on Global Literacy*, September 2016, p. 4, available at https://www.cfr.org/content/newsletter/files/CFR_NatGeo_ASurvey onGlobalLiteracy.pdf. Also cited in Deborah Perlstein, "Foreign Policy Isn't Just Up To Trump," *The Atlantic*, 23 November 2019, available at https://www.theatlantic.com/ideas/archive/2019/11/congresss-constitutional-role-us-foreign-policy/602485/.

Although Congress has only declared war 11 times in U.S. history during five conflicts,[44] the United States has been involved in more than 100 military conflicts around the globe, in most cases with the president introducing U.S. armed forces into active combat without prior congressional authorization or a formal declaration of war by Congress.[45] To this day, Congress has sought to impose constraints on the president's ability unilaterally to inject U.S. armed forces abroad in areas of hostility.[46]

While the president has the constitutional authority to make treaties and ambassadorial appointments, as noted above, those actions are subject to the "advice and consent" of the Senate, which means the Senate gets to debate and approve (or reject) them.[47] Cabinet officials and other presidential appointments are also subject to Senate confirmation.

In general, the most significant power of the legislature is what James Madison referred to in *Federalist 58* as the "power over the purse," which Madison argued may be "the most complete and effectual weapon with which any constitution can arm the immediate representatives of the people, for obtaining a redress of every grievance, and for carrying into effect every just and salutary measure."[48] This "power over the purse" is a reflection of the Congress'

---

[44] Those conflicts were the War of 1812, the War with Mexico, the Spanish-American War, World War I, and World War II.

[45] Barbara Salazar Torreon and Sofia Plagakis, "Instances of Use of United States Armed Forces Abroad, 1798-2020," Congressional Research Service, CRS Report R42738, 13 January 2020, available at https://www.everycrsreport.com/files/20200113_R42738_a0ad25a6589 0e572ed70eb734fe4ed8df893338a.pdf.

[46] See discussion of the War Powers Resolution in Chapter Six.

[47] In popular parlance, the Senate's "advice and consent" role is often confused with treaty ratification. Only the executive branch can ratify treaties, but the Senate must first approve them before the instruments of ratification can be deposited with the appropriate governing body.

[48] James Madison, *Federalist 58*.

ability to fund (or not to fund) the workings of government. Article I, Section 9 of the Constitution states, "No money shall be drawn from the Treasury but in consequence of appropriations made by law." This ability to provide or withhold funding in such amounts as Congress determines based on its own priorities is an essential element of the checks and balances in the American system of government. (It also helps explain the phone call I received from LTG O'Neill referenced in Chapter One.)

In many areas, the Constitution leaves much room for interpretation, and members of Congress have not been shy about deploying their interpretations of what the Founders actually meant in ways that unsurprisingly support their own arguments. For example, during debate over the Affordable Care Act ("Obamacare") in 2013 — a dispute that led to a government shutdown — Republican Senators argued that the Founding Fathers would have opposed Obamacare while Democratic Senators invoked the Founders' names to argue just the opposite.[49]

The Federalist Papers

Every student of constitutional government should be aware of *The Federalist Papers*. The papers were a series of 85 essays published in various New York newspapers written by Alexander Hamilton, James Madison, and John Jay. These three Founding Fathers participated in the

---

[49] In a 21-hour speech on the Senate floor, Senator Ted Cruz (R-TX) invoked the names of 27 signers of the Declaration of Independence when arguing against Obamacare. See David A. Fahrenthold, "Founding Fathers weigh in on Obamacare (with the help of today's statesmen)," *The Washington Post*, 1 October 2013, available at https://www.washingtonpost.com/politics/founding-fathers-weigh-in-on-obamacare-with-the-help-of-todays-statesmen/2013/10/01/377cebd2-2ad3-11e3-b139-029811dbb57f_story.html.

Constitutional Convention in 1787 and sought to make the case for ratification of the U.S. Constitution to a citizenry that was not uniformly supportive of the new nation's framework for governance. It is widely believed that Hamilton wrote most of these essays under the pseudonym "Publius." Madison wrote more than two dozen and Jay only five. Three of the essays are thought to have been written collaboratively. *The Federalist Papers*, though admittedly difficult to read in the language of the time, provide the best guide to how the Framers interpreted the Constitution when they wrote it and how the public understood the document when it was ratified.

Several of the papers are worth highlighting here. For example, in *Federalist 45*, Madison argued that the primary purpose of the Union was security and that the powers in the Constitution for the federal government were few and "exercised principally on external objects as war, peace, negotiation, foreign commerce, where main use of taxation will be." Madison argued that the states would enjoy an "advantage" over the federal government because while the powers of federal government would be exercised "in times of war and danger," most of the powers reserved for the states involved actions taken during "times of peace and security," which it was assumed would be more prevalent.

Perhaps the most-cited paper is *Federalist 10*, in which Madison argues against "the violence of faction." In Madison's view, factions—i.e., disruptive groups of citizens animated by passion over an issue that is exercised to the detriment of the greater civic good—can be controlled better in a republic than a democracy. He argued that the diversity of opinions in the Union would be the best bulwark against the tyranny of one view over another. Madison's belief in the utility of the "checks and balances" system of government established in the Constitution is perhaps best expressed in *Federalist 51*, where he writes, "If men were angels, no government would be necessary."

Hamilton's views of the role of the president and the executive branch are best explained in *Federalist 69* and *Federalist 74*. In *Federalist 69*, Hamilton contrasts the president's power with those of the king of England. He argues that the president's powers are "nominally the same with that of the king of Great Britain, but in substance much inferior to it." He notes that the English king is a "perpetual" hereditary monarch who cannot be impeached, tried, or removed from office. While the president can veto legislation, his veto can be overridden, unlike the British monarch whose ruling is "absolute."

Hamilton explains that the president is the Commander in Chief of the armed forces largely to preserve unity of command. In *Federalist 74* he argues: "Of all the care or concerns of government, the direction of war most peculiarly demands those qualities which distinguish the exercise of power by a single hand." However, the Congress has the sole authority to declare war and provide for the armed forces. This is because the decision to take the nation to war was considered to be so serious as to require an affirmation by the people themselves through their duly elected representatives.[50] As Madison wrote to Thomas Jefferson in 1798, "The constitution supposes, what the History of all Governments demonstrates, that the Executive is the branch of power most interested in war, and most prone to it. It has accordingly with studied care vested the question of war to the Legislature."[51]

Other powers were given to the president for reasons of practicality. For example, the president was granted the power to receive ambassadors and ministers because it was

---

[50] See, for example, Louis Fisher, *Presidential War Power*, (Lawrence: University Press of Kansas, 1995), pp. 1-4. Also see Joseph Story, *Commentaries on the Constitution of the United States*, 1833, Vol. III, Chapter XXI, available at https://www.constitution.org/js/js_321.htm.

[51] Cited in Tom Woods, "Presidential War Powers: The Constitutional Answer," available at https://libertyclassroom.com/warpowers/.

easier for the president to do so than to convene the full Congress (a time-consuming enterprise in the early days of the Republic). In addition, the power of the pardon was granted exclusively to the president because, as Hamilton wrote in *Federalist 74*, "one man appears to be a more eligible dispenser of the mercy of government, than a body of men."

Though not as prolific as Madison or Hamilton, John Jay wrote several papers, including *Federalist 64*, in which he explains the powers of the Senate. The Senate was considered to be the more prominent body of Congress, as Senators were older, held longer terms, and were originally elected by their state's legislators. This latter requirement — later changed in 1913 by the 17th Amendment to the Constitution, which provided for their direct election — was intended to free Senators from the pressures of public opinion so they would be better able to concentrate on their duties at hand. In essence, Senators were conceived of as "ambassadors" to the federal government. Indeed, Madison argued in *Federalist 62* that "the nature of the senatorial trust" requires "greater extent of information and stability of character."

The Senate has a particularly important role in foreign and national security affairs. Jay argued there were advantages to vesting treaty-making power in the hands of two bodies (the president and the Senate) that were not directly elected by the people. He noted:

As the select assemblies for choosing the President, as well as the State legislatures who appoint the senators, will in general be composed of the most enlightened and respectable citizens, there is reason to presume that their attention and their votes will be directed to those men only who have become the most distinguished by their abilities and virtue, and in whom the people perceive just grounds for confidence.... the President and senators so chosen will always be of the number of those who best understand our national interests, whether considered in relation to the several States or to foreign nations.... With such men the power of making treaties may be safely lodged.[52]

Jay argued that vesting treaty powers in older, wiser Senate members means the people "will not be liable to be deceived by those brilliant appearances of genius and patriotism, which, like transient meteors, sometimes mislead as well as dazzle." Interestingly, although the Constitution vests treaty-making power in the hands of both the president and the Senate (which must provide its advice and consent by two-thirds vote), it is silent on the process for changing, abrogating, or withdrawing from treaties. Nevertheless, Jay argued that "treaties are made, not by only one of the contracting parties, but by both; and consequently, that as the consent of both was essential to their formation at first, so must it ever afterwards be to alter or cancel them." In reality, however, the courts have upheld the president's broad authority to revoke treaties unilaterally.[53]

---

[52] John Jay, "The Powers of the Senate," *Federalist 64*, 7 March 1788, available at https://avalon.law.yale.edu/18th_century/fed64.asp.

[53] For example, in 1979 the U.S. Court of Appeals for the District of Columbia upheld the decision by President Carter to abrogate the U.S. mutual defense treaty with Taiwan. See Graham Hovey, "Appeal Court Backs Carter on Taiwan: Upholds His Abrogation of Treaty Without Consent of Congress, *The New York Times*, 1 December 1979, available at https://www.nytimes.com/1979/12/01/archives/appeal-court-backs-carter-on-taiwan-upholds-his-abrogation-of.html. More recently, in 2002 President George W. Bush withdrew the United States from the 1972 U.S.-Soviet Anti-Ballistic Missile (ABM) Treaty and, in 2019, President Donald J. Trump withdrew the United States from the 1987 U.S.-Soviet Intermediate-range Nuclear Forces (INF) Treaty. In neither case was prior congressional approval sought or obtained.

In *Federalist 75*, Hamilton argued that treaties are contracts among nations: "They are not rules prescribed by the sovereign to the subject, but agreements between sovereign and sovereign. The power in question seems therefore to form a distinct department, and to belong, properly, neither to the legislative nor to the executive." Consequently, he argued, that "the joint possession of the power in question, by the President and Senate, would afford a greater prospect of security, than the separate possession of it by either of them."

Hamilton was dismissive of the role of the House of Representatives in treaty making, stating that the weight of the evidence:

> ...will apply with conclusive force against the admission of the House of Representatives to a share in the formation of treaties. The fluctuating and, taking its future increase into the account, the multitudinous composition of that body, forbid us to expect in it those qualities which are essential to the proper execution of such a trust. Accurate and comprehensive knowledge of foreign politics; a steady and systematic adherence to the same views; a nice and uniform sensibility to national character; decision, SECRECY [emphasis in original], and despatch, are incompatible with the genius of a body so variable and so numerous.... The greater frequency of the calls upon the House of Representatives, and the greater length of time which it would often be necessary to keep them together when convened, to obtain their sanction in the progressive stages of a treaty, would be a source

of so great inconvenience and expense as alone
ought to condemn the project.[54]

Historical Trends

As should be evident by now to the reader, the Congress
has a clear and significant role in the formulation of U.S.
foreign and national security policy. Yet that role is not
uniformly acknowledged and has been subject to
interpretation and challenge over the years. Clearly, Edwin
Corwin's description, cited earlier, is exactly right.

James Lindsay notes that struggle between the executive
and legislative branches over who controls the direction of
U.S. foreign and defense policy has generally been the
historical norm, with rare exceptions—such as the
immediate post-World War II period when the fear of
communism served as a unifying force. During this
roughly two-decade period, Congress was generally
deferential to the executive branch. This deference was
shattered, as Lindsay notes, by the Vietnam War.[55]

Throughout history there have been notable examples
of Congress deferring to the wishes of the Chief Executive
or challenging the decisions of the president. Some issues
remain not only controversial but subject to judicial or other
challenges even to this day.

During the Civil War, President Abraham Lincoln was
faced with riots, militia actions, and threats to the integrity
of the Union, including Maryland's threat to secede.
Consequently, he suspended the writ of *habeas corpus*
without congressional approval as a "necessary measure"

---

[54] Alexander Hamilton, "The Treaty-Making Power of the Executive,"
Federalist 75, (undated), available at
https://avalon.law.yale.edu/18th_century/fed75.asp.

[55] Lindsay, *Congress and the Politics of U.S. Foreign Policy*, op. cit., pp. 24-
26.

in response to an armed rebellion.[56] *Habeas corpus* means that detainees can seek relief from unlawful imprisonment. Article I, Section 9 of the Constitution states: "The privilege of the writ of *habeas corpus* shall not be suspended, unless when in cases of rebellion or invasion the public safety may require it." More recently, this became an issue when President George W. Bush suspended the writ of *habeas corpus* in order to detain persons considered "enemy combatants" as part of the Global War on Terror.[57] The issue of which branch of government has the authority to act on *habeas corpus* cases has been the subject of numerous judicial reviews.

The Senate's role in treaty-making is considered to be one of the most powerful tools it has to influence foreign policy. Yet, as noted previously, this power is shared with the president and has not been without its share of controversy.

The Constitution vests the president with the power to make treaties, subject to the advice and consent of the Senate ("provided two-thirds of the Senators present concur"). In the early days, President George Washington negotiated a treaty with the Creek Indians but was unsure how to interpret the Senate's "advice and consent" rule. Believing that it required him to appear in person before the Senate prior to negotiating the treaty, Washington did so; however, his presence was met with confusion and uncertainty among the Senators present, with some advocating for a delay so that Washington's proposed

---

[56] Robert Longley, "Why Bush and Lincoln Both Suspended Habeas Corpus," ThoughtCo., 22 August 2019, available at https://www.thoughtco.com/bush-lincoln-both-suspended-habeas-corpus-3321847.

[57] Ibid.

action could be studied by a committee.[58] As a consequence, Washington grew increasingly agitated, shouting, "This defeats every purpose of my coming here."[59] After this experience, Washington reportedly declared he "would be damned if he went there again."[60] This was the only time a president traveled to the Senate in person to seek its advice and consent on a treaty. Subsequently, all future treaties were sent to the Senate after they had already been negotiated.

A historical review of how the Senate exercised its important treaty role shows periods when the Senate was in no mood to consent to ratification of treaties simply because the president requested it. As Lindsay notes, during the 27-year period from 1871 to 1898, no major treaty submitted to the Senate for its advice and consent was approved.[61] In an 1898 letter to historian Henry Adams during the Spanish-American War, Secretary of State John Hay wrote, "I have told you many times that I did not believe another important treaty would ever pass the Senate" and that "the man who makes the Treaty of Peace with Spain will be lucky if he escapes lynching."[62] President William McKinley was, however, able to obtain Senate approval of

---

[58] See a description of Washington's initial experience at "George Washington and the Indians," 22 September 2011, available at http://nativeamericannetroots.net/diary/1077.

[59] "Irritating the President," United States Senate, available at https://www.senate.gov/artandhistory/history/minute/The_Senate_Irritates_President_George_Washington.htm.

[60] Steven Knott, "George Washington: Domestic Affairs," The Miller Center, University of Virginia, available at https://millercenter.org/president/washington/domestic-affairs.

[61] Lindsay, *Congress and the Politics of U.S. Foreign Policy*, op. cit., p.15.

[62] William Roscoe Thayer, *The Life and Letters of John Hay*, Vol. 2, (Boston and New York, Houghton Mifflin Company, 1915), p. 170, available at https://archive.org/details/lifelettersofjoh02thayer/page/170.

the peace treaty with Spain by the slimmest of margins — one vote.[63]

To Consult or Not to Consult?

In general, the president may improve the chances of gaining congressional approval for executive branch policies by involving the legislative branch in discussions on major national security issues prior to acting. Examples include President James Madison naming Senator James A. Bayard, Sr. to the delegation negotiating the Treaty of Ghent that ended the War of 1812 and President Clinton involving Senators in discussions over enlarging the North Atlantic Treaty Organization (NATO). This, of course, does not guarantee success and is not without risk.

Other presidents have not been as fortunate in their dealings with Congress. President Woodrow Wilson traveled to Paris personally to negotiate the terms of the Treaty of Versailles, which ended military hostilities against Germany in World War I. But in doing so he insisted on attaching the League of Nations Covenant to it, which Congress had opposed. Senator Henry Cabot Lodge, then Chairman of the Senate Foreign Relations Committee and an opponent of the League of Nations, thought this was a mistake. Indeed, one of Wilson's key mistakes is thought to have been "his failure to engage in bipartisan consultations on issues of war and peace." Instead of working with Lodge and other critics, Wilson "antagonized" them.[64] The result was overwhelming congressional rejection of the peace treaty. President Harry Truman did not tell Congress

---

[63] Lindsay, *Congress and the Politics of U.S. Foreign Policy*, op. cit., p.15.

[64] Richard Striner, *Woodrow Wilson and World War One: A Burden Too Great to Bear*, (Rowman & Littlefield, Lanham, Maryland and Plymouth, England, 2014), available at https://historynewsnetwork.org/article/155810.

before dispatching troops to Korea in 1950 to counter North Korea's invasion of the South.[65] And President Richard Nixon's decisions on war and peace issues, taken without congressional consultation, led to sharp criticism, with some scholars referring to his administration as an "imperial presidency."[66]

Indeed, Congress played essentially no role in a number of presidential decisions involving the use of military force, including President Reagan's decision to deploy U.S. Marines to Lebanon or to invade Grenada ("Operation Urgent Fury") in 1983; his decision to mine Nicaraguan harbors in 1984; and the bombing of Libya in 1986. Nor was Congress involved in President George H. W. Bush's decision to invade Panama ("Operation Just Cause") in 1989.

In sum, the history of national security decision making is one where Congress has been at times deferential to the executive branch and at other times strongly assertive in exercising its constitutional prerogatives. This includes instances involving policy decisions related to WMD, considered by numerous administrations on a bipartisan basis to be one of the most consequential national security issues. Some of these issues are explored in more detail in subsequent chapters.

---

[65] Lindsay, *Congress and the Politics of U.S. Foreign Policy,* op. cit., p. 19.

[66] In 1973, American historian Arthur M. Schlesinger, Jr. published *The Imperial Presidency,* questioning the exercise of foreign policy by the Chief Executive and arguing it had often exceeded its constitutional authorities.

CHAPTER THREE

THE ORGANIZATION AND OPERATION OF
THE LEGISLATIVE BRANCH

Although its workings remain a mystery to many, Congress does conduct its business according to a well-defined set of rules and procedures.[67] Because we have a bicameral legislature, the House and Senate operate under different guidelines, though many of their procedures are similar. The organization of both bodies is also similar and based upon a committee structure. Since 1789, Congress has used committees to carry out its day-to-day legislative business. Yet much has changed since the early days of the Republic and from time to time Congress has felt the need to adapt its procedures to contemporary realities. Some of the most significant changes to the organization and operation of the legislative branch occurred as a result of the Legislative Reorganization Act of 1946 (hereafter referred to as the "LRA").

The LRA represented one of the most comprehensive reforms of Congress, and its provisions were crafted in bipartisan fashion by a joint committee co-chaired by Senator Robert LaFollette, Jr (R-WI) and Representative Almer Stillwell "Mike" Monroney (D-OK). It emerged out of concern that after the Great Depression and World War II, the balance of federal power was shifting away from Congress and toward the president. The Congress had

---

[67] This Chapter provides only an overview of congressional organization and operations. For a much more definitive and authoritative description and explanation of congressional procedures see Walter J. Oleszek, *Congressional Procedures and the Policy Process*, 9th Edition, (CQ Press, SAGE Publications, Los Angeles, London, New Delhi, Singapore, and Washington, D.C., 2014).

given President Franklin Delano Roosevelt broad authority through his "New Deal." During FDR's first 100 days in office, Congress approved every major program he requested, including creation of the Tennessee Valley Authority and reforms to the banking, monetary, housing, and transportation systems. This standard subsequently became the benchmark by which future presidents would be judged in their first 100 days.[68]

Congressional deference to the president's wishes led to concerns that the legislative branch was becoming too lethargic and unable to act with the necessary dispatch. In part, this was attributed to congressional processes that were seen as antiquated and increasingly irrelevant to contemporary requirements. Hence, the LRA was born.

One of the most comprehensive discussions of the LRA can be found in George B. Galloway's seminal article in the March 1951 issue of *The American Political Science Review*. In it, Galloway identifies 10 main objectives of the act as follows:

1. To streamline and simplify congressional committee structure.
2. To eliminate the use of special or select committees.
3. To clarify committee duties and reduce jurisdictional disputes.
4. To regularize and publicize committee procedures.
5. To improve congressional staff aids.
6. To reduce the work load on Congress.
7. To strengthen legislative oversight of administration.
8. To reinforce the power of the purse.

---

[68] Kenneth T. Walsh, "The First 100 Days: Franklin Roosevelt Pioneered the 100-Day Concept," *U.S. News and World Report*, 12 February 2009, available at https://www.usnews.com/news/history/articles/2009/02/12/the-first-100-days-franklin-roosevelt-pioneered-the-100-day-concept.

9. To regulate lobbying.
10. To increase the compensation of members of Congress and provide them retirement pay.[69]

The LRA did reduce the total number of committees by 58 percent—in the House the number of standing committees was reduced from 48 to 19 while Senate committees were reduced from 33 to 15. Some of the committees that were eliminated were seen as less useful than others, or what one former Massachusetts governor referred to as "ornamental barnacles on the ship of state."[70] Special committees were seen as unnecessary because they did not have legislative authority to act on individual bills and because it was assumed their duties could be fulfilled by other committees.

In addition, the act created roughly parallel committee structures in both the House and Senate with the intent of facilitating joint actions and results. Committee responsibilities were defined in ways intended to minimize jurisdictional disputes, and committees were required for the first time to keep records of their hearings and other activities. Among other requirements, each conference report (which provides the compromise outcome between House and Senate committee versions of a bill) had to include a "Statement of Managers" explaining the final outcome of negotiations over the bill.[71]

Importantly, the LRA "marked the birth of a full-fledged congressional staff."[72] It provided administrative

---

[69] George B. Galloway, "The Operation of the Legislative Reorganization Act of 1946," *The American Political Science Review*, (Vol. 45, No. 1, March 1951), pp. 41-68.

[70] Attributed to Alvan T. Fuller, in Galloway, Ibid., p. 43.

[71] Galloway, op. cit., pp. 47-49.

[72] This quote, attributed to Ernest Griffith, a former director of what is today known as the Congressional Research Service, is cited in Galloway, op. cit., p. 56.

assistants for Senators, increased the size of the Office of Legislative Counsel, and expanded the Legislative Research Service (which later became the Congressional Research Service). It also authorized the hiring of Professional Staff Members for committees and limited the number of committee assignments for each member.[73] These latter changes were an attempt to redistribute the workload among the committees more judiciously, as even in the 1950s the workload was said to be "beyond effective legislative control."[74]

The LRA's move to strengthen oversight of programs carried out by the executive branch was intended to foster closer cooperation between both branches of government. Whether it achieved the desired effect, however, is debatable. Indeed, over the years increasing congressional oversight has been seen by some executive branch officials as an attempt to "micromanage" the activities of whatever administration is in power. Perhaps unsurprisingly, this has often led to an "us versus them" or "hide and seek" mentality where members of Congress believe they are forced to uncover details that they believe are being withheld from them. This tension is particularly apparent when Congress is controlled by one political party and the White House by another, and unfortunately detracts from the cooperative relationships that could more effectively facilitate the creation and implementation of sound policy. In today's highly charged partisan political environment, this tension is all too evident.

The LRA also required Congress to put forth its own legislative budget and to report on its own expenditures.[75] It also sought to strengthen the rules on lobbying by requiring registered lobbyists to file quarterly financial

---

[73] Galloway, op. cit., pp. 54, 56-57.

[74] Ibid., p. 58.

[75] Ibid., pp. 62-65.

statements, although there was controversy over whether these rules applied to all lobbyists or just those whose "principal purpose" was to influence legislation.[76] Perhaps most importantly in the eyes of members, the LRA raised congressional salaries by 25 percent, allowed members a tax-exempt expense allowance, and extended retirement coverage to them.[77] In short, the 1946 LRA represented a major step toward reforming the organization and operation of Congress in ways that made it more relevant to contemporary circumstances.

In time, it became apparent that, even with the reforms embodied in the 1946 LRA, Congress was not keeping up with the pace of technological and societal change in the country. Additional reforms were therefore needed.[78] In 1970, another Legislative Reorganization Act was passed that made extraordinary changes to Congress' operating procedures. For the first time, in an effort to improve transparency, television cameras were allowed to broadcast committee hearings (presaging the birth and expansion of today's C-SPAN). Electronic voting was also instituted in the House. Senate rules were changed to allow committee meetings to occur at the same time the full Senate was in session (until then, Senate committees could not meet to conduct business when the full Senate was in session because of the need for a quorum). In addition, the role of the minority in making staff committee selections was increased. And the Legislative Research Service became

---

[76] Ibid., pp. 65-67.

[77] Ibid., pp. 67-68.

[78] Former Secretary of Defense and General James Mattis (USMC, Ret.), under whom I worked at the Pentagon in 2017 and 2018, was fond of saying that the Department of Defense needed to operate at "the speed of relevance." Many saw Congress as unable or unwilling to operate in such a manner.

what is today known as the Congressional Research Service (CRS), and its role was expanded.[79]

How a Bill Becomes a Law... Really

For those of us old enough to remember the children's television series *Schoolhouse Rock!*, an episode more than 40 years ago sought to explain in animated cartoon fashion how a bill becomes a law. The episode, "I'm Just a Bill," set to a catchy tune, chronicles the fate of a lowly bill patiently waiting to be signed into law and the various hurdles that must be overcome before that stage of legislative nirvana can be reached. Our friend "Bill" laments the fact that "it's a long, long journey" to go from bill to law, including "a long, long wait" in committee. Fortunately for Bill, he is one of the lucky ones who eventually makes it to the president's desk where he gets signed into law.[80] This 1976 episode famously became an instant classic – so much so that *Saturday Night Live* (SNL) parodied the original episode in 2014 with its own version of "How A Bill Does Not Become A Law."[81]

Despite this overly simplified explanation of the legislative process, most bills in fact must pass through various committees of jurisdiction, be voted on in their

---

[79] For additional details on the impact of the 1970 LRA, see Judy Schneider, Christopher M. Davis, and Betsy Palmer, "Reorganization of the House of Representatives: Modern Reform Efforts," Congressional Research Service, CRS Report RL31835, 20 October 2003, available at https://archives-democrats-rules.house.gov/archives/RL31835.pdf.

[80] A YouTube video of the *Schoolhouse Rock!* Episode of "I'm Just A Bill" can be found at https://www.youtube.com/watch?v=OgVKvqTItto, and the lyrics are available at http://www.schoolhouserock.tv/Bill.html.

[81] The SNL parody is available at https://www.youtube.com/watch?v=JUDSeb2zHQ0.

respective chambers, and (if approved) be reconciled in a House-Senate "conference."[82]

Both chambers of Congress have the authority to decide how many committees and subcommittees they should have. There are three types of committees: **Standing**, **Select**, and **Joint**.[83] At the time of this writing, in the 116th Congress there are 20 standing committees in the House, three select committees, and four joint committees (with members of both the House and Senate). One committee dealing with the "solvency of multi-employer pension plans" is considered a "joint select" committee.[84] In the Senate, there are 17 standing committees and two select committees. There is also one "Special Committee on Aging."[85] There are also 104 House subcommittees and 70 Senate subcommittees. The sheer number of committees virtually ensures that, despite the 1946 LRA's intent to minimize jurisdictional disputes by clearly delineating responsibilities, disputes over jurisdiction will occur.

Standing committees are those that are considered permanent and which are identified in the rules of each chamber. Both the House and Senate operate under their own set of rules. Within their respective guidelines each committee adopts its own rules on how to organize itself and how to conduct its day-to-day business. The House Armed Services Committee, for example, posts its rules online with details of, among other things, when the committee meets; what falls within the jurisdiction of the various subcommittees; how legislation shall be referred for consideration; how hearings shall be publicized; what time

---

[82] The "conference" process is described in more detail in connection with discussion of the annual National Defense Authorization Act in Chapter Seven.

[83] Despite the 1946 LRA's desire to eliminate select committees, a number of such committees remain.

[84] See https://www.house.gov/committees.

[85] See https://www.senate.gov/committees/.

limits are established for members to ask questions of witnesses; and how far in advance of a hearing witness statements must be provided.[86]   Similarly, the Senate Armed Services Committee (SASC) posts its rules, which differ in some ways from its House committee counterpart.[87]

Both the HASC and SASC are standing committees, in that they are permanent bodies with legislative jurisdiction and the authority to conduct oversight functions and authorize budgets. Yet these are not the only committees with jurisdiction over national security and foreign policy matters. In fact, there are nearly two dozen committees in the House and Senate with some degree of jurisdiction over these issues, including the homeland security committees, intelligence committees, and appropriations committees, to name but a few. The sheer number of committees makes it important to delineate clearly their individual responsibilities and authorities to avoid bogging down legislative actions over jurisdictional disputes, though this has not been a uniformly successful process.

Select committees (sometimes called "special" committees in the Senate) can be either permanent or temporary. Unlike standing committees, their charters are not written into the standing rules of the House and Senate and their members are chosen by party leaders, not by party

---

[86] See "Rules of the Committee on Armed Services 116th Congress," available at https://armedservices.house.gov/committee-rules.

[87] For example, the HASC rules stipulate that "The Committee shall meet every Wednesday at 10:00 a.m., when the House of Representatives is in session…" while the SASC rules state that "The regular meeting days of the Committee shall be Tuesday and Thursday, unless the Chairman, after consultation with the Ranking Minority Member, directs otherwise." The SASC rules are available at https://www.armed-services.senate.gov/about/rules.

caucuses. Otherwise, they operate in a manner similar to standing committees.[88]

Joint committees are composed of Senators and House members and may also be either permanent or temporary. Though the number of joint committees has fluctuated over time, their number has remained relatively small. Supporters of joint committees have argued that they promote common approaches and unified congressional actions. They are also thought to foster collaboration among congressional staffs. Joint hearings are also deemed useful for streamlining the legislative process and promoting bicameral comity. Opponents of such joint endeavors, however, have argued that they undermine the independence and prerogatives of the separate chambers, and raise unnecessary protocol issues (e.g., who has seniority at a joint hearing, who sits where, or who gets to ask questions first). As a practical matter, opponents argue that because the House and Senate schedules are different, the ability to conduct legislative business jointly is somewhat constrained.[89]

Today, there are approximately two dozen committees that claim some degree of jurisdiction in the area of national security. Even committees that generally do not have national security responsibilities can, on occasion, insert themselves into the national security legislative process. Strong committee chairmen have been known to use the power of their chairmanship to wrest jurisdiction of defense-related matters away from other committees, while members who are considered issue leaders on specific topics can drive consideration of those topics toward

---

[88] A brief but excellent description of the various types of committees can be found in the Congressional Research Service report on "Committee Types and Roles," 2 May 2017, available at https://www.everycrsreport.com/files/20170502_98-241_c52611f19d487a44b3c3c3b335bebd1d84390697.pdf.

[89] Galloway, op. cit., pp. 41-46.

committees that normally would lack legislative authority to consider them.

A striking example of this occurred in the 1970s when Rep. Al Gore (D-TN), a member of the House Science and Technology Committee, injected the committee into the debate over nuclear arms control issues by insisting that concern over "nuclear winter" (i.e., a reference to the devastating climate effects of a nuclear exchange between the United States and Soviet Union) was a science and technology issue. Similarly, in the 1980s, Sen. Chuck Grassley (R-IA) used his influence on the Judiciary Committee to involve the committee in the debate over defense funding. He did this by focusing on charges of "waste, fraud, and abuse" in defense contracting.[90] At the time, charges of "gold plating" reinforced concerns over reports the Pentagon was buying $600 toilet seats and $400 hammers. Because contractor overcharging carried criminal penalties, the Judiciary Committee earned a key role in the defense budget debate.

The issue of export controls and technology transfer is another area where normal committee jurisdictional lines were adjusted. In the 1990s, concerns over the export of sensitive space-related technology and high-performance computing capabilities to China led to major congressional legislative actions (discussed in more detail in Chapter Fourteen). The protection of sophisticated U.S. technologies from illicit export to unauthorized end users fell squarely within the jurisdictional purview of the Foreign Affairs Committee in the House (then named the House International Relations Committee or HIRC). However, due to difficulties passing an annual authorization bill, the House Armed Services under the chairmanship of Rep. Floyd D. Spence (R-SC), with HIRC concurrence, included provisions in its annual authorization bill significantly

---

[90] Lindsay, op. cit., p. 54.

changing the statutory rules governing the export of sensitive technologies. The HASC even created a new position within the Office of the Under Secretary of Defense for Policy—a Deputy Under Secretary of Defense for Technology Security Policy—to assist "in supervising and directing the activities of the Department of Defense relating to export controls" and "in developing policies and positions regarding the appropriate export control policies and procedures that are necessary to protect the national security interests of the United States."[91] This position was later repealed in a subsequent NDAA.

There are exceptions to every rule but, in general, before a bill becomes a law it must pass through the appropriate committee or committees of Congress. In reality, this is easier said than done. Committees are the graveyards of bills, with more dying in committee than passing. Every year since 2001, Rep. Barbara Lee (D-TX) has introduced legislation to create a federal "Department of Peacebuilding" in order to "target the root causes of domestic and international violence and promote policies to create [a] sustainable, peaceful world."[92] The bill has gone nowhere. As our friend "Bill" from *Schoolhouse Rock!* noted: "I'm one of the lucky ones. Most bills never even get this far. I hope they decide to report on me favorably, otherwise I may die."

---

[91] *Strom Thurmond National Defense Authorization Act for Fiscal Year 1999,* Public Law 105-261, October 17, 1998, Section 1521, available at https://www.congress.gov/105/plaws/publ261/PLAW-105publ261.pdf.

[92] "Congresswoman Barbara Lee Renews Call for Department of Peacebuilding," Press release, 16 February 2017, available at https://lee.house.gov/news/press-releases/congresswoman-barbara-lee-renews-call-for-department-of-peacebuilding. She introduced the bill again on 8 February 2019. See "Department of Peacebuilding Act of 2019 Introduced!," The Peace Alliance, available at https://peacealliance.org/department-of-peacebuilding-act-of-2019-introduced/.

The Big Eight

In the area of national security, there are eight main committees with primary jurisdiction and responsibility. (See Figure 1) While there are multiple other committees whose jurisdictions touch on national security matters, these eight are considered to be the primary ones. They are:

- House Committee on Armed Services (HASC)
- Senate Committee on Armed Services (SASC)
- House Committee on Foreign Affairs (HFAC)
- Senate Committee on Foreign Relations (SFRC)
- House Committee on Appropriations (HAC), particularly the Subcommittee on Defense (HAC-D)
- Senate Committee on Appropriations (SAC), particularly the Subcommittee on Defense (SAC-D)
- House Permanent Select Committee on Intelligence (HPSCI)
- Senate Select Committee on Intelligence (SSCI)

Figure 1. The "Big Eight" Committees and Their Jurisdictional Responsibilities[93]

Committee	Responsibilities
House Committee on Armed Services (HASC)	Defense policy generally; ongoing military operations; organization and reform of DoD and the Department of Energy (DOE); counter-drug programs; security cooperation and humanitarian assistance activities (except special operations-related activities) of the DoD; acquisition and industrial base policy; technology transfer and export controls; joint interoperability; detainee affairs and policy; force protection policy; and interagency reform as it pertains to the DoD and the nuclear weapons programs of the DOE.

[93] This information is primarily taken from the individual committees' websites.

Committee	Responsibilities
Senate Committee on Armed Services (SASC)	Aeronautical and space activities peculiar to or primarily associated with development of weapons systems or military operations; common defense; DoD, the Departments of the Army, Navy, and Air Force, generally; maintenance and operation of the Panama Canal, including administration, sanitation, and governance of the Canal Zone; military research and development; national security aspects of nuclear energy; naval petroleum reserves, except those in Alaska; pay, promotion, retirement, and other benefits and privileges of members of the armed forces, including overseas education of civilian and military dependents; selective service system; and strategic and critical materials necessary for the common defense.
House Committee on Foreign Affairs (HFAC)	Oversight and legislation relating to: foreign assistance (including development assistance, Millennium Challenge Corporation, the Millennium Challenge Account, HIV/AIDS in foreign countries, security assistance, and Public Law 480 programs abroad); national security developments affecting foreign policy; strategic planning and agreements; war powers, treaties, executive agreements, and the deployment and use of U.S. armed forces; peacekeeping, peace enforcement, and enforcement of United Nations or other international sanctions; arms control and disarmament issues; the International Development Finance Corporation, the U.S. Agency for International Development; activities and policies of the State,

Committee	Responsibilities
House Committee on Foreign Affairs (HFAC) **continued**	Commerce, and Defense Departments and other agencies related to the Arms Export Control Act and the Foreign Assistance Act, including export and licensing policy for munitions items and technology and dual-use equipment and technology; international law; promotion of democracy; international law enforcement issues, including narcotics control programs and activities; international cyber issues; U.S. Agency for Global Media; embassy security; international broadcasting; public diplomacy, including international communication and information policy, and international education and exchange programs.
Senate Committee on Foreign Relations (SFRC)	Acquisition of land and buildings for embassies and legations in foreign countries; U.S. boundaries; diplomatic service; foreign economic, military, technical, and humanitarian assistance; foreign loans; international activities of the American National Red Cross and the International Committee of the Red Cross; international aspects of nuclear energy, including nuclear transfer policy; international conferences and congresses; international law as it relates to foreign policy; International Monetary Fund and other international organizations established primarily for international monetary purposes (except that, at the request of the Committee on Banking, Housing, and Urban Affairs, any proposed legislation relating to such subjects reported by the SFRC shall be referred to the Committee on Banking, Housing, and Urban

Committee	Responsibilities
Senate Committee on Foreign Relations (SFRC) **continued**	Affairs); intervention abroad and declarations of war; measures to foster commercial intercourse with foreign nations and to safeguard American business interests abroad; national security and international aspects of U.S. trusteeships; ocean and international environmental and scientific affairs as they relate to foreign policy; protection of U.S. citizens abroad and expatriation; relations of the United States with foreign nations generally; treaties and executive agreements, except reciprocal trade agreements; United Nations and its affiliated organizations; World Bank group, the regional development banks, and other international organizations established primarily for development assistance purposes.
House Committee on Appropriations (HAC), Subcommittee on Defense (HAC-D)	Appropriation of funding for: Departments of Army, Navy (including Marine Corps), Air Force; Office of Secretary of Defense; defense agencies (except DoD-related accounts and programs under the Subcommittee on Military Construction and Veterans Affairs, and the Army Corps of Engineers (Civil Works)); Central Intelligence Agency; intelligence community agencies and organizations; and the Office of the Director of National Intelligence.

Committee	Responsibilities
Senate Committee on Appropriations (SAC), Subcommittee on Defense (SAC-D)	Appropriation of funding for: Basic Allowance for Housing; Central Intelligence Agency; Central Intelligence Agency Retirement and Disability System Fund; Defense Advanced Research Projects Agency; defense agencies; Defense Finance and Accounting Service; defense health; Defense Intelligence Agency; Defense Investigative Service; Defense Logistics Agency; Defense Security and Cooperation Agency; Departments of the Air Force, Army, and Navy (including the Marine Corps); Office of the Secretary of Defense; environmental restoration; facilities sustainment; intelligence community; Missile Defense Agency; National Geospatial-Intelligence Agency; National Guard and Reserve Components; National Reconnaissance Office; and the National Security Agency.
House Permanent Select Committee on Intelligence (HPSCI)	Intelligence oversight of: Office of the Director of National Intelligence; Central Intelligence Agency; Defense Intelligence Agency; DoD; DOE; Departments of Homeland Security, Justice, State, and Treasury; Drug Enforcement Administration; Federal Bureau of Investigation; National Geospatial-Intelligence Agency; National Reconnaissance Office; National Security Agency; Office of Naval Intelligence; Twenty-Fifth Air Force; U.S. Army Intelligence and Security Command; U.S. Coast Guard intelligence; and Marine Corps intelligence activity.

Committee	Responsibilities
Senate Select Committee on Intelligence (SSCI)	Intelligence oversight of: Office of the Director of National Intelligence and the Director of National Intelligence; Central Intelligence Agency and the Director of the Central Intelligence Agency; Defense Intelligence Agency; National Security Agency; intelligence activities of other agencies and subdivisions of DoD; intelligence activities of the Department of State; and intelligence activities of the Federal Bureau of Investigation.

The Armed Services committees have jurisdiction over most issues related to DoD. This includes oversight of its programs, organization, and management; personnel policy; weapons procurement; operations and maintenance; research and development; and defense issues related to other nations. Both the HASC and SASC have multiple subcommittees that deal with various aspects of defense policy and programs. They are both authorization committees; they authorize spending for DoD programs but do not actually provide funding.

The actual dollars are provided by the appropriations committees, which have significant budgetary power; these committees are responsible for approving the budgets of all federal agencies. While there are more than a dozen appropriations bills that must be passed annually to keep the government functioning, the DoD budget is handled by the Subcommittees on Defense (HAC-D and SAC-D). When the appropriations committees fail to pass a budget on time, the result can be a government shutdown and the furlough of "non-essential" federal workers. Alternatively, the Congress can pass a Continuing Resolution (CR), which continues to fund the government at prior year levels but generally prohibits increases in funding or new program starts. The use of CRs — which can last anywhere from a day to a full year — has expanded in recent years as Congress has faced increased difficulty passing budgets on time.

Article I, Section 9 of the U.S. Constitution states: "No Money shall be drawn from the Treasury, but in Consequence of Appropriations made by Law." This means that every federal agency and department of government must rely on receiving funding from Congress to carry out its authorized responsibilities. Without such funding, the business of government shuts down. This includes the salaries of those working for the government, as evidenced by various personnel furloughs in recent years.

For almost three months after the start of the current fiscal year (2020), the DoD was operating without a congressionally passed defense authorization or appropriation bill. That meant DoD was conducting its activities under yet another CR, which prohibited the department from moving forward with new programs and generally restricted levels of spending to the prior year's amounts. Given that much of what DoD requires to defend the nation is determined by the actions of foreign entities — including nations and actors abroad who seek to threaten U.S. security, U.S. interests, and the safety of Americans — artificially constraining the resources available to the department increases the risk that the nation will be ill-prepared to confront unanticipated security challenges that may suddenly emerge.

In recent years, the number of CRs affecting defense has expanded dramatically. The uncertainty surrounding when critical defense resources will ultimately be provided and how much Congress will approve plays havoc with DoD planning and programs. Secretary of Defense Mark Esper has stated that "every day under a CR is a day we're competing with Russia and China with one hand tied behind our back…. In fact, we continue to lose nearly $5 billion in buying power for every quarter we remain in a CR. This must end."[94] Deputy Secretary of Defense David Norquist released extensive contingency guidance on how DoD should plan to continue operations during a lapse in congressional appropriations.[95] As the former Comptroller and Chief Financial Officer of DoD, he has a full appreciation of the impacts of a CR and what DoD needs to do to continue to perform its vital national security missions. Yet, many in DoD and elsewhere in government do not. Understanding this process and its implications is an essential first step toward developing possible solutions.

There is often confusion between the work of the authorization and appropriations committees. Though analogies are never exact, I tend to explain the differences by comparing them to the different roles played by bank personnel. Let's say John is looking for a home equity loan to build a pool in his back yard. He visits the bank to ask for a $10,000 loan. John's credit worthiness is reviewed by a loan officer who will either approve or reject John's application. This is the equivalent of an authorization. If approved, John will receive a check from the cashier in the amount approved by the loan officer – in essence, he receives an appropriation. Only after John receives the appropriated funds does he have the money necessary to pay for his pool.

---

[94] Secretary of Defense Mark T. Esper, "Keynote Address at the Reagan National Defense Forum," 7 December 2019, available at https://www.defense.gov/Newsroom/Transcripts/Transcript/Article /2038129/keynote-address-by-secretary-of-defense-mark-t-esper-at-the-reagan-national-def/.

[95] Deputy Secretary of Defense David L. Norquist, "Memorandum on Guidance for Continuation of Operations During a Lapse of Appropriations," August 26, 2019, available at https://media.defense.gov/2019/Sep/26/2002187450/-1/-1/1/GUIDANCE-FOR-CONTINUATION-OF-OPERATIONS-DURING-A-LAPSE-IN-APPROPRIATIONS.PDF.

Occasionally, however, the cashier will write a check for less (or sometimes more!) than the loan officer approves. When the appropriated amount differs from what has been authorized, the authorizers will often revise the numbers in the authorization bill to match the appropriated totals.[96]

My introduction to the predominance of the appropriators came after the HAC-D approved an amount for a program within my portfolio of responsibility that was significantly less than the HASC had authorized. This led me to call my staff counterpart on the HAC-D to seek an explanation for the discrepancy, which I thought was surely a mistake on their part. "Oh, it's no mistake, Dave," I was informed. "Our chairman doesn't like that program, so we're not appropriating the amount you authorized." Had I collaborated with my HAC-D counterpart beforehand, this embarrassing disconnect between the authorization and appropriations committees might have been averted. Another lesson learned.

The other significant difference between authorization and appropriation bills is that the former provides policy guidance and direction to the various agencies and departments while the latter is generally limited to providing funding. For DoD, the annual National Defense Authorization Act or NDAA (discussed in Chapter Seven) establishes guidance on what and how the DoD can spend its appropriated funds. For example, controversial issues

---

[96] Various Congressional Research Service reports explain in detail the relationship between authorization and appropriation bills. See, for example, James V. Saturno, Bill Heniff Jr., and Megan S. Lynch, "The Congressional Appropriations Process: An Introduction," Congressional Research Service, CRS Report R42388, 30 November 2016, available at https://www.senate.gov/CRSpubs/8013e37d-4a09-46f0-b1e2-c14915d498a6.pdf. Also see "Authorization of Appropriations: Procedural and Legal Issues," Congressional Research Service, CRS Report R42098, 30 November 2016, available at https://www.everycrsreport.com/files/20161130_R42098_b097157b210 6f87ce334741931f819fc94c13a00.pdf.

like establishment of the Space Force, whether or not to close the Guantanamo Bay detention facility in Cuba, or policy regarding transgender members of the military are thrashed out in the NDAA and often add significantly to the time it takes to resolve differences between the House and Senate and come to closure on a final version of the bill. In this regard, the appropriators have an arguably easier task — their bill is shorter and may take less time to complete by avoiding many of the controversial and politically partisan issues of the day that tend to clog the NDAA process.

Two other committees with substantial foreign and national security policy responsibilities are the Senate Foreign Relations and House Foreign Affairs Committees. These committees are concerned mostly with foreign policy issues and have responsibility for international agreements and treaties. Consequently, when a nuclear arms treaty like New START (the 2010 "new" Strategic Arms Reduction Treaty) goes before the Senate for its advice and consent prior to ratification, it is not the Senate Armed Services Committee but rather the Senate Foreign Relations Committee that has primary jurisdiction in making a recommendation to the Senate on whether or not to approve it.

The last two committees comprising the "Big Eight" are the two intelligence committees, the House Permanent Select Committee on Intelligence and the Senate Select Committee on Intelligence. Because of the nature of their work, much day-to-day business involves classified material that has a direct bearing on U.S. national security. The HPSCI and SSCI have oversight and budgetary authority regarding many of the nation's top-secret intelligence programs.

Other committees with some degree of authority for national security policy include the House Committee on Homeland Security and Senate Committee on Homeland

Security and Governmental Affairs, both of which were organized after the terrorist attacks of September 11, 2001 to provide oversight of the newly created Department of Homeland Security. In addition, the critical issue of export controls is overseen in the Senate by the Senate Committee on Banking, Housing, and Urban Affairs. Consequently, it can be challenging for those not deeply steeped in congressional processes to determine which committee has responsibility for what national security issue.

Trends in Committee Influence

When it comes to national security policy, the Armed Services and Appropriations committees are generally considered to be the powerhouse committees among the "Big Eight," as they have oversight responsibility of, and establish policies and priorities for, a department whose annual budget exceeds $700 billion. The annual NDAA is considered a "must pass" bill as it authorizes funding for DoD, and Congress has passed an NDAA every year for the past 59 consecutive years. Because the NDAA is considered so critical, members often seek to attach amendments to it that might not pass Congress if offered separately as stand-alone legislation. Hence, some refer to the NDAA as a "Christmas tree" bill and member-sponsored provisions as "ornaments."[97]

With the passage of time and the advent of new technology, the HASC and SASC produced authorization bills of increasing size and complexity. The movement from typewriters and carbon paper, to word processors, to

---

[97] Katherine Q. Seelye, "Senators Add the Ornaments and Trimmings," *The New York Times*, 20 December 2009, available at https://www.nytimes.com/2009/12/20/health/policy/20prescription s.html.

computerized workstations allowed edits and changes to bills to be made more quickly and frequently.

Versions of the NDAA during the early days of the Cold War lacked specificity. For example, a 1959 version of the NDAA noted simply that the "Secretary of the Air Force may procure guided missiles and 24,000 serviceable aircraft."[98] Today's NDAA is nearly a thousand pages long and contains detailed specific guidance for each of the military services. Also, in 1959, then-Chairman of the SASC, Sen. Richard Russell (D-GA) successfully sponsored legislation requiring that all appropriations for aircraft, missiles, and naval ships receive prior authorization. As Sen. Russell explained, this "would put us in the policy area where, in my judgment, the Armed Services Committee should be."[99]

Over the next quarter century, the number of specific line-item authorizations in the DoD budget grew substantially in order "to reduce the area of discretionary power of the Office of the Secretary of Defense... and to strengthen legislative control of programs."[100] Clearly, the

---

[98] Cited in the *Congressional Record*, Vol. 105, Part 11, 30 July 1959, p. 14767, available at
https://books.google.com/books?id=EzTskz97FxoC&pg=PA14767&lpg=PA14767&dq=secretary+of+the+air+force+may+procure+guided+missiles+and+24,000+serviceable+aircraft&source=bl&ots=ObOHB-qQhZ&sig=ACfU3U2PYov-OH_Vxlvw1JCtGSVONuGRLQ&hl=en&sa=X&ved=2ahUKEwjn3JDpvKnmAhUsT98KHc6JBnUQ6AEwAXoECAoQAQ#v=onepage&q=secretary%20of%20the%20air%20force%20may%20procure%20guided%20missiles%20and%2024%2C000%20serviceable%20aircraft&f=false.

[99] See "A Brief History of the Committee: The Russell Era, 1955-1968," The Center for Legislative Archives, National Archives, available at https://www.archives.gov/legislative/finding-aids/reference/senate/armed-services/1955-1968.html.

[100] James M. Lindsay, "Congress and Defense Policy," *American Defense Policy*, Seventh Edition, edited by Peter L. Hayes, Brenda J. Vallance, and Alan R. Van Tassel, (The Johns Hopkins University Press, Baltimore and London, 1997), p. 84, available at https://books.google.com/books?id=evo4nKODKDsC&pg=PA84&lpg

role of the HASC and SASC assumed greater importance and influence as they increased their oversight and guidance of DoD. Nevertheless, criticisms over the relevance of the authorization committees continue to be heard today, especially in cases where the appropriations committees choose not to follow the authorizer's lead.

The House and Senate Appropriations Committees are perhaps the most consequential committees of Congress, as any program requiring money (i.e., every program) must go through the appropriations committees. The HAC and SAC are more budget oriented than their authorization counterparts, but occasionally they can affect national security policy in dramatic ways.

A couple of examples should suffice. The fiscal year 1985 appropriations bill (signed into law on October 12, 1984), imposed a moratorium on U.S. anti-satellite testing pursuant to certain conditions, restrictions, and presidential certifications.[101] The moratorium was championed by Rep. Joseph P. Addabbo (D-NY), then-Chairman of the HAC-D.[102]

The 2001 *Nuclear Posture Review*, promulgated by the George W. Bush Administration, called for the development of several nuclear weapons initiatives, including a Robust Nuclear Earth Penetrator (RNEP) that

---

=PA84&dq=%22to+strengthen+legislative+control+of+programs%22&s
ource=bl&ots=Imzl8D3udf&sig=ACfU3U0D-dkun-qRfp9enhvsQ-
37PVja0A&hl=en&sa=X&ved=2ahUKEwjwg-
mR1KnmAhXSVN8KHd1XCSUQ6AEwAHoECAMQAQ#v=onepage&
q=%22to%20strengthen%20legislative%20control%20of%20programs%2
2&f=false.

[101] See Section 8100 of Public Law 98-473, 12 October 1984, available at https://www.govinfo.gov/content/pkg/STATUTE-98/pdf/STATUTE-98-Pg1837.pdf.

[102] "Anti-Satellite Missile Gets New Restrictions," *CQ Almanac 1984*, available at https://library.cqpress.com/cqalmanac/document.php?id=cqal84-1152023.

could hold an adversary's hard and deeply buried targets at risk. Because nuclear weapons programs are funded by the DOE's National Nuclear Security Administration (NNSA), an entity created by the fiscal year 2000 NDAA, programs like RNEP required the approval of the House Appropriations Committee's Energy and Water Subcommittee. At the time, the Chairman of the Subcommittee, Rep. David Hobson (R-OH), repeatedly refused to approve appropriations for such activities, arguing that "The development of new weapons for ill-defined future requirements is not what the Nation needs at this time."[103] As a consequence of the Energy and Water Subcommittee's refusal to fund the program, RNEP was never developed or procured and a key aspect of the Bush Administration's nuclear program remained unimplemented.

The importance of the appropriations committees was summed up by former HAC Chairman Norman Dicks (D-WA) when he said of the HAC, "It's where the money is. And money is where the clout is."[104] Indeed, the appropriators and authorizers are often seen as competitors in setting national security priorities. The expansion of

---

[103] See "Rep. David Hobson on Administration's Nuclear Weapons Initiatives," quoted by Richard M. Jones, American Institute of Physics, 24 March 2005, available at https://www.aip.org/fyi/2005/rep-david-hobson-administrations-nuclear-weapons-initiatives.

[104] Cited in Steven S. Smith, Jason M. Roberts, and Ryan J. Vander Wielen, *The American Congress*, Ninth edition (Cambridge University Press, New York, 2015), p. 101, as quoted in Christopher J. Deering and Steven S. Smith, "Committees in Congress," Third edition (Congressional Quarterly Press, Washington, D.C., 1997), p. 67, available at https://books.google.com/books?id=HTgZCgAAQBAJ&pg=PA101&dq=where+the+money+is+and+money+is+where+clout+is%22+norm+dicks&hl=en&newbks=1&newbks_redir=0&sa=X&ved=2ahUKEwjSj_uG26nmAhVLvFkKHVOeBVoQ6AEwAHoECAQQAg#v=onepage&q=where%20the%20money%20is%20and%20money%20is%20where%20clout%20is%22%20norm%20dicks&f=false.

authorizations for individual line items has sometimes been viewed with suspicion by appropriators, as it creates a perception that the authorization committees are encroaching on the appropriator's turf. Likewise, with controversial issues complicating and delaying completion of the annual NDAA, the authorizers occasionally see the appropriators as stepping on their toes by deciding on appropriations amounts before they are authorized or appropriating amounts different than those already authorized.

Unlike the major roles played by the authorization and appropriations committees, the foreign affairs committees have not traditionally enjoyed the same level of influence in charting American national security policy. James Lindsay notes that the SFRC and HFAC have been "remarkably ineffective in shaping U.S. foreign policy."[105] He recounts the inability of the SFRC to get the Senate to approve a foreign assistance authorization bill every year from 1985 until 1991 and quotes former SFRC Chairman Sen. Richard Lugar (R-IN) as saying, "The committee as a whole is not really a major player in this business."[106]

The ineffectiveness of the HFAC to get an authorization bill passed has previously been recounted in connection with the debate over export controls and the adoption by the HASC of export control provisions in the NDAA that would normally fall within the purview of the HFAC. Control over the export of sensitive military technologies is governed by the International Trafficking in Arms Regulations, or ITAR, and the licensing of military exports to third countries is the responsibility of the State Department. Hence, as the House committee of jurisdiction overseeing the State Department's budget and programs, the HFAC should have a major role to play in working with

---

[105] Lindsay, *Congress and the Politics of U.S. Foreign Policy*, op. cit., p.55.
[106] Ibid.

the executive branch to ensure that critical U.S. military technologies do not wind up in the hands of unauthorized end users or adversaries.

Because the treaty approval process is one way the Senate can influence major national security policies, the SFRC has a larger role to play than the HFAC. This has further contributed to the perception that the HFAC lacks gravitas. In the 1940s, one member referred to it as "a dump heap, where service was a chore rather than a privilege."[107] In 1990, Rep. Dante Fascell (D-FL), then-Chairman of the HFAC, described it as "almost irrelevant."[108]

By contrast, the intelligence committees (HPSCI and SSCI) play a significant role in national security issues, though much of their work remains outside the public eye due to the classified nature of their activities. Because of this, neither HPSCI nor SSCI receive the same level of public scrutiny that the other "Big Eight" committees receive, though their activities can have just as much influence on U.S. national security. In addition, because of the unique nature of their work, the intelligence committees rely heavily on information shared by the executive branch.

There have been times when the work of the intelligence committees has emerged into the public spotlight. Usually, this is after a major intelligence failure or when noteworthy covert actions have gone awry, when Congress is looking for someone to blame and what lessons there are to be learned. Notable intelligence failures include the "Bay of Pigs" invasion of Cuba in 1961; the Iranian revolution in 1978 that overthrew the pro-U.S. Shah of Iran; the "Iran-Contra" affair during the Reagan Administration, in which the administration was accused of trading arms for hostages; the collapse of the Soviet Union in 1991; and the terrorist attacks on the United States on September 11, 2001.

---

[107] Ibid., p. 56.

[108] Ibid., p. 57.

Each of these events served as a catalyst for congressional actions, sometimes in support of the administration, sometimes in opposition.

Congress' relative passivity regarding intelligence oversight during the early days of the Cold War gave way to a more assertive approach after revelations of misconduct by the intelligence community in the 1970s, including concerns over the use of intelligence agencies to conduct domestic surveillance of Americans opposed to the Vietnam War. The SSCI was established in 1976 and was followed by the HPSCI in 1997. As select committees, they operate somewhat differently from the other standing committees. Their charters are not contained in the standing rules of the House and Senate, and their members are chosen by their respective party leaderships.

Chamber Action

These "Big Eight" committees conduct the bulk of the national security workload on Capitol Hill. Of course, any bill that makes it through committee must also be passed on the House and Senate floor, where the rules are different for each chamber. Any Senator can offer an amendment on the Senate floor, which allows for relatively open debate. By contrast, the House, with its much larger membership, has a Rules Committee, which produces a "rule" that includes amendments found to be in order, and the rule is approved or disapproved by the whole House. This helps structure the legislative debate and keeps the process from getting bogged down. It is an especially useful tool for advancing House floor action on a "Christmas tree" bill like the NDAA by limiting the number of "ornaments" that can be hung on the bill.

Most civics students learn that there are 100 Senators and 435 members of the House of Representatives. In fact, there are actually 441 House members, as six members do not represent states. Along with the 50 states, the House has *non-voting* Delegates from the Commonwealth of the Northern Mariana Islands, Puerto Rico, Guam, American Samoa, the U.S. Virgin Islands, and the District of Columbia (D.C.). Anyone living in or around Washington, D.C. will probably have noticed the distinctive D.C. automobile license plates that read "Taxation Without Representation," a feature in the nation's capital since November 2000 and originally intended as a protest against the lack of congressional voting representation of D.C. residents.[109]

The House also relies heavily on a procedure known as "Suspension of the Rules," whereby generally non-controversial bills are passed expeditiously. This includes, for example, the naming of post offices or federal buildings. House rules allow for such a procedure to occur if certain requirements are met.[110]

An additional parliamentary device intended to facilitate legislative action occurs when the House "resolves" itself into something called "The Committee of the Whole House on the State of the Union," or more succinctly, "The Committee of the Whole." Because bills are generally debated and amended in committee, and because committee rules differ from those that govern the workings of the entire House, the Committee of the Whole is a procedure that allows the entire House to act as though it were a committee.[111]

C-SPAN aficionados may notice, while viewing House proceedings, that sometimes the person in the Speaker's

---

[109] In August 2017, the phrase was changed to "End Taxation Without Representation." See https://dmv.dc.gov/service/end-taxation-without-representation-tags.

[110] A summary of these rules can be found at https://archives-democrats-rules.house.gov/archives/suspend_rules.htm.

[111] See "Committee of the Whole: An Introduction," Congressional Research Service, CRS Report RS20147, 15 May 2013, available at https://www.everycrsreport.com/files/20130515_RS20147_4f74c68b25 6cc2492e02046f879ee60da04b1545.pdf.

chair is referred to as "Mr. Speaker" or "Madam Speaker," while at other times the chairperson is addressed as "Mr. Chairman" or "Madam Chairman." Astute observers will understand that the latter means that the House is considering legislation as the Committee of the Whole while the former form of address means that the House is conducting its business under the rules of the full chamber. Another way of knowing whether the proceedings are being conducted by the full House or in the Committee of the Whole is to notice the placement of the mace located to the right of the Speaker's chair. The mace is raised when the House is conducting its business and lowered when the House resolves itself into the Committee of the Whole, though this is not always visible to television viewers.

The House mace is considered to be "a symbol of the authority of the Sergeant at Arms of the House of Representatives" with a long and distinguished tradition.[112] According to the rules of the House, the Sergeant at Arms presents the mace to separate the warring parties and to enforce order on the House floor when members become unruly.[113] Though fisticuffs and genuine knock-down, drag-outs generally do not occur on the House floor, occasionally members can get unruly.[114] I only witnessed

---

[112] "Whereas: Stories From the People's House," History, Art & Archives, U.S. House of Representatives, 4 December 2017, available at https://history.house.gov/Blog/Detail/15032450168.

[113] Karen L. Haas, *Rules of the House of Representatives, One Hundred Fourteenth Congress*, 6 January 2015, p. 2, available at http://clerk.house.gov/legislative/house-rules.pdf.

[114] The most serious confrontation on the House floor is reported to have taken place in 1858 during debate over the Kansas Territory's Constitution. See "The Most Infamous Floor Brawl in the History of the U.S. House of Representatives," History, Art & Archives, U.S. House of Representatives, (undated), available at https://history.house.gov/Historical-Highlights/1851-1900/The-most-infamous-floor-brawl-in-the-history-of-the-U-S--House-of-Representatives/.

this once on the House floor when, during a 1995 debate over Bosnia policy, Rep. Jim Moran (D-VA) shoved Rep. Randy "Duke" Cunningham (R-CA) out the door into the Speaker's Lobby.[115] Rep. Robert Dornan (R-CA) and Rep. George Miller (D-CA) were also involved in the altercation, which was broken up by Capitol Police. The last time the Sergeant at Arms prepared to remove the mace from its pedestal to restore decorum in the chamber was in 1994 when Rep. Maxine Waters (D-CA) accused Rep. Peter King (R-NY) of "badgering" a hearing witness.[116]

Types of Legislation

There are four distinct types of legislation Congress considers: **Bills,** **Joint** **Resolutions,** **Concurrent** **Resolutions,** and **Simple Resolutions.**   Each is briefly described below.[117]

Simply put, **Bills** are legislative proposals, i.e., proposals intended to become laws. They are numbered sequentially at the beginning of each session of Congress. House bills are preceded with "H.R." (House of Representatives) and Senate bills with "S."   Most bills

---

[115] Tony Perry, "Lawmaker Conciliatory After Fight in Congress," *Los Angeles Times*, 22 November 1995, available at https://www.latimes.com/archives/la-xpm-1995-11-22-mn-6126-story.html.

[116] *Congressional Record*, Volume 140, Number 102, 29 July 1994, available at https://www.govinfo.gov/content/pkg/CREC-1994-07-29/html/CREC-1994-07-29-pt1-PgH27.htm.

[117] Additional detail on the different types of legislation can be found in the "House Office of the Legislative Counsel Guide to Legislative Drafting," available at https://legcounsel.house.gov/HOLC/Drafting_Legislation/Drafting_ Guide.html; the Senate explanation of "Types of Legislation" is available at https://www.senate.gov/legislative/common/briefing/leg_laws_acts. htm.

considered by Congress are "public bills," which impact the general public, but on occasion Congress will consider "private bills" that only affect individual citizens or organizations. Identical versions of a bill must be passed in both chambers before it can be presented to the president for his signature or veto.

Joint Resolutions may originate in either the House ("H.J. Res.") or Senate ("S.J. Res.") and generally deal with specific limited matters, such as the designation of a federal holiday. Since they also must be passed by both houses of Congress and signed by the president, there is essentially no legislative difference between a joint resolution and a bill. However, a congressional declaration of war is generally done through a joint resolution.

Concurrent Resolutions ("H. Con. Res." and "S. Con. Res.") differ slightly from bills and joint resolutions, in that they do not carry the same force of law and need not be signed by the president to take effect. They are generally used to make changes to congressional rules governing the operation of both chambers, or to convey the views of both houses of Congress on a particular issue. For example, concurrent resolutions can authorize the convening of a joint session of Congress or allow the Capitol rotunda to be used for a specific purpose.

Finally, **Simple Resolutions** ("H. Res." and "S. Res.") convey the views of either the Senate or the House, but not both. They may be used to amend chamber rules or to declare sympathy on the passing of a former member. They require neither the approval of both chambers nor the signature of the president. Consequently, they do not have the force of law. Simple resolutions are also used in the House to bring Articles of Impeachment against a sitting president. H. Res. 755, passed by the House Judiciary Committee in December 2019, was for the purpose of

"Impeaching Donald John Trump, President of the United States, for high crimes and misdemeanors."[118]

In today's technological society where the use of social media is ubiquitous, passions can easily be inflamed by groups who support or oppose a particular piece of legislation. However, often the general public cannot and does not distinguish between bills and resolutions, and the actual import of a lobbying campaign may be less than meets the eye.

For example, the Armenian Council of America encouraged citizens to "Call Your Senator Today!" in an effort to pass S. Res. 150, a resolution condemning the "Armenian Genocide" by Turkey.[119] While consideration of such a resolution has become an annual ritual on Capitol Hill, this simple resolution merely expresses the sentiment of the Senate that it is U.S. policy to commemorate this event. As passed, it does not carry the force of law or require any particular action be taken by the president or the executive branch. The resolution, originally introduced in April 2019 by Sen. Robert Menendez (D-NJ), Chairman of the Senate Foreign Relations Committee, was referred to his committee for action, but languished without action due to administration concerns until the full Senate moved to consider it and passed it unanimously on December 12, 2019.[120] An identical resolution (H. Res. 296) passed the House overwhelmingly by a vote of 405-11 in October 2019.

---

[118] H. Res. 755, 10 December 2019, available at https://www.congress.gov/bill/116th-congress/house-resolution/755/text.

[119] "Help Pass S. Res.150 – Call Your Senator Today!," *Massis Post*, 19 November 2019, available at https://massispost.com/2019/11/help-pass-s-res-150-call-your-senator-today/.

[120] Humeyra Pamuk, "U.S. Senate passes resolution recognizing Armenian genocide, angering Turkey," Reuters, 12 December 2019, available at https://www.reuters.com/article/us-usa-turkey-armenia/u-s-senate-unanimously-passes-resolution-recognizing-armenian-genocide-idUSKBN1YG2DZ.

Unlike these simple resolutions, a bill imposing sanctions on Turkey for its invasion of northern Syria in October 2019 (H.R. 4695) passed the House by a veto-proof bipartisan margin of 403-16. This bill carries a stronger impact than H. Res. 296 and would prohibit the transfer of certain U.S. defense articles to Turkey as well as bar senior Turkish officials from entering the United States.

Once a bill is signed by the president, it becomes an "enacted" Public Law and is given a sequential "P.L." number. Accordingly, "P.L. 115-88" refers to the 88th bill signed by the president during the 115th Congress. Often, the enactment of a bill into law is accompanied by a "signing statement," in which the president expresses his views on the provisions of the bill he has just signed. In recent years, the proliferation of signing statements by presidents of both parties has led to increased controversy over whether the Chief Executive is attempting to unilaterally interpret the legal requirements in the bill by using these statements to convey his views on how they will or will not be implemented.[121]

The Importance of Congressional Staff

The Congress could not function without a large cadre of staffers who support both individual Senators and members and the various committees. There are literally thousands of staffers working on Capitol Hill, and that number has grown significantly over the years. As a general rule, the larger the committee, the larger the staff. The HASC alone, for example, has nearly 60 members — that number is well more than half of the entire Senate. And the committee staff has grown as well, though there have been efforts to cut back on the size (and budgets) of committees and staff.

---

[121] A discussion of signing statements can be found in Chapter Six.

Committee staffs are divided between those supporting the majority and the minority, with the majority holding an edge proportional to the balance of power among the members. The HASC, in particular, has sought to adhere to a tradition of bipartisanship, including at the staff level, even during times of great partisan divide. Collegiality and cooperation are important when preparing a bill like the NDAA, which authorizes funding for the entire DoD. The majority and minority staffs must work well together to support the members' objective of adequately providing for the needs of our uniformed service personnel and their civilian counterparts.

Just prior to my joining the HASC staff, the committee was chaired by Rep. Ron Dellums (D-CA), a liberal member from Oakland representing a constituency with a significant anti-military bias. Despite his credentials as a declared "peace activist,"[122] Dellums ran the HASC in a fair and truly bipartisan manner, earning the respect of both his Democratic and Republican colleagues. I believe he was also the only HASC Chairman who, having successfully crafted the NDAA in committee, voted *against* moving the bill to the House floor — as a show of solidarity with his constituents.

Even after the "Republican Revolution" of 1994, the new committee Chairman, Rep. Floyd D. Spence (R-SC), sought to keep the HASC truly bipartisan in its operation, without a bright line dividing majority and minority staffs as House leadership sought. This earned the HASC the reputation as being perhaps the most bipartisan committee in the House, a circumstance that facilitated action on the NDAA.

Two other congressional bodies have traditionally large staffs: The Government Accountability Office (GAO – formerly known as the General Accounting Office) and the

---

[122] Ronald V. Dellums and H. Lee Halterman, *Lying Down With the Lions: A Public Life from the Streets of Oakland to the Halls of Power*, (Beacon Press, Boston, MA, 2000), p. 6.

Congressional Research Service (CRS – formerly known as the Legislative Research Service). The GAO is the investigative arm of Congress and has a staff of more than 3,000. CRS is the research arm of Congress with a staff of about 700 or so.[123] Both organizations have seen a decline in staff over time, but they remain well-resourced to support members by conducting analyses and writing reports on various topics at the request of members and committees.[124]

There are those who believe that the large size of congressional staffs removes decision-making power from the members and concentrates it in the hands of unelected and unaccountable subordinates. The letter then-Rep. Mark Green (D-WI) received from one of his constituents regarding my role in funding decisions for the Cooperative Threat Reduction program (cited in Chapter One) is an example of this. On the other hand, many members recognize that staff support is essential to their ability to understand complex issues and effectively exercise their legislative responsibilities. In the words of former Rep. Charles Whalen Jr (R-OH).:

---

[123] See Lee Drutman and Steven Teles, "Why Congress Relies on Lobbyists Instead of Thinking for Itself," *The Atlantic*, 10 March 2015, available at https://www.theatlantic.com/politics/archive/2015/03/when-congress-cant-think-for-itself-it-turns-to-lobbyists/387295/. Also see Frederick M. Kaiser, "GAO: Government Accountability Office and General Accounting Office," Congressional Research Service, CRS Report RL30349, 10 September 2008, pp. 11-13, available at https://www.everycrsreport.com/files/20080910_RL30349_4ca46f5803 80ac76857b3e32e4be3937b331909a.pdf.

[124] It is difficult to overstate the importance and influence of the Congressional Research Service. In response to a Point of Order raised by House Judiciary Committee Ranking Member Doug Collins (R-GA) during the committee's debate on Articles of Impeachment against President Trump, Committee Chairman Jerold Nadler ruled against the Point of Order based on his conversations with CRS.

It must be remembered that [staff] do not exercise a Svengali-like influence over their "bosses." Rarely, if ever, is a representative moved to sponsor a proposition with which he disagrees. What staff expansion has done, however, is broaden a congressman's participation both in his field of specialization... and in those areas where he has little personal knowledge, expertise, or committee involvement.[125]

Because of the important role that congressional staff play, a job on the Hill is an excellent way to help shape and influence the course of American policy, as well as a good steppingstone to other careers in the federal government. Indeed, many senior DoD leaders began their government careers as I did—working on the Hill as congressional staffers. This includes former Secretaries of Defense, Deputy Secretaries of Defense, Under Secretaries of Defense, and Assistant Secretaries of Defense.

"Knowledge is power," as the saying goes. And having knowledge of how Congress works allows those in government or seeking government jobs to be more effective public policy practitioners.

---

[125] Charles Whalen Jr., *The House and Foreign Policy: The Irony of Congressional Reform*, (University of North Carolina Press, Chapel Hill, NC, 1982), pp. 59-60, quoted in Lindsay, *Congress and the Politics of U.S. Foreign Policy*, op. cit., p. 74.

CHAPTER FOUR

THE ORGANIZATION AND OPERATION OF THE EXECUTIVE BRANCH

As previously noted, Article II of the Constitution explicitly enumerates relatively few powers of the president. Yet the powers the president has in the area of national security are consequential.

In the United States, the president performs multiple functions, including serving as the Chief of State and Head of Government.[126] The former role is mostly ceremonial, such as when the president welcomes foreign dignitaries to State dinners, while the Head of Government role is more substantive. This is significantly different than in other countries where the two roles are often separate and held by different individuals.

In a parliamentary system like the United Kingdom, the hereditary monarch (Queen Elizabeth at present) serves as the ceremonial Chief of State. In Germany, the President (Frank-Walter Steinmeier) serves as the Chief of State but the Chancellor (currently Angela Merkel) is the Head of Government. Among other functions, the Chief of State can call the legislature into session. This position is seen as non-partisan and above politics. On the other hand, the Head of Government role is considered a political position. The Head of Government serves as the leader of the party in power and supervises the entire government bureaucracy, with the ability to call for early elections. In the U.S.

---

[126] Amos A. Jordan, William J. Taylor, Jr., Michael J. Meese, and Suzanne C. Nielsen, "Presidential Leadership and the Executive Branch," *American National Security*, Sixth Edition, (The Johns Hopkins University Press, Baltimore, MD, 2009), p. 77.

presidential system, the president can call for a special session of Congress (such as during the State of the Union address) but cannot call for an early election.

The president also oversees and commands a huge national security bureaucracy as Commander in Chief. This includes the Department of Defense, as well as other federal agencies and departments with national security responsibilities. Yet, as previously noted, only the Congress has the authority to declare war and authorize the funds needed to support U.S. military action, and the president's decision to deploy troops into areas of active conflict without prior congressional authorization has often led to disputes over whether such actions are constitutional or not.

In addition, the president is the nation's chief diplomat with the constitutional power to appoint and receive ambassadors.   He is viewed as the nation's chief spokesperson and is often referred to as the "leader of the free world."   Importantly, the president is responsible for allocating the resources of the federal government through preparation of an annual budget request, which then gets submitted to Congress for action.   Submission of the president's budget request (referred to as the "PB") is one example of the president's ability to initiate legislation.   In addition to initiating legislation, the president must also execute the laws Congress passes in accordance with the Constitution's requirement to "take Care that the Laws be faithfully executed."[127]

When it comes to national security, the president is considered to have three main functions: that of Resource Allocator, Policy Planner, and Coordinator and Monitor of Operations.[128]   These functions are fundamental to the

---

[127] Ibid., pp. 77-78.

[128] These three functions are described in Keith C. Clarke and Lawrence J. Legere, eds., *The President and the Management of National Security,*

execution of the president's national security responsibilities.

The ability to allocate resources across all agencies of the federal government is an essential aspect of determining any administration's priorities. How much money is budgeted for the operations of the Department of Defense vice the Department of State, for example, can reflect an administration's views on the importance of military preparedness vice diplomacy. Critics of the Trump Administration, citing what they assert is a shortchanging of fiscal resources for the State Department while defense spending has increased, have accused President Trump of favoring military over diplomatic solutions.[129]

The president's national security budget request communicates the president's national security priorities. It is prepared by the Office of Management and Budget (OMB), the largest organization within the Executive Office of the President (EOP), following negotiations with DoD and other federal departments and agencies. OMB, through its budget oversight role, is the implementation and enforcement arm of presidential policy.[130]

The policy planning role is one that is associated with major administration initiatives and that usually involves

---

(Praeger, New York, NY, 1969), p. 19, cited in Jordan, et al., *American National Security*, op. cit., p. 78.

[129] See, for example, Courtney McBride, "Trump Keeps the Pressure on State Department Spending," *The Wall Street Journal*, 11 March 2019, available at https://www.wsj.com/articles/trumps-keeps-the-pressure-on-state-department-spending-11552326475. Also see Zeeshan Aleem, "Trump wants to gut the State Department by 25 percent. You read that right.," Vox, available at https://www.vox.com/policy-and-politics/2018/2/12/17004372/trump-budget-state-department-defense-cuts. Aleem states, "Combined with the administration's proposed increase in military spending, the budget vividly illustrates that Trump sees military force—and not diplomacy—as the most effective way of preventing conflicts and advancing America's national security interests."

[130] Jordan, et al., *American National Security*, op. cit., pp. 78, 95.

multiple federal agencies and departments. For example, after World War II the Marshall Plan—named after retired General and former Secretary of State George C. Marshall—was a major initiative that provided substantial amounts of aid to help the nations of Europe get back on their feet and anchored solidly in the democratic camp. Other policy planning initiatives include enlargement of the NATO alliance, which took place in various tranches after German reunification in 1990, and the development of strategies to counter the nuclear weapons programs of countries like North Korea and Iran.

Many of these activities, including those involving the provision of foreign assistance, are coordinated by the State Department, which has had a separate Policy Planning Staff since 1947. The president's policy planning role allows the administration to develop both short-term and long-range plans and strategies designed to advance U.S. national security interests.

In addition, the president uses the interagency process to coordinate and monitor the implementation of policies established by his administration. This coordinating activity, which brings together multiple federal agencies and departments, is necessary to ensure that the large government bureaucracy is fully aware of the administration's approach to national security issues and is consistent in how it explains U.S. policy to domestic and foreign audiences. Often this function is managed by the president's National Security Advisor and the National Security Council (NSC) staff. Monitoring the implementation of these policies is also essential to ensure the policy remains relevant, appropriate, and responsive to dynamic events overseas.

The White House Organization

Over the years, the size of the White House staff has fluctuated dramatically. President Herbert Hoover relied on a relatively small number of advisers, including three secretaries, one military assistant, one naval aide, and 20 clerks. By contrast, Presidents George W. Bush and Barack Obama had a staff of more than 400 working in the White House, in addition to more than 100 other staffers detailed from other government agencies. [131]

Presidents generally have a great deal of flexibility in organizing their staff. For example, the position of National Security Advisor (known formally today as "Assistant to the President for National Security Affairs") did not exist until President Eisenhower created it in 1953. Likewise, a Chief of Staff is not required, though this position has been filled on a regular basis since at least 1979. The Chief of Staff is considered the highest-ranking staff employee within the EOP and oversees the rest of the White House staff, the scheduling of appointments, and other important functions on behalf of the president.[132]

Other key White House staff positions include the Director of OMB, the President's Homeland Security Advisor (formally the "Assistant to the President for Homeland Security and Counterterrorism"), the Counsel to the President, the Presidential Press Secretary, and, as noted earlier, the Assistant to the President for National Security Affairs.

---

[131] Ibid., p. 81. Also see Mark Cancian, "Limiting Size of NSC Staff," Center for Strategic and International Studies, 1 July 2016, available at https://www.csis.org/analysis/limiting-size-nsc-staff.

[132] Ibid., pp. 79-81.

Executive Branch Agencies

A host of federal agencies with three-letter acronyms make up the executive branch. In the national security area, they include the Departments of Defense (DoD), State (DoS), and Homeland Security (DHS). Within DoD, the Office of the Secretary of Defense (OSD) plays a major role in coordinating with the rest of the federal government on national security policies and actions, while the Joint Staff, in support of the Joint Chiefs of Staff (JCS), plays an important role in developing military strategy and supporting the work of the geographic and functional combatant commands.

The State Department is the primary agency responsible for the conduct of American diplomacy abroad, with the Secretary of State serving as the president's principal adviser and spokesperson on foreign policy matters. State is a relatively small (compared to DoD in terms of budget and personnel) organization with a labyrinth of offices handling both regional and functional accounts. At times, the State and Defense Departments have been at odds over policy decisions while at other times there has been a great deal of synchronization between the two. During my last tour at the Pentagon serving as Deputy Under Secretary of Defense for Policy, then-Secretary of Defense James Mattis spoke regularly to the Secretary of State to coordinate policy positions. I rarely, if ever, attended a meeting in Secretary Mattis' office with a foreign delegation without the presence of a State Department official at the table — a condition upon which Mattis insisted. He was a strong advocate for the importance of the work of our State Department colleagues, often arguing that the purpose of the U.S. military was to create negotiating space for America's diplomats and telling

Congress, "If you don't fund the State Department fully, then I need to buy more ammunition ultimately."[133]

The Department of Defense is by far the largest of the national security agencies in government. The Pentagon building alone is the workplace for more than 25,000 employees and is said to be the largest office building in the world. It occupies more than six-and-one-half million square feet and is surrounded by 30 miles of access highways and 67 acres of parking space.[134]

The Secretary of Defense oversees the Department of Defense and is the principal advisor to the president on DoD matters. Within OSD, there are numerous Under Secretaries, Assistant Secretaries, and Deputy Assistant Secretaries responsible for national security policy. The organizational titles and responsibilities of these offices do not always correspond exactly to their State Department counterparts. For example, DoS has an Under Secretary for Arms Control and International Security Affairs and, within that organization, an Assistant Secretary for Arms Control, Verification and Compliance. In DoD, the Under Secretary of Defense for Policy oversees arms control policy issues, but compliance issues fall under the Under Secretary for Acquisition and Sustainment.

In addition, the JCS—and the Joint Staff that supports them—are responsible for assessing the military implications of various policy courses of action. By statute, the Chairman of the JCS is the principal military adviser to both the Secretary of Defense and the president. The other chiefs are the military leaders of their respective services. In

---

[133] Alex Lockie, "Mattis once said if State Department funding gets cut 'then I need to buy more ammunition'," *Business Insider*, 27 February 2017, available at https://www.businessinsider.com/mattis-state-department-funding-need-to-buy-more-ammunition-2017-2.

[134] Michaila Hancock, "Pentagon: the world's largest office building - in infographics," *Architects' Journal*, 27 August 2015, available at https://www.architectsjournal.co.uk/news/pentagon-the-worlds-largest-office-building-in-infographics/8688204.article.

1986, the Goldwater-Nichols Act elevated the role of the JCS by explicitly granting each service chief the right to provide military advice directly to the president rather than through the Chairman or Secretary of Defense as had been customary until then.[135] Goldwater-Nichols also placed the Secretary of Defense in the reporting chain between the commanders of the various geographic and functional combatant commands and the president.[136]

The Department of Homeland Security was an outgrowth of the September 11, 2001 terrorist attacks and was formally established in 2002. While the homeland security effort was intended "to prevent terrorist attacks within the United States, reduce America's vulnerability to terrorism, and minimize the damage and recover from attacks that do occur,"[137] the DHS mission statement today simply says the department "will safeguard the American people, our homeland, and our values."[138]

DHS was formed by consolidating nearly two dozen agencies and offices under the new organization. This includes the Transportation Security Administration (TSA), Federal Emergency Management Agency (FEMA), Secret Service, Customs and Border Patrol (CBP), and the Coast Guard.[139] DoD often provides support to elements of DHS, such as providing National Guard units to assist CBP with security along the southern border or defense support to civil authorities like FEMA after a natural disaster.

---

[135] Jordan, et al., *American National Security*, op. cit., p. 93.

[136] With the creation of the Space Force in 2019, there are now 11 geographical and functional combatant commands.

[137] Assistant Secretary of Defense for Homeland Defense and Global Security, "Frequently Asked Questions: Homeland Defense," available at https://policy.defense.gov/OUSDP-Offices/ASD-for-Homeland-Defense-Global-Security/Homeland-Defense-Integration-DSCA/faqs/.

[138] Department of Homeland Security Mission Statement, available at https://www.dhs.gov/photo/dhs-mission-statement.

[139] Jordan, et al., *American National Security*, op. cit., p. 126.

Although DHS has been in existence for nearly two decades, it is still a relatively new agency and the division of authorities between DHS and DoD occasionally requires written agreements between the two departments delineating their respective responsibilities.[140]

Finally, the intelligence community provides decision makers with the information necessary to help them make informed decisions on national security matters. The intelligence community, or "IC" ("eye see"), is not a homogeneous body but a collection of 16 separate intelligence agencies and entities, including the Central Intelligence Agency (CIA), National Reconnaissance Organization (NRO), National Geospatial-Intelligence Agency (NGA), National Security Agency (NSA), Defense Intelligence Agency (DIA), and the intelligence arms of the State and Treasury departments and the various military services. The role of the IC is to collect, analyze, produce, and disseminate information to those with a need to know.

The CIA was established by the National Security Act of 1947 and until recently its director was dual-hatted as both the head of the agency and the Director of Central Intelligence, a title that encompassed coordinating the activities of the other intelligence entities.[141] In 2004, Congress passed the "Intelligence Reform and Terrorism Prevention Act," creating the position of Director of

---

[140] For example, DoD and DHS signed a Memorandum of Agreement (MOA) on cybersecurity in 2010 and a Memorandum of Understanding (MOU) on cyber defense in 2018. See "Memorandum of Agreement Between The Department of Homeland Security and The Department of Defense Regarding Cybersecurity," September 2010, available at https://nsarchive2.gwu.edu/NSAEBB/NSAEBB424/docs/Cyber-037.pdf, and Jared Serbu, "DoD, DHS reach accord on new steps to cooperate in cyber defense," *Federal News Network*, 16 November 2018, available at https://federalnewsnetwork.com/cybersecurity/2018/11/dod-dhs-reach-accord-on-new-steps-to-cooperate-in-cyber-defense/.

[141] Jordan, et al., *American National Security*, op. cit., p. 157.

National Intelligence (DNI) to serve as "head of the intelligence community" and to "act as the principal adviser to the President, to the National Security Council, and the Homeland Security Council for intelligence matters related to the national security."[142] As President George W. Bush stated at the time:

> The DNI will have the authority to order the collection of new intelligence, to ensure the sharing of information among agencies and to establish common standards for the intelligence community's personnel. It will be the DNI's responsibility to determine the annual budgets for all national intelligence agencies and offices and to direct how these funds are spent. These authorities vested in a single official who reports directly to me will make all our intelligence efforts better coordinated, more efficient, and more effective.[143]

Policy Making and Coordination Structures

The National Security Council staff has the responsibility of developing U.S. national security policy and strategy for approval by the president, integrating all elements of national power to achieve U.S. strategic objectives, and overseeing the implementation of U.S. national security policies and programs by the various federal departments and agencies to ensure compliance with the

---

[142] Section 1011 of Public Law 108-458, "Intelligence Reform and Terrorism Prevention Act of 2004," 17 December 2004, available at https://www.govinfo.gov/content/pkg/PLAW-108publ458/pdf/PLAW-108publ458.pdf.

[143] Statement by President George W. Bush on Signing the Intelligence Reform and Terrorism Prevention Act, 17 December 2004, available at https://georgewbush-whitehouse.archives.gov/news/releases/2004/12/20041217-1.html.

administration's stated goals. The NSC staff traditionally brings together representatives from the main federal entities, including the IC, in meetings that take place at the Principal, Deputy, Under Secretary, and Assistant Secretary levels. These meetings often include agencies that may play only minor roles in the national security issues under discussion. Along with DoD and State, they can include the Departments of Commerce, Justice, and the Treasury, OMB, the Agency for International Development (USAID), and the U.S. Mission to the United Nations, among others.

In the Trump Administration, National Security Presidential Memorandum (NSPM)-4 established the organization of the National Security Council and Homeland Security Council (HSC—a parallel committee focused on homeland security matters). Although the nomenclature has varied from administration to administration, NSPM-4 continued the tradition of organizing meetings around a Principals Committee (PC), Deputies Committee (DC), and various Policy Coordinating Committees (PCCs). PC meetings involve Cabinet-level officials and are generally chaired by the National Security Advisor while DC meetings are usually chaired by the Deputy National Security Advisor with participants at the sub-Cabinet level.[144]

The National Security Council was created by the National Security Act of 1947. Although PC, DC, and PCC meetings are often referred to as "NSC" meetings, the NSC itself consists of only four statutory members: the President, Vice President, and Secretaries of State and Defense. Other department and agency heads attend regularly, some by invitation depending on the topic. The Director of National Intelligence and the Chairman of the Joint Chiefs of Staff are considered "statutory advisors" to the NSC.[145]   The

---

[144] National Security Presidential Memorandum-4, 4 April 2017, available at https://fas.org/irp/offdocs/nspm/nspm-4.pdf.
[145] Ibid.

difference between a PC meeting and an NSC meeting is the presence of the president. If the president attends a meeting with the principals, it is automatically considered an NSC meeting. If the president does not attend, it is a PC meeting.

The role of the NSC has fluctuated over the years. It can serve as an "honest broker," soliciting the opinions of the various agencies in order to present their respective views to the president to inform the decision-making process, or as an advocate, seeking to rally interagency support around a particular course of action. It is also responsible for communicating the views of the president to the interagency in order to ensure compliance with presidential policy directives and consistent messaging among the various government agencies.

At times, the NSC has become an operational arm of U.S. national security policy, for example, when during the Reagan Administration some NSC staff members became involved in operations involving the funneling of aid to anti-Communist resistance fighters in Latin America and seeking the release of U.S. hostages in the Middle East.[146] As Robert O'Brien, President Trump's National Security Advisor, has noted[147]:

> ...the NSC staff at the White House was intended to coordinate policy rather than run it. My job as the national security adviser is to distill and present to the president the views and options that come from the various departments and agencies. The NSC then ensures that those agencies actually execute the

---

[146] See Rep. Ed Jenkins and Robert H. Brink, "The National Security Council and the Iran-Contra Affair," *Georgia Journal of International and Comparative Law*, Vol. 18:19, 1988, pp. 19-44, available at https://digitalcommons.law.uga.edu/cgi/viewcontent.cgi?referer=http s://www.google.com/&httpsredir=1&article=1636&context=gjicl.

[147] O'Brien is President Trump's fourth National Security Advisor, succeeding LTG Michael Flynn (USA, Ret.), LTG H.R. McMaster (USA, Ret.), and Amb. John Bolton.

president's decisions. This is the "honest broker" model of the national security adviser, best personified by Brent Scowcroft, who held the post during both the Gerald Ford and George H.W. Bush administrations.

After consulting several of my predecessors and analyzing the NSC's current configuration, I have determined that the agency can and should be streamlined, and am in the process of restoring the NSC to its historical mission.

With the president's approval, we will reduce the NSC staff, making it more effective by reaffirming its mission to coordinate policy and ensure policy implementation.[148]

Though Congress has the power to create executive branch agencies, establish presidential and Cabinet-level reporting requirements, and withhold or condition funding for administration programs, its powers over the Executive Office of the President are not unlimited. During the impeachment process for President Trump over the suspension of military assistance to Ukraine, members of the president's inner circle of advisers, including the National Security Advisor, Deputy National Security Advisor, and director of OMB, refused to testify under subpoena before the HPSCI when the administration asserted "executive privilege" to prevent their appearance

---

[148] Robert C. O'Brien, "Here's how I will streamline Trump's National Security Council," *The Washington Post*, 16 October 2019, available at https://www.washingtonpost.com/opinions/robert-c-obrien-heres-how-i-will-streamline-trumps-national-security-council/2019/10/16/2b306360-f028-11e9-89eb-ec56cd414732_story.html.

and to withhold documents from the committee.[149]   The matter was referred to the courts for judicial resolution and again demonstrates the nature of the "struggle" between the executive and legislative branches of government.[150]

Issues that raise separation of powers concerns are often controversial and subject to challenge among the parties and adjudication in the courts.   The outcome of these disputes can have enormous consequences for the setting of U.S. national security policy.

---

[149] A letter on 8 October 2019 to House leadership from Pat A. Cipollone, Counsel to President Trump, stated that the House's impeachment inquiry "is constitutionally invalid and violates basic due process rights and the separation of powers." The letter is available here: https://games-cdn.washingtonpost.com/notes/prod/default/documents/7cb26618-e770-45ef-9c45-bdd5554ce201/note/9608d380-f0df-4e07-8b08-8f326b723626.pdf#page=1. Also, in a 15 October 2019 letter to House committee chairmen, Robert R. Hood, Assistant Secretary of Defense for Legislative Affairs stated that because of "legal and practical concerns" and the administration's stated objections, "the Department is unable to comply with your request for documents at this time." The full letter is available here: https://www.scribd.com/document/430591053/Pentagon-Letter-To-House-Democrats-On-Trump-Impeachment-Inquiry#download&from_embed.

[150] Some form of "executive privilege," which has been described as "the right of the President and high-level executive branch officers to withhold information from Congress, the courts, and ultimately the public," has been invoked by multiple presidents since the days of George Washington. See Mark J. Rozell, "Executive Privilege and the Modern Presidents: In Nixon's Shadow," *Minnesota Law Review*, Vol. 83, 1999, p. 1069, available at https://scholarship.law.umn.edu/cgi/viewcontent.cgi?article=2893&context=mlr. Also see Chris Calabrese, "When Presidents use executive privilege," *Constitution Daily*, National Constitution Center, 24 March 2017, available at https://constitutioncenter.org/blog/when-presidents-use-executive-privilege.

Limitations on the Exercise of Presidential Power

There are a multitude of constraints on the exercise of presidential power, to include the tension with Congress mentioned above as a result of the ongoing struggle for primacy in directing U.S. policy. Other constraints are not the result of congressional impetus or actions, but rather a consequence of other factors.[151]

For example, presidential decision making is often influenced by domestic public opinion. After all, presidents are directly accountable to the American people, and there is always an element of politics in presidential decision making, especially for a president seeking re-election; however, this is arguably more prevalent in domestic policy matters than with respect to national security policy. Presidential scholars have cited a weakening of the presidency as U.S. involvement in the Vietnam War dragged on and public opinion turned decidedly, and occasionally violently, against the war. President Nixon's resignation after the Watergate scandal is considered to have been one of the presidency's low points in contemporary American history. Public opinion also shifted substantially against President George W. Bush after the U.S. invasion of Iraq and the overthrow of Saddam Hussein, when the vast caches of weapons of mass destruction Saddam was thought to be hiding, and which was one of the expressed reasons for military action, were not found and U.S. casualties mounted following a rise in attacks by insurgents seeking to force the removal of U.S. forces from the region.

---

[151] The categorization of constraints that follows in this section is drawn from "Presidential Leadership and the Executive Branch," Chapter 4, in Jordan, et al., *American National Security*, op. cit., pp. 97-101.

Outside interest groups can also have a significant influence on presidential decision making. This, of course, is not unique to the executive branch, as scores of lobbyists, contractors, and non-governmental organizations (NGOs) also seek to influence congressional decision making.[152] In the 1990s, for example, various business groups argued strenuously for the administration to grant China permanent "Most Favored Nation" status—a preferential trade designation that would have opened the Chinese market to greater penetration by U.S. companies and businesses.

Perhaps not well recognized, but important nevertheless, is the effect the policies of past administrations can have on presidential decision making. President John F. Kennedy's decision to launch the ill-fated Bay of Pigs operation in Cuba in 1961 was enabled by planning conducted by his predecessor, President Eisenhower, and a desire not to look weak in dealing with the threat of a communist country 90 miles off the coast of Florida. President Barack Obama carried over many of the policies of his predecessor, George W. Bush, with respect to the "Global War on Terror." This included renditions of suspected terrorists, drone strikes, and keeping open the U.S. detention facility at Guantanamo Bay, Cuba.

Execution of the president's decisions can also be thwarted by a government bureaucracy predisposed toward inaction as a consequence of disagreements with administration policies. The U.S. government is a vast bureaucracy where actions can be slow-rolled or stymied by a variety of activities and behaviors. Selective "leaking" by anonymous sources often occurs in an effort to engender negative public opinion (as well as congressional opposition) to specific policies or plans. For example, portions of the classified Bush Administration's 2001

---

[152] The role of external actors in the congressional decision-making process is discussed in more detail in Chapter Nine.

Nuclear Posture Review and a draft of the Trump Administration's 2018 *Nuclear Posture Review* were leaked — with the apparent intent to generate opposition to the policies presented in those documents. More recently, the term "deep state" has entered the political lexicon to reflect a belief that unelected bureaucrats opposed to the president's policies are conspiring to overturn administration actions.[153]

Within the vast apparatus of government there is no unanimity on issues. Occasionally, officials at the State Department are at odds with their Defense Department counterparts. This, in part, is what the NSC process is intended to resolve. There are also instances where career civil servants hold different views from political appointees within their own agency. These internal executive branch disagreements often complicate the process of executing the president's stated policies and decisions.

There are also times when a president's actions are bounded by the actions of other countries. The Obama Administration felt the need to "reset" U.S. relations with Russia after Moscow's military conflict with Georgia in 2008 led to a marked deterioration in the relationship between the Kremlin and the George W. Bush Administration. President Obama's approach led to negotiation of the "New START" arms control treaty with Russia in 2010, intended to restore a degree of "stability" in the bilateral U.S.-Russia relationship. Moreover, the desire to seek as many coalition partners as possible prior to launching military actions — as evidenced in the 1991 Gulf War and in the subsequent military operations in Afghanistan and Iraq — often affects how the president exercises his role as Commander in Chief. The increasingly prevalent quest to obtain allied support for U.S. military operations can be a strong factor

---

[153] Charles S. Clark, "Deconstructing the Deep State," *Government Executive,* available at https://www.govexec.com/feature/gov-exec-deconstructing-deep-state/.

in determining under what conditions a president will commit the nation's armed forces to war, and whether U.S. military forces will remain engaged in areas of conflict without a certain level of allied and coalition support.

In these cases, the Congress will often seek to assert its influence as well on presidential decision making by reminding the Chief Executive that only Congress has the constitutional authority to declare war. This long-standing debate is part of the "struggle for the privilege of directing American foreign policy" that resonates to this day.

CHAPTER FIVE

HOW AND WHY CONGRESS SHAPES POLICY

What is it that drives members of Congress to take particular actions? What motivates them to support or oppose certain policies? Is it simple partisanship that determines where members come down on specific issues? The answers to these questions are more complicated than one might think.

Former Chairman of the Senate Foreign Relations Committee, Sen. Arthur H. Vandenberg (R-MI), is credited with coining the phrase "politics stops at the water's edge," meaning that American foreign policy interests and U.S. dealings with other nations should not be riven by partisan disagreements. This maxim is often cited by politicians of all political stripes to argue that foreign and national security policy is too important to be politicized or subjugated to the whims of any political "faction" over the common good. Some argue, however, that the "Vandenberg rule" has been "honored more in its breach than in its observance."[154]

Among the many drivers and motivators of congressional action are three in particular that deserve mention here: 1) constituent interests; 2) reelection prospects; and 3) personal beliefs and values.

Clearly, members of Congress are elected to represent the views of their constituents, and woe be to the member

---

[154] Owen Berger, "Does Politics Really Stop 'At the Water's Edge'?," *Nations & States*, 11 February 2016, available at https://nationsandstates.com/2016/02/11/does-politics-really-stop-at-the-waters-edge/.

who forgets or ignores this simple reality. However, occasionally the views of individual state or district constituents may not align with others' perceptions of the greater good, and members of Congress will need to decide whether to support the needs of the nation or the desires of the electorate that put them in the position to decide such weighty matters in the first place.

Members do take seriously the need to protect and advocate on behalf of the people in their district. They will often raise parochial issues in congressional hearings, even when the topic under discussion is clearly one of national rather than local importance. Questioning the Secretary of Defense at a budget hearing over the status of a military housing project in a member's district or about environmental remediation efforts at a particular military installation in a Senator's home state is a relatively common occurrence. In part, it allows individual members to raise issues their constituents care about directly to the most senior levels of government. It also sends a message to constituents that the member takes the interests of his electors seriously.

Members also focus on the economic aspects of national security policy. Numerous weapons systems are produced with parts manufactured in multiple congressional districts. The workforce involved in the F-35 Joint Strike Fighter program is distributed among 46 states.[155] The jobs benefit of "spreading the wealth" of the defense contracting process to multiple states helps ensure broad-based congressional support for critical (and sometimes non-critical) defense programs.

Occasionally, members will reflect the dominant mood of the general public on a particular issue if they perceive that the views of the average people in their district are not being adequately represented. This is often referred to as

---

[155] See https://www.f35.com/global/participation/united-states-who-we-are.

"populism." There have been numerous "populist" movements in American history that were portrayed as representing the interests of the "common man" in contrast to the "elite." The contemporary "Tea Party" movement, patterned after the Boston Tea Party of the American Revolution, reflected a conservative focus on shrinking the size of the federal government and the amount of money it spends.[156] The "Occupy" movement, which led to major protests against perceived economic and political injustice and resulted in the "occupation" of public buildings, parks, and institutions from New York to California, including on Wall Street, became a worldwide phenomenon. Rep. Nancy Pelosi (D-CA) expressed her support for the Occupy Wall Street movement, declaring, "I support the message to the establishment, whether it's Wall Street or the political establishment and the rest, that change has to happen."[157]

During election seasons, third-party candidates often appeal to populist sentiments. In 1912, President Theodore ("Teddy") Roosevelt ran for re-election on a progressive platform that advocated for populist reforms, arguing, "We believe that unless representative government does absolutely represent the people it is not representative government at all."[158] Robert La Follette, Sr. likewise stoked the flames of populist sentiment in 1924 when he ran for president as leader of the Progressive Party, having earlier

---

[156] "Tea Party Movement," *Encyclopædia Britannica*, updated 11 November 2019, available at https://www.britannica.com/topic/Tea-Party-movement.

[157] Jessica Desvarieux, "Pelosi Supports Occupy Wall Street Movement," ABC News, 9 October 2011, available at https://abcnews.go.com/Politics/pelosi-supports-occupy-wall-street-movement/story?id=14696893.

[158] Thomas Curwin, "Review: Theodore Roosevelt whipped up a frenzy of populism in 1912. We're still living with the consequences.," *Los Angeles Times*, 16 July 2016, available at https://www.latimes.com/books/reviews/la-ca-jc-cowan-people-rule-20160706-snap-story.html.

spoken out against U.S. involvement in World War I, a position he believed resonated among the populace.[159] More recently, David Duke, a former Grand Wizard of the Knights of the Ku Klux Klan, ran as the Populist Party's nominee for president in 1988, while Henry "Ross" Perot ran as an independent candidate for president in 1992, playing on popular disillusionment with the establishment party candidates.

The effect of populism on politics was a concern of the Founders, which is one reason Madison believed that a republic could better govern and control the "violence of faction" than a democracy. It also helps explain why the Senate was given a larger role in foreign policy decisions than the House, as Senators at the time were chosen by their state legislatures rather than by popular vote and served for longer terms, thereby minimizing the risk of having their views contaminated by "populist" appeals.

A telling example of how the views of local constituents may not always align with national priorities and how members of Congress can be conflicted in their approach to important national security issues can be found in the debate over the Panama Canal Treaty signed by President Jimmy Carter in 1977. Sen. Edward Zorinsky (D-NE), a supporter of the treaty, found himself at odds with his constituents, who favored maintaining U.S. control over the Canal Zone. Sen. Zorinsky invited President Carter to Nebraska to speak to his constituents, but they were not swayed. In the end, Zorinsky voted with his constituents and against the treaty.[160]

---

[159] "Robert M. La Follette," *Encyclopædia Britannica*, available at https://www.britannica.com/biography/Robert-M-La-Follette/Antiwar-position.

[160] Recounted in Lindsay, *Congress and the Politics of U.S. Foreign Policy*, op. cit., p. 33. Despite the fact that polls showed 60 percent of Americans against the treaty, the Senate approved it by a two-thirds majority.

Although members of Congress generally do not want to take the risk of offending their constituents, they also do not want to be seen as putting the nation at risk or being unpatriotic by supporting or opposing policies simply to curry favor with their constituents.   When first-term Congresswoman Elissa Slotkin (D-MI) announced to her constituents that she would vote in favor of impeaching President Trump, the reaction was strong and highly charged along partisan lines. In the face of the raw emotions on display when she announced her decision, she declared that "if this district sees fit to elect someone else, then I will accept that and walk away with my head held high that I've made decisions based on principle, and not political calculus."[161] As the lone Republican to cast a vote to remove President Trump from office, Sen. Mitt Romney (R-UT) noted that "there are people in my party and in my state who will strenuously disapprove of my decision," but that disregarding "my oath before God" would "expose my character to history's rebuke and the censor of my own conscience."[162]

The desire to get reelected is certainly a motivation for many in Congress, though as the example above suggests, it is not always determinative. Most Americans do not pay close attention to national security policy, which often involves events in other countries. Of greater concern are domestic policy issues that affect the everyday lives of average citizens. Few members of Congress are elected on foreign or national security platforms and most run for

---

[161] Sheryl Gay Stolberg, "Slotkin, Backing Impeachment, Draws Instant Protests, and Applause," *The New York Times*, 16 December 2019, available at
https://www.nytimes.com/2019/12/16/us/politics/slotkin-impeachment.html.

[162] See "Full transcript of Sen. Mitt Romney's Senate impeachment trial remarks," *The Salt Lake Tribune*, 5 February 2020, available at
https://www.sltrib.com/news/politics/2020/02/05/full-transcript-sen-mitt/.

office focusing on issues that more directly affect their constituents. This arguably gives members more flexibility to vote their conscience when it comes to national security issues.

Of course, there are exceptions to every rule, and occasionally foreign and national security policy concerns do rise to a level where they affect not only popular opinion but national elections, especially if they involve issues of war and peace. As popular sentiment turned increasingly against the war in Vietnam, a greater number of anti-war Senators were elected to office.[163] Both Presidents George H. W. Bush and George W. Bush saw their political futures affected by military conflicts—though the former's success in expelling Iraqi forces from Kuwait in the 1991 Gulf War was not enough to get him reelected while the latter saw public support turn against him despite the overthrow of Saddam Hussein, in part because of the failure to find large caches of WMD in Iraq and the growing number of U.S. casualties.

Members of Congress use various tactics to grab the headlines in ways that keep their names visible to their constituents. Political "grandstanding" to gain favorable attention is not uncommon. An iconic example of this occurred in 1987 when several members of Congress—in protest of Toshiba's illegal sale of submarine technology to the Soviet Union—stood outside the U.S. Capitol building with sledgehammers and smashed a Toshiba "boombox."[164] Members will also often take credit for sponsoring

---

[163] An interesting analysis of the reasons for this can be found in Paul Burstein and William Freudenburg, "Ending the Vietnam War: Components of Change in Senate Voting on Vietnam War Bills," *American Journal of Sociology*, Vol. 82, Number 5 (March 1977), pp. 991-1006.

[164] Lindsay, *Congress and the Politics of U.S. Foreign Policy*, op. cit., pp. 36, 136-137. Also see David Skidmore, "Rep. Bentley: None Dare Call It Toshiba," Associated Press, 2 July 1987, available at https://apnews.com/c5f3c744b7b368b7a83b895f43872afe.

legislation intended to improve the lives of citizens or strengthen U.S. national security. Those seeking reelection frequently target their constituents with information highlighting the number of bills they sponsored to make their voters' lives better. In the area of national defense, it is not uncommon for members to highlight their successes in facilitating military funding decisions that bring jobs to their states or districts.

Some members may be motivated, at least in part, by ties to a particular ethnic community. The three currently serving House members of Armenian descent, for example, were all co-sponsors of H. Res. 296, the "Armenian Genocide" Resolution that passed overwhelmingly in the House. Two of the three (Democrats Anna Eshoo and Jackie Speier) represent districts in California, which has the highest concentration of residents of Armenian descent in the nation. The third (Democrat Anthony Brindisi) represents a district in New York State, which ranks third in the number of Armenian Americans. Similarly, a bill praising Greece and condemning Turkey for its purchase of the S-400 air defense system from Russia, and a bill to end the arms embargo on Cyprus, were both co-sponsored by Rep. Gus Bilirakis (R-FL), a Greek American and member of the Congressional Hellenic-Israeli Alliance.[165]

Another driver of congressional behavior is a desire to seek higher office. Many members of Congress and Senators have sought to burnish their national security credentials in order to run for president. During the 2016 presidential campaign, former Senator Hillary Clinton (D-NY) declared that "as a member of the Armed Services Committee, I worked to maintain the best-trained, best-equipped, strongest military, ready for today's threats and tomorrow's.... I've stood up to adversaries like Putin and

---

[165] The first is H.R. 2913, the "Eastern Mediterranean Security and Energy Partnership Act of 2019" and the second is H.R. 4558, the "End the Cyprus Arms Embargo Act of 2019."

reinforced allies like Israel. I was in the Situation Room on the day we got bin Laden."[166] Former Senators Barack Obama and Joe Biden were elected president and vice president in 2008 and 2012. In a 2008 speech to the Democratic National Convention, Sen. Biden criticized the Bush Administration's foreign policy and highlighted the expertise he gained from serving in Congress, saying: "I've been on the ground in Georgia, Iraq, Pakistan, Afghanistan, and I can tell you in no uncertain terms: This administration's policy has been an abysmal failure."[167] The field of candidates running in the 2020 presidential race included at least seven current or former Senators and 10 current or former members of the House. Other members of Congress have "graduated" from the Hill to serve in Cabinet-level positions, such as the current Secretary of State Michael Pompeo and former Secretary of State John Kerry.

Although foreign and defense policy expertise is not usually determinative in national elections, having substantive background and experience in national security matters can be a net plus for members seeking to advance up the career ladder.

An additional factor that influences congressional behavior is the core set of values and beliefs a member holds. How members view the world and the U.S. role in it heavily influences their stand on foreign and national security policy issues. Those who believe "that government

---

[166] Sam Frizell, "Transcript: Read the Full Text of Hillary Clinton's Campaign Launch Speech," *Time*, 13 June 2015, available at https://time.com/3920332/transcript-full-text-hillary-clinton-campaign-launch/.

[167] "Transcript – Joseph R. Biden's Convention Speech," *The New York Times*, 27 August 2008, available at https://www.nytimes.com/2008/08/27/us/politics/27text-biden.html.

is best that governs least"[168] may support national security policies that align with libertarian principles. Some who think American policies have been responsible for much of the world's problems may favor large cuts in U.S. defense spending and oppose the development of new military capabilities. Others who fall in what has been termed the "America First" camp may question policies that are perceived as ceding American sovereignty to international institutions such as the United Nations.

Arguments over whether the United States should accede to the International Criminal Court, for example, often illustrate the tension between those who believe in the value of international frameworks and agreements and those who place primacy on ensuring that national sovereignty is not compromised by granting authority over U.S. actions to unaccountable international bodies. Sen. Ted Cruz (R-TX) has argued that the UN has "no power to bind the United States, and no President of the United States, Republican or Democrat, has the authority to give away our sovereignty."[169] This debate reflects a dichotomy between those who subscribe to a "realist" view of the international system and those who take an "idealist" view.[170] Elements

---

[168] Attributed in various forms to Thomas Jefferson, John Locke, or Henry David Thoreau. See Eugene Volokh, "Who first said, 'The best government is that which governs least'? Not Thoreau.," *The Washington Post*, 6 September 2017, available at
https://www.washingtonpost.com/news/volokh-conspiracy/wp/2017/09/06/who-first-said-the-best-government-is-that-which-governs-least-not-thoreau/.

[169] "Ted Cruz on Foreign Policy," *On The Issues*, citing a statement during the Republican primary debate, 16 September 2015, available at https://www.ontheissues.org/International/Ted_Cruz_Foreign_Policy .htm.

[170] For an excellent discussion of the differences between "realists" and "idealists" and how their contrasting views affect their respective national security approaches, see Keith B. Payne, "Realism, Idealism, Deterrence, and Disarmament," *Strategic Studies Quarterly*, Volume 13, Issue 3, Fall 2019, pp. 7-37, available at

of this debate can also be found in the arguments of those who support an "isolationist" or "interventionist" foreign policy.

Fundamental beliefs that shape a member's worldview have also been evident in major national security debates involving U.S. defense posture and arms control. There are those who believe nuclear weapons pose the greatest threat to humanity and must ultimately be eliminated. They see nuclear arms control agreements as an important tool for regulating strategic competition between Russia and the United States and a necessary first step toward eventual elimination of nuclear weapons. Senators Robert Menendez (D-NJ), Edward Markey (D-MA), and others have been highly critical of the Trump Administration for withdrawing the United States from the landmark 1987 Intermediate-range Nuclear Forces (INF) Treaty as a result of Russian cheating and for what they perceive as an abandonment of arms control efforts more generally.[171]

Others believe that peace and stability are best assured, not by paper agreements with a party that has a history of violating its obligations, but by maintaining American strength. Ronald Reagan's maxim of "peace through strength" is often cited by those who place more faith in the power of American military might than the power of persuasion or diplomacy when it comes to keeping the peace and deterring aggression by adversaries.[172] Lengthy

---

https://www.airuniversity.af.edu/Portals/10/SSQ/documents/Volume-13_Issue-3/Payne.pdf.

[171] Sen. Markey, for example, called the decision "the absolute wrong approach" that would lead to "a tit-for-tat arms race that everyone will lose." See Press Release, "Senator Markey Blasts President Trump's INF Treaty Decision," 4 December 2018, available at https://www.markey.senate.gov/news/press-releases/senator-markey-blasts-president-trumps-inf-treaty-decision.

[172] The debate between the value of diplomacy versus military strength to keep the peace has gone on for decades, even finding its way into the nation's science fiction culture. In 1967, for example, an episode in the

congressional debates took place in the 1970s and 1980s between "hawks" and "doves" over arms control and defense policy. Since the end of the Cold War, many of these issues have garnered less attention among the general public, but for some members of Congress few issues are as serious as these.

Other factors, of course, come into play as influencers of congressional behavior and actions. Among them are party loyalty, religious beliefs, and pressure campaigns conducted by external interest groups—including those with money to contribute to campaign coffers. (The role of external interest groups is discussed in more detail in Chapter Nine.)

Tools for Influencing Policy

Congressional scholars often refer to two types of legislation: "substantive legislation" and "procedural legislation." In the foreign policy realm, the first "specifies what the content of policy will be" while the latter "targets the structures and procedures by which foreign policy is made."[173] Congress influences foreign and national security policy through both types of legislative actions.

---

original "*Star Trek*" television series entitled, "A Taste of Armageddon," had the Enterprise's chief engineer Montgomery Scott ("Scotty") disparaging diplomatic efforts to end a 500-year-long war between two planets with the comment, "The best diplomat I know is a fully activated phaser bank." See "A Taste of Armageddon" transcript, 23 February 1967, available at http://www.chakoteya.net/StarTrek/23.htm.

[173] Lindsay, *Congress and the Politics of U.S. Foreign Policy*, op. cit., p. 99.

The Treaty-Making Process

One of the most significant and substantive ways Congress can influence foreign and national security policy is through its role in the treaty process. International treaties carry the force of law, so they bind the United States legally. Arms control treaties, like other types of treaties, are negotiated by the executive branch but require the "advice and consent" of the Senate. This means that Senators can have an outsized influence on major administration foreign policy initiatives.

After President Obama signed the New START arms control treaty in 2010, the Senate, in its Resolution of Ratification, included numerous conditions, declarations, and understandings defining its interpretation of the treaty and how it should be implemented. In order to obtain the necessary Senate votes for approval in the face of strong Senate concern over the U.S. nuclear weapons program, the administration pledged to carry out an extensive nuclear modernization effort. In the end, the Senate approved the treaty by a vote of 71-26.[174] Unlike the actual treaty text, a Senate Resolution of Ratification is not legally binding, though the conditions and interpretations the Senate places on its consent to ratification may lead to legal challenges down the road if the administration acts in a manner that conflicts with the Senate's understanding of the agreement.[175]

As previously noted, only the Senate was given the power to vote on the ratification of treaties. The House was considered to be too lacking in stature and too subject to the

---

[174] The Resolution of Ratification, passed on 22 December 2010, can be found at https://2009-2017.state.gov/documents/organization/154123.pdf.

[175] See, for example, discussion of the Reagan Administration's "broad interpretation" of the ABM Treaty referenced in Chapters One and Eleven.

whims of popular opinion to be entrusted with this grave responsibility. In *Federalist 64*, John Jay argued that treaty-making power should "be exercised by men the best qualified for the purpose" and that Senators, "whose reputation for integrity inspires and merits confidence," were best suited to the task. "With such men the power of making treaties may be safely lodged," Jay argued.[176]

President Washington's Senate encounter over the treaty with the Creek Indians, recounted in Chapter Two, is only one example of how the Founders' decision to split treaty-making power between the Chief Executive and the Senate is a reflection of the constitutional "struggle" between the president and Congress. Over the years, the Senate has swung, pendulum-like, between approving treaties as negotiated and aggressively challenging or modifying them. James Lindsay notes that during the first two centuries of the Republic, the Senate showed relative deference toward the president, approving 90 percent of the treaties presented to it by the requisite two-thirds vote.[177] With more than 1,500 treaties approved since the nation's early days, this is a sizable collection of agreements establishing the parameters of U.S. relations with other countries.

Nevertheless, the Senate has occasionally been strongly assertive in refusing to go along with the president's treaty desires. Between 1789 and 1992, the Senate refused to act on more than 100 treaties, leaving them in ratification purgatory. Moreover, during this same time period, Senators soundly rejected nearly two dozen treaties, including the treaty of Versailles that ended World War I (the first instance of Senatorial rejection of a peace treaty), the establishment of the World Court, and the UN

---

[176] John Jay, *Federalist 64*, "The Powers of the Senate From the New York Packet," 7 March 1788, available at
https://avalon.law.yale.edu/18th_century/fed64.asp.

[177] Lindsay, *Congress and the Politics of U.S. Foreign Policy*, op. cit., p. 79.

Convention on the Law of the Sea.[178] Some treaties were only approved by the Senate after many years of languishing without action. The Geneva Protocol (formally called "The Protocol for the Prohibition of the Use in War of Asphyxiating, Poisonous or other Gases, and of Bacteriological Methods of Warfare") was signed in 1925 but not ratified by the United States until half a century later in 1975.

The Senate has also seen fit to modify or amend treaties before consenting to their ratification. Until 1868, a two-thirds vote was required to modify a treaty. Senators then rewrote the rules of the Senate to allow treaties to be amended by majority vote. The 1977 Panama Canal Treaty was amended by the Senate to affirm America's right to intervene if the security of the canal was threatened. Some amendments are considered "killer amendments" if they so fundamentally change the nature of the underlying agreement that the other parties to it or the U.S. Administration would refuse to agree. One such amendment would have allowed U.S. forces to remain in the Canal Zone for 20 years after sovereignty had been transferred to Panama. A proposed amendment to the INF Treaty would have required President Reagan to certify that the Soviet Union was in compliance with all its other treaty obligations before the INF Treaty could take effect. More than 40 treaties had been rejected by 1992 as a result of such "killer amendments."[179]

---

[178] Ibid., p. 79. Also see Robert C. Byrd, *The Senate 1789-1989, Historical Statistics 1789-1992*, Wendy Wolff, editor, Volume 4 (U.S. Government Printing Office, Washington, D.C., 1993), p. 730, available at https://books.google.com/books?id=2AJP1fQkiMQC&pg=PA730&lpg =PA730&dq=ellen+collier+senate+rejection+of+treaties&source=bl&ots =GZo8YsD7TE&sig=ACfU3U1jcZtDRuREfOm5naiYc9Bc0WqWBA&hl= en&sa=X&ved=2ahUKEwj8h9_YxszmAhUQjVkKHcQxAxkQ6AEwAH oECAgQAQ#v=onepage&q=ellen%20collier%20senate%20rejection%20 of%20treaties&f=false.

[179] Lindsay, *Congress and the Politics of U.S. Foreign Policy,* op. cit., p. 81.

It is generally difficult to withdraw from a legally binding treaty once ratified. Most treaties, including arms control treaties, contain a "supreme interests" clause that allows a party to withdraw from its obligations if conditions change such that its supreme interests are jeopardized by continued adherence. However, this clause is infrequently exercised. There are only two instances in recent years where the United States withdrew from arms control treaties. The first is when President George W. Bush withdrew from the 1972 U.S.-Soviet ABM Treaty (mentioned in Chapter One); the second is when President Trump withdrew from the aforementioned INF Treaty in 2019. In neither case did the United States abrogate the agreement or violate its terms. Instead, the United States complied with the withdrawal provisions as stipulated in the treaties by giving six months' advance notice to the other party (Russia).

Although the Constitution requires Senatorial consent to treaties, it is silent on the process for withdrawing from them. In the two cases mentioned above, some in Congress argued that if the Senate has a constitutional right to weigh in before a treaty can enter into force, it should also have the right to do so before a president can unilaterally withdraw from it. Those who subscribe to this view sometimes cite Thomas Jefferson's statement that "Treaties being declared, equally with the laws of the United States, to be the supreme law of the land, it is understood that an act of the legislature alone can declare them infringed and rescinded." This argument, however, does not enjoy universal acceptance among legal scholars and has not been upheld by the courts.[180]

---

[180] See, for example, Russell Feingold, "Donald Trump can unilaterally withdraw from treaties because Congress abdicated responsibility," NBC Think, 7 May 2018, available at https://www.nbcnews.com/think/opinion/donald-trump-can-

Similarly, some have criticized presidential decisions to make unilateral agreements on national security issues by arguing such agreements can only be made as a consequence of the Senate's treaty-making power. For example, some in Congress were highly critical of the Clinton Administration's 1994 "Agreed Framework" with North Korea, which was intended to prevent Pyongyang from developing nuclear weapons but was not a formal treaty.[181] Critics of the Obama Administration's 2015 Iran nuclear deal argued that the agreement not only was flawed but should have been submitted to the Senate for its advice and consent. Two prominent critics of the Obama Administration's national security policies argued:

> ...agreements that extend beyond a president's time in office or make long-term commitments of U.S. sovereignty must undergo the Article II treaty process. An enduring non-aggression pact, or even a unilateral commitment not to use American force on a lasting basis, demands the participation of other branches of government. Together with ending economic sanctions (which Iran will demand), these commitments would work a significant change in the U.S.–Iran relationship that is tantamount to a peace treaty. Peace agreements should receive Senate approval. Only the cooperation of the executive and legislative branches of government over time can ensure that

---

unilaterally-withdraw-treaties-because-congress-abdicated-responsibility-ncna870866.

[181] Glenn Kessler, "History lesson: Why did Bill Clinton's North Korea deal fail?," *The Washington Post*, 9 August 2017, available at https://www.washingtonpost.com/news/fact-checker/wp/2017/08/09/history-lesson-why-did-bill-clintons-north-korea-deal-fail/.

the U.S. will live up to restrictions on its sovereignty.[182]

In a 2013 letter to Vice President Joe Biden, Chairman of the House Armed Services Committee's Strategic Forces Subcommittee, Rep. Mike Rogers (R-AL), wrote that the Obama Administration's plans for additional nuclear weapons reductions required congressional consent. He noted that years before, then-Senator Biden had stated "with the exception of the SALT 1 agreement, every significant arms control agreement during the past three decades has been transmitted to the Senate pursuant to the Treaty Clause of the Constitution" and that "we see no reason whatsoever to alter this practice."[183]

Executive Agreements

One way a president can seek to avoid extensive congressional interference in the process of negotiating agreements with foreign countries is to conclude an "executive agreement." This kind of agreement can be concluded either by the president alone (a "sole executive agreement") or with the approval of Congress (a "legislative-executive agreement"). Neither the Constitution nor *The Federalist Papers* mention executive agreements, yet they have become increasingly common in the conduct of foreign affairs as they do not require a two-thirds vote of approval by the Senate.

---

[182] John R. Bolton and John Yoo, "Advice on 'Advice and Consent,'" *National Review*, 31 December 2014, available at https://www.nationalreview.com/2014/12/advice-advice-and-consent-john-r-bolton-john-yoo/.

[183] Cited in Josh Rogin, "No Word From Russia as Obama Will Announce U.S. Nuclear Reductions," *Daily Beast*, 11 July 2017, available at https://www.thedailybeast.com/no-word-from-russia-as-obama-will-announce-us-nuclear-reductions?ref=scroll.

The president has the authority as the nation's Chief Executive and Commander in Chief to negotiate executive agreements. Though attempts have been made to clarify the criteria for negotiating treaties vice executive agreements, scholars believe there is no substantive difference between them, other than the role Congress plays in their approval.[184]

Understandably, the use of executive agreements has not always been looked upon favorably by congressional overseers of administration policy. From time to time, Congress has attempted to limit the president's ability to use executive agreements as a means of constraining the unilateral exercise of presidential power. In the 1950s and 1960s, multiple attempts to limit presidential authority to negotiate executive agreements unilaterally failed. In 1972, Congress passed the Case-Zablocki Act, which required the president to notify Congress of executive agreements within two months after implementation, yet the president's ability to negotiate such agreements remained relatively unconstrained.[185]

In some cases, executive agreements are required by law, such as for trade agreements and agreements on civil nuclear cooperation with other countries (so-called "123" agreements).   In other cases, the president has sole discretion whether to conclude an agreement as an executive agreement or a treaty.   Examples of executive agreements include: a U.S. military basing agreement with the UK in 1940; the 1945 Yalta and Potsdam agreements at the end of World War II; the Vietnam peace accord in 1973; the Sinai agreements in 1975; a U.S.-Russia chemical weapons destruction agreement in 1990 (done as a legislative-executive agreement with congressional approval); and the North American Free Trade Association

---

[184] Lindsay, *Congress and the Politics of U.S. Foreign Policy,* op. cit., p. 82.
[185] Ibid., pp. 83-84.

(NAFTA) agreement in 1993. The aforementioned Iran nuclear deal (formally the "Joint Comprehensive Plan of Action") was described by the Obama Administration as neither a treaty nor an executive agreement but a series of "political commitments."[186]

In short, the president has tremendous flexibility in negotiating agreements with other countries; however, the Congress has repeatedly sought to bound the limits of that flexibility in ways that enhance its own ability to set the parameters of U.S. foreign and national security policy.

Procedural Actions

Besides substantive legislative action on treaties, the Congress can also use procedural legislation to enact its national security priorities. One way of doing this is through the creation of executive branch agencies to focus on congressional agenda items of interest.

In 1961, Congress (with support of the Kennedy Administration) created the Arms Control and Disarmament Agency (ACDA) "to strengthen the national security of the United States by formulating, advocating, negotiating, implementing and verifying effective arms control, nonproliferation, and disarmament policies, strategies, and agreements."[187] At the height of the Cold War, ACDA was seen as an independent voice for arms control efforts to manage the strategic arms competition with the Soviet Union. It was disestablished in 1999, though

---

[186] Matthew Weybrecht, "State Department Affirms That Iran Deal Is Only a Political Commitment," *Lawfare*, 28 November 2015, available at https://www.lawfareblog.com/state-department-affirms-iran-deal-only-political-commitment.

[187] See ACDA mission statement in the National Archives Federal Register, available at https://www.federalregister.gov/agencies/arms-control-and-disarmament-agency.

there are some today who favor its reincarnation to address contemporary nuclear arms control issues.[188]

More recently, the National Nuclear Security Administration (NNSA) was established by Congress in the National Defense Authorization Act for Fiscal Year 2000 (despite the Clinton Administration's opposition to the NNSA's charter and responsibilities).[189] The NNSA, a semi-autonomous entity within the Department of Energy (DOE) whose administrator reports directly to the Secretary of Energy, was created in the wake of congressional concerns over lax nuclear security at DOE and the theft of U.S. nuclear secrets by China. NNSA is "responsible for enhancing national security through the military application of nuclear science." It is also charged with maintaining the efficacy of the U.S. nuclear stockpile and working to reduce the threat of the proliferation of weapons of mass destruction.[190]

Additionally, as noted in Chapter Three, Congress created the position of Deputy Under Secretary of Defense for Technology Security Policy to focus on the congressional priority of ensuring sensitive U.S. military technology did not fall into the hands of potential U.S. adversaries. And more recently, Congress eliminated the Office of the Under Secretary of Defense for Acquisition, Technology, and Logistics (AT&L), dividing its responsibilities into two separate entities—the Under Secretary of Defense for

---

[188] See, for example, Rebecca Davis Gibbons, "Bring back the Arms Control and Disarmament Agency," *The Hill*, 3 October 2019, available at https://thehill.com/opinion/national-security/463757-bring-back-the-arms-control-and-disarmament-agency.

[189] See William J. Clinton, "Statement on Signing the National Defense Authorization Act for Fiscal Year 2000," 5 October 1999, available at https://www.presidency.ucsb.edu/documents/statement-signing-the-national-defense-authorization-act-for-fiscal-year-2000.

[190] National Nuclear Security Administration, "About NNSA," available at https://www.energy.gov/nnsa/about-nnsa.

Acquisition and Sustainment (A&S) and the Under Secretary of Defense for Research and Engineering (R&E).

These procedural actions are part of Congress' effort to ensure it is not always at a disadvantage in its struggle with the executive branch to direct American national security policy.

CHAPTER SIX

THE EBB AND FLOW OF CONGRESSIONAL INFLUENCE AND EXECUTIVE POWER

Discerning which branch of government predominates in crafting U.S. national security policy is not always easy. Much depends on the specific issues under consideration. On various issues and at various times, Congress has sought to be more assertive in exercising its authorities on key national security questions, though greater assertiveness has not always translated into greater influence.

For members of Congress, there is always some risk in challenging the president on national security policy. In part, this is due to a popular belief that the president knows best what is in the national security interest. Moreover, the cacophony of competing voices on Capitol Hill does not engender confidence among the general public that Congress is a more capable arbiter of American national security interests than the president. However, members who challenge the president on foreign and national security policy may do so in the belief that disagreements on such weighty issues with which the public is generally unfamiliar will place them at less risk than disagreements on domestic policy, which is usually of more interest to constituents.

In the formulation and guidance of foreign and national security policy, the president is generally assumed to hold an advantage over Congress. In President Theodore Roosevelt's words, the president commands the "bully pulpit," a phrase coined to express the president's ability to drive an agenda.[191]   As the Commander in Chief of the nation's armed forces, the president is considered to be the single authority responsible for the affairs of state and the security of the country. As the head of state and the head of government, the president can initiate foreign policy decisions, including those involving the use of military force abroad.

The importance of leaving such weighty decisions in the hands of a single authority was articulated by Alexander Hamilton in *Federalist 70* where he wrote, "That unity is conducive to energy will not be disputed. Decision, activity, secrecy, and despatch will generally characterize the proceedings of one man in a much more eminent degree than the proceedings of any greater number; and in proportion as the number is increased, these qualities will be diminished."[192]   As President Woodrow Wilson would later note: "The initiative in foreign affairs, which the President possesses without any restriction whatever, is virtually the power to control them absolutely."[193]

Congress' ability to influence national security policy has ebbed and flowed depending on the circumstances and the issue under consideration.   James Lindsay has characterized Congress' role in foreign policy as one of "timidity," noting that "the doubts members have about

---

[191] See "Federal Power: Theodore Roosevelt," Bill of Rights Institute, available at https://billofrightsinstitute.org/educate/educator-resources/lessons-plans/presidents-constitution/federal-power-theodore-roosevelt/.

[192] Alexander Hamilton, "The Executive Department Further Considered," *Federalist 70*, available at https://avalon.law.yale.edu/18th_century/fed70.asp.

[193] Cited in Donald R. Wolfensberger, "Woodrow Wilson, Congress & Foreign Policy: The Education of a Neophyte - An Introductory Essay," Seminar at the Woodrow Wilson International Center for Scholars, 17 October 2011, available at https://www.wilsoncenter.org/sites/default/files/Cong-FP-intro-essay.pdf.

their competence in foreign policy stem partly from their lack of experience."[194]   Indeed, the number of members of Congress with military experience has steadily decreased since the 1970s, with only 96 veterans serving in the 116th Congress in 2019.[195] Some analysts believe that those members who are veterans are more likely to favor an assertive congressional posture in national security matters and more willing to challenge the president's proclivities to act unilaterally.[196]

In some cases, Congress must act affirmatively before national security decisions can be implemented.   The Senate's treaty role is one example of this.   In other cases, the president can implement decisions taken unilaterally unless the Congress acts to block or prohibit them.   The implementation of "123 agreements" on civil nuclear cooperation negotiated by the executive branch, for example, takes effect automatically unless Congress moves to block them.

Some scholars also see a difference in Congress' ability to influence national security policy depending on whether the issue is of long-term or short-term consequence. James Lindsay refers to the difference between longer-term "strategic policy," which Congress can more readily influence due to its ability to write legislation and make

---

[194] Lindsay, *Congress and the Politics of U.S. Foreign Policy*, op. cit., pp. 141-142.

[195] Leo Shane, III, "Veterans in the 116th Congress, by the numbers," *Military Times*, 20 November 2018 (updated on 18 December 2018), available at https://www.militarytimes.com/news/pentagon-congress/2018/11/21/veterans-in-the-116th-congress-by-the-numbers/.

[196] See, for example, Danielle Lupton, "Having fewer veterans in Congress makes it less likely to restrain the president's use of force," *The Washington Post*, 10 November 2017, available at https://www.washingtonpost.com/news/monkey-cage/wp/2017/11/10/fewer-veterans-serve-in-congress-every-term-that-makes-congress-less-likely-to-rein-in-the-presidents-use-of-force/.

structural changes that limit the president's flexibility, and shorter-term "crisis policy," where the president can utilize his or her authority as Commander in Chief to deploy military forces to deal with an urgent crisis or contingency with less risk of congressional meddling or second-guessing.[197]

The Congressional Research Service has identified six distinct ways in which the president can make foreign policy and six ways the Congress can craft foreign policy.[198] However, the delineation is not always neat and clean. While the president's actions can spark a congressional reaction that nullifies or seriously constrains the president's objectives, Congress' actions can likewise prompt a reaction by the Chief Executive that can have unanticipated consequences for the implementation of congressional programs and priorities.

Recent history shows the ebb and flow of congressional activism with respect to the foreign and national security decision-making process. Some scholars believe the passage of the Gulf of Tonkin Resolution in 1964 was "the nadir of congressional influence over foreign policy."[199] This resolution stated: "Congress approves and supports the determination of the President, as Commander in Chief,

---

[197] Lindsay, *Congress and the Politics of U.S. Foreign Policy,* op. cit., pp. 147-156.

[198] The president can make foreign policy by 1) responding to foreign events; 2) submitting legislative proposals; 3) negotiating international agreements; 4) making policy statements; 5) implementing policy actions; and 6) acting independently of Congress. The Congress can make foreign policy by 1) passing resolutions and policy statements; 2) imposing legislative mandates; 3) applying pressure; 4) restricting or cutting off funding; 5) providing informal advice; and 6) exercising oversight. For a detailed description of these roles, see "Foreign Policy Roles of the President and Congress," Congressional Research Service, CRS Report RL30193, 1 June 1999, available at https://www.everycrsreport.com/files/19990601_RL30193_2046177bba d4fcb65cba6f9025d53bf6479d2afd.pdf.

[199] Lindsay, *Congress and the Politics of U.S. Foreign Policy,* op. cit., p. 23.

to take all necessary measures to repel any armed attack against the forces of the United States and to prevent further aggression."[200] This action essentially gave the president a free hand to build up U.S. forces in Vietnam. In the 1970s, however, Congress began to exercise its foreign and defense policy authority more aggressively.

Congressional activism in arms control policy, for example, ebbed and flowed in the 1970s, as the Senate debated the first two strategic arms limitation treaties (SALT I and SALT II). SALT I, concluded by the Nixon Administration in 1972, was overwhelmingly approved by the Senate by a vote of 88 to 2. SALT II, however, was extremely controversial and President Carter withdrew it from Senate consideration after the Soviet invasion of Afghanistan in 1979, though opponents of the treaty, including Senator Henry "Scoop" Jackson (D-WA), concluded that it did not have the votes to pass anyway. Jackson called SALT II "a license for a massive buildup in strategic arms" that placed the United States at a strategic disadvantage vis-à-vis the Soviet Union. In a report on the treaty, the Senate Armed Services Committee concluded it "is not in the national security interests of the United States."[201]

Other strategic nuclear force issues garnered significant congressional attention.   For example, U.S. nuclear targeting policy in the 1970s was an issue that generated significant interest in the Senate. One analyst stated that the Senate "attempted to become informed about the details of proposed U.S. [nuclear] policy" and "did not passively

---

[200] Transcript of Tonkin Gulf Resolution (1964), available at https://www.ourdocuments.gov/doc.php?flash=false&doc=98&page=transcript.

[201] Robert G. Kaiser, "Senate Committee Says SALT Not in America's Best Interest," *The Washington Post*, 21 December 1979, available at https://www.washingtonpost.com/archive/politics/1979/12/21/senate-committee-says-salt-not-in-americas-best-interest/4052ff7e-8ddd-465a-b586-2533449e0a2e/.

support the executive's proposals but actively debated, questioned, and challenged them."[202]   Decades later, the Senate again demonstrated it was not a "rubber stamp" for executive branch arms control priorities when in 1999 it voted down the Comprehensive Test Ban Treaty (CTBT) — an agreement that would have permanently banned nuclear testing. Sen. Jesse A. Helms (R-NC) called the CTBT "the most egregious treaty ever submitted to the Senate for advice and consent," while then-Senate Minority Leader Thomas A. Daschle (D-SD) called the rejection "a terrible, terrible mistake."[203]

More recently, however, concerns have again been raised over the appropriate balance of power between the executive and legislative branches. In a February 2020 open letter to the Senate, a bipartisan group of 70 former Senators argued that "Congress is not fulfilling its constitutional duties" and is "ceding its powers to the executive." They blamed the "partisan gridlock that is all too routine in recent decades" for allowing the executive branch "to effectively 'legislate' on its own terms through executive order and administrative regulation," noting, "The Senate's abdication of its legislative and oversight responsibilities erodes the checks and balances of the separate powers that are designed to protect the liberties on which our democracy depends."[204]

---

[202] Alan Platt, *The U.S. Senate and Strategic Arms Policy, 1969-1977*, (Westview Press, Boulder, Colorado), 1978, pp. 91-92.

[203] Helen Dewar, "Senate Rejects Test Ban Treaty," *The Washington Post*, 14 October 1999, p. A1, available at https://www.washingtonpost.com/wp-srv/politics/daily/oct99/senate14.htm.

[204] "70 former U.S. senators: The Senate is failing to perform its constitutional duties," *The Washington Post*, 25 February 2020, available at https://www.washingtonpost.com/opinions/former-us-senators-the-senate-is-failing-to-perform-its-constitutional-duties/2020/02/25/b9bdd22a-5743-11ea-9000-f3cffee23036_story.html.

Judicial Branch Actions

Sometimes the struggle between the executive and legislative branches is referred to the courts for resolution. This usually happens when the Congress feels that the Chief Executive has overstepped his constitutional authorities.[205] Occasionally, cases get elevated all the way to the U.S. Supreme Court; however, the Supreme Court has generally ruled in favor of the president.

In an often cited 1936 case, Supreme Court Justice George Sutherland noted that "the President [operates] as the sole organ of the federal government in the field of international relations."[206] The high court's deference to executive authority has been in evidence repeatedly since then. In 1979, for example, the Supreme Court justified its dismissal of a legal challenge to President Carter's decision to end the U.S.-Taiwan mutual defense treaty by saying its action was necessary "because it involves the authority of the President in the conduct of our country's foreign relations."[207]

---

[205] During the House's impeachment inquiry against President Trump, the White House asserted executive privilege ("absolute immunity") in refusing to allow officials to testify when subpoenaed to appear by Congress. Despite the Congress' insistence that refusal to appear was evidence of "obstruction," the president's former National Security Advisor John Bolton and Deputy National Security Advisor Charles M. Kupperman appealed to the courts for a ruling on whether they were compelled to testify under subpoena. See, for example, the letter to Pat. A. Cipollone, Counsel to the President, from Steven A. Engel, Assistant Attorney General, Office of Legal Counsel, Department of Justice, 25 October 2019, available at https://www.justsecurity.org/wp-content/uploads/2019/11/ukraine-clearinghouse-white-house-letter-to-kupperman-10.25.19.pdf.

[206] United States v. Curtiss-Wright Export Corp., 299 U.S. 304 (1936), available at https://supreme.justia.com/cases/federal/us/299/304/. Also cited in Lindsay, *Congress and the Politics of U.S. Foreign Policy*, op. cit., p. 144.

[207] Ibid.

In some cases, the courts have ruled that lawsuits challenging the actions of the president were "nonjusticiable," meaning that they involved matters that were inherently political rather than legal and did not merit judicial decision. Various lawsuits challenging the constitutionality of the Vietnam War were brought before the judicial branch of government, only to be dismissed as nonjusticiable; not one made it as far as the Supreme Court.[208] Scholars have interpreted the courts' actions as giving the president a decided advantage over Congress when it comes to setting the course of American foreign and national security policy.

War Powers

One of the most contentious areas of national security policy where Congress and the president frequently clash is over the use of military force abroad. As previously noted, Congress has the sole authority to declare war but has only done so a handful of times, while the president has sent U.S. troops into harm's way around the globe more than a hundred times.

In debate during the Constitutional Convention in 1787, James Madison argued that the Constitution should grant Congress the authority to "declare war," and not to "make war," since the president should have the power "to repel sudden attacks."[209] The issue of who has authority to commit U.S. military forces to hostilities is hotly debated even today. For example, the ongoing struggle to ensure the lasting defeat of the Islamic State of Iraq and Syria (ISIS) is being waged under congressional authorizations for the

---

[208] Ibid.

[209] See "The Heritage Guide to the Constitution," available at https://www.heritage.org/constitution/#!/articles/1/essays/49/declare-war.

use of military force dating back to 2001 and 2002. Various members of Congress have complained that those resolutions, adopted after the September 11, 2001 terrorist attacks, were intended to authorize military actions against al-Qaeda, not ISIS, and that the ongoing war against terrorism should be approved by Congress through a new Authorization for the Use of Military Force (AUMF) resolution.[210]

Opposition to the president's use of military force without prior congressional authorization has traditionally been bipartisan, with many in Congress seeing such action as usurping Congress' constitutional mandate to declare war. President Obama's decision to conduct air strikes against Libya in 2011, intended to prevent a potential massacre of civilians by Libyan strongman Col. Muammar Gadhafi's forces, prompted a bipartisan lawsuit by Reps. Walter Jones (R-NC), Dennis Kucinich (D-OH), and eight other members of Congress. Rep. Kucinich argued that President Obama should be impeached as a result.[211] The air strikes also led the House to pass various resolutions of disapproval, including H. Res. 292, which declared that the "President has failed to provide Congress with a compelling rationale" for military intervention in Libya and stated that the "President shall not deploy, establish, or maintain the presence of units and members of the United States Armed

---

[210] Senators Tim Kaine (D-VA) and Rand Paul (R-KY) have been among the Senate's most vocal supporters of a new AUMF that would give congressional blessing to ongoing U.S. military operations against ISIS. See "Kaine Statement On 17th Anniversary of 2002 AUMF," available at https://www.kaine.senate.gov/press-releases/kaine-statement-on-17th-anniversary-of-2002-aumf, and statement by Sen. Paul during debate on the National Defense Authorization Act for Fiscal Year 2018, available at https://fas.org/irp/congress/2017_cr/paul-aumf.html.

[211] Jennifer Epstein, "Kucinich: Libya action 'impeachable'," *Politico*, 21 March 2011, available at https://www.politico.com/story/2011/03/kucinich-libya-action-impeachable-051668.

Forces on the ground in Libya unless the purpose of the presence is to rescue a member of the Armed Forces from imminent danger."[212]

Support for the president's action was also notably bipartisan, with former George W. Bush Administration lawyer John Yoo arguing that President Obama's action was "firmly in the tradition of American foreign policy. Throughout our history, neither presidents nor Congress have acted under the belief that the Constitution requires a declaration of war before the U.S. can conduct military hostilities abroad.... For once, Mr. Obama has the Constitution about right."[213]

In an attempt to wrest power from the executive branch during what was seen as President Nixon's "imperial presidency," Congress passed the War Powers Resolution in 1973, overriding President Nixon's veto with the necessary two-thirds majority in both chambers. Some believed this legislation would restore a balance of power between Congress and the president on matters of war and peace. Yet even today, nearly half a century after its passage, the War Powers Act remains highly controversial and hotly debated. Some argue it is unconstitutional; that it is imprecise and lacks clarity; and that it has failed to live up to its billing as a result of the failure of multiple presidents to abide by its requirements. Former Senate Armed Services Committee Chairman Sam Nunn stated that "The War Powers Act has never worked, will not work. My general thinking is we need to move much more to a

---

[212] H. Res. 292, "Declaring that the President shall not deploy, establish, or maintain the presence of units and members of the United States Armed Forces on the ground in Libya, and for other purposes," 3 June 2011, available at https://www.congress.gov/bill/112th-congress/house-resolution/292.

[213] John Yoo, "Antiwar Senator, War-Powers President," *The Wall Street Journal*, 25 March 2011, available at https://www.wsj.com/articles/SB10001424052748704050204576218540505216146.

consultative mechanism so that the President consults with the Congress before making these decisions and not after that."[214]

In general, the act does not prevent the president from deploying U.S. troops overseas. Its basic provisions, however, require Congress to be notified within 60 days of the president introducing military forces into an area of "hostilities" (undefined) or where hostilities are "imminent" (extendable for another 30 days). The president must remove those forces after that time if the Congress does not declare war, with certain exceptions.[215]

The statutory requirement to remove U.S. forces according to the timetable established by the War Powers Act has traditionally not been adhered to by presidents of either party. After President Reagan sent U.S. Marines to Lebanon in 1982 it took Congress nine months to direct the president to "obtain statutory authorization from Congress" for any substantial increase in their numbers.[216] After the bombing of the Marine barracks in Beirut in October 1983, Congress finally invoked the War Powers Act. However, enforcement of the act has always been difficult.

There are numerous examples where Congress has failed to prevent the president from introducing U.S. forces into hostilities and failed to obtain their withdrawal according to the timelines established by the War Powers Act. President Harry Truman introduced U.S. forces to Korea without obtaining prior congressional approval. The

---

[214] Adam Clymer, "Democrats Study Amending War Powers Act," *The New York Times*, 24 October 1993, available at https://www.nytimes.com/1993/10/24/world/democrats-study-amending-war-powers-act.html.

[215] The War Powers Resolution is available at https://avalon.law.yale.edu/20th_century/warpower.asp.

[216] See S. 639, Lebanon Emergency Assistance Act of 1983, 27 June 1983, available at https://www.congress.gov/bill/98th-congress/senate-bill/639.

Bay of Pigs invasion of Cuba in 1961 and the invasion of Cambodia in 1970 followed a similar pattern. As noted previously, during times of crisis or national emergency, the president often has the upper hand when it comes to the use of military force, as the Congress is often reluctant to second-guess the president.

In the 1991 Persian Gulf War, President George H. W. Bush requested congressional authorization to use force to expel Saddam Hussein from Kuwait only after a five-month troop buildup in Saudi Arabia had occurred. At the same time, however, he argued such authorization was unnecessary, stating, "If I don't get the votes, I'm going to do it anyway. And if I get impeached, so be it."[217] Congressional criticism was muted by the success of Operation Desert Storm.

Strong congressional support was also evident for President George W. Bush's decision to respond to the September 11, 2001 terrorist attacks. A joint resolution passed by Congress authorized the president "to use all necessary and appropriate force against those nations, organizations, or persons he determined planned, authorized, committed, or aided the terrorist attacks... or harbored such organizations or persons."[218] This 2001 AUMF was followed in 2002 by another AUMF authorizing the president to use the U.S. armed forces "as he determines to be necessary and appropriate" to "defend the national security of the United States against the continuing threat

---

[217] Quoted in Kate Keller, "An Unlikely Hardliner, George H. W. Bush Was Ready to Push Presidential Powers," *Smithsonian Magazine*, 14 May 2018, available at
https://www.smithsonianmag.com/history/unlikely-hardliner-george-h-w-bush-was-ready-push-presidential-powers-180969017/.

[218] Public Law 107-40, "Joint Resolution to authorize the use of United States Armed Forces against those responsible for the recent attacks launched against the United States," available at
https://www.congress.gov/107/plaws/publ40/PLAW-107publ40.pdf.

posed by Iraq."[219] An opinion by the Bush Administration's Office of Legal Counsel in 2002 stated that "the President's constitutional authority to undertake military action to protect the national security interests of the United States is firmly established in the text and structure of the Constitution and in executive branch practice. Thus, to the extent that the President were to determine that military action against Iraq would protect our national interests, he could take such action based on his independent constitutional authority; no action by Congress would be necessary."[220]

These and other examples demonstrate the difficulty Congress has had in constraining the president's freedom of action to deploy U.S. forces abroad. The effectiveness of the War Powers Act has been undermined by Congress' general reluctance to second-guess the president on critical national security issues; the executive branch's assertion that the act is an unconstitutional infringement on the president's constitutional authorities as Commander in Chief; the lack of definitional clarity in the act itself; and the general deference of the judicial branch to presidential prerogatives.

Despite these difficulties, some in Congress continue to insist that congressional authorization is necessary prior to deploying U.S. troops in harm's way. In defending President Donald Trump's decision to bomb Syrian chemical weapons sites in retaliation for the Bashar Hafez al-Assad regime's use of chemical weapons on its own citizens, the Department of Justice's Office of Legal Counsel stated, "The President could lawfully direct airstrikes on

---

[219] Public Law 107-243, "Authorization For Use of Military Force Against Iraq Resolution of 2002," available at https://www.congress.gov/107/plaws/publ243/PLAW-107publ243.pdf.

[220] Jack Goldsmith, "The Ease of Writing an OLC Opinion in Support of Military Action Against North Korea," *Lawfare*, 14 September 2017, available at https://www.lawfareblog.com/ease-writing-olc-opinion-support-military-action-against-north-korea.

facilities associated with Syria's chemical weapons capability because he had reasonably determined that the use of force would be in the national interest and that the anticipated hostilities would not rise to the level of a war in the constitutional sense."[221] This was challenged by Sen. Tim Kaine (D-VA), who argued, "The ludicrous claim that this president can magically assert 'national interest' and redefine war to exclude missile attacks and thereby bypass Congress should alarm us all. This is further proof that Congress must finally take back its authority when it comes to war."[222]

More recently, the January 2020 U.S. airstrike in Iraq that killed Qassem Soleimani, the military leader of Iran's Islamic Revolutionary Guard Corps Quds Force, again brought congressional concerns over war powers into stark relief. Sen. Richard Blumenthal (D-CT) stated, "The present authorizations for use of military force in no way cover starting a possible new war."[223] Sen. Tom Udall (D-NM) accused President Trump of "bringing our nation to the brink of an illegal war with Iran without any congressional approval as required under the Constitution of the United States. Such a reckless escalation of hostilities is likely a violation of Congress' war making authority...."[224] Sen.

---

[221] See Steven A. Engel, Office of Legal Counsel, Department of Justice, "April 2018 Airstrikes Against Syrian Chemical-Weapons Facilities," 31 May 2018, available at
https://www.justice.gov/olc/opinion/file/1067551/download.

[222] Charlie Savage, "Trump Had Power to Attack Syria Without Congress, Justice Dept. Memo Says," *The New York Times*, 1 June 2018, available at
https://www.nytimes.com/2018/06/01/us/politics/trump-war-powers-syria-congress.html.

[223] Leo Shane III, "Killing of top Iranian military commander elicits praise, worry from Congress," *Military Times*, 2 January 2020, available at https://www.militarytimes.com/news/pentagon-congress/2020/01/03/killing-of-top-iranian-leader-elicits-praise-worry-from-congress/.

[224] Ibid.

Rand Paul (R-KY) took to Twitter to comment, "If we are to go to war w/Iran the Constitution dictates that we declare war. A war without a Congressional declaration is a recipe for feckless intermittent eruptions of violence w/ no clear mission for our soldiers."[225] And House Speaker Nancy Pelosi (D-CA) criticized the president's action, saying it was conducted "without an Authorization for Use of Military Force (AUMF) against Iran. Further, this action was taken without the consultation of the Congress."[226]

In response to the president's action, Sen. Kaine introduced a resolution, supported by Sen. Mike Lee (R-UT), that would require a congressional authorization or formal declaration of war before the United States initiates any hostilities with Iran. He stated that the resolution "would not prevent the United States from defending itself from imminent attack, nor would it prevent us from authorizing military action against Iran. It would merely require that war against Iran cannot occur until there are a public debate and congressional vote in favor of it."[227] A non-binding resolution to limit the actions of the president on Iran, filed by Rep. Elissa Slotkin (D-MI), passed the House on January 9, 2020 along mostly partisan lines by a

---

[225] Paul Kane and Mike DeBonis, "Lawmakers reignite old debate over war powers," *The Washington Post*, 4 January 2020, available at http://thewashingtonpost.newspaperdirect.com/epaper/viewer.aspx.

[226] Statement by House Speaker Nancy Pelosi, 2 January 2020, available at https://www.speaker.gov/newsroom/1220.

[227] Sen. Tim Kaine, "Congress needs to show some courage, follow the Constitution and vote on war with Iran," FoxNews.com, 8 January 2020, available at https://www.foxnews.com/opinion/tim-kaine-congress-constitution-vote-iran. A modified version of this resolution passed the Senate on February 13, 2020 with rare bipartisan support by a 55-45 vote, demonstrating that the assertion of congressional prerogatives occasionally trumps partisan politics. See Catie Edmondson, "In Bipartisan Bid to Restrain Trump, Senate Passes Iran War Powers Resolution," *The New York Times*, 13 February 2020, available at https://www.nytimes.com/2020/02/13/us/politics/iran-war-powers-trump.html.

224-194 vote.   On January 30, 2020, the House passed another resolution sponsored by Rep. Ro Khanna (D-CA) that would prohibit the president from spending federal funds to carry out military strikes against Iran (except in self-defense or to prevent an imminent attack on the United States) without prior congressional approval.[228] The same day, a separate resolution introduced by Rep. Barbara Lee (D-CA) that would repeal the 2002 AUMF also passed the House along mostly partisan lines, despite a White House veto threat should it pass the Senate and wind up on the president's desk.[229]   On May 6, 2020, President Trump vetoed S.J. Res. 68, sponsored by Sen. Kaine, which declared U.S. armed forces to be in a state of "hostilities" with Iran, and which directed the president to "terminate" the use of U.S. forces "unless explicitly authorized by a declaration of war or specific authorization for use of military force against Iran."[230] The following day, the Senate, by a 49-44 vote, failed to achieve the necessary two-thirds majority to override the president's veto.

Also in the Senate, a resolution introduced by Sens. Rand Paul and Jeff Merkley (D-OR) states, "Neither the [2001] Authorization for Use of Military Force... nor the

---

[228] Catie Edmondson, "House Votes to Repeal 2002 Military Authorization in Bid to Rein in Trump on Iran," *The New York Times*, 30 January 2020, available at https://www.nytimes.com/2020/01/30/us/politics/House-military-authorization-iran-trump.html.

[229] Office of Management and Budget, The White House, "Statement of Administration Policy: H.R. 2456 (House Amendment to Senate Amendment to H.R. 550) – Repeal of the Authorization for Use of Military Force Against Iraq of 2002," 27 January 2020, available at https://www.whitehouse.gov/wp-content/uploads/2020/01/SAP_HR-2456.pdf.

[230] See S.J. Res. 68, available at https://www.congress.gov/bill/116th-congress/senate-joint-resolution/68/text. Also see The White House, "Presidential Veto Message to the Senate for S.J. Res. 68," 6 May 2020, available at https://www.whitehouse.gov/briefings-statements/presidential-veto-message-senate-s-j-res-68/.

Authorization for Use of Military Force Against Iraq Resolution of 2002... may be interpreted as a statutory authorization for the use of military force against the Islamic Republic of Iran."[231] Senate Minority Leader Chuck Schumer (D-NY) stated, "The president does not have the authority for a war with Iran. If he plans a large increase in troops and potential hostility over a longer time, the administration will require congressional approval and the approval of the American people."[232]   Sen. Tammy Duckworth (D-IL) stated there is "no question that the President—any President—does not have Constitutional authority to draw the United States into a war without prior Congressional approval.   This solemn duty is solely for Congress to decide..."[233]

On the other hand, some in Congress praised the airstrike as justified given Soleimani's involvement in military attacks on Americans in the region. Sen. Lindsay Graham called it a "bold action" against "one of the most ruthless and vicious members of the Ayatollah's regime. He had American blood on his hands."[234] Sen. Ben Sasse (R-NE) declared, "Gen. Soleimani has killed hundreds and hundreds of Americans, and was actively plotting more. This commander-in-chief — any C-in-C. — has an

---

[231] See text at
https://www.merkley.senate.gov/imo/media/doc/Merkley%20Iran%20Resolution.pdf.

[232] Cited in Alexander Bolton, "Kaine introduces resolution to block war with Iran," *The Hill*, 3 January 2020, available at
https://thehill.com/homenews/senate/476702-kaine-introduces-resolution-to-block-war-with-iran.

[233] WICS/WRSP Staff, "Illinois lawmakers respond to U.S. killing of Iranian general," NewsChannel 20, available at
https://newschannel20.com/news/local/illinois-lawmakers-respond-to-us-killing-of-iranian-general.

[234] Ryan Saavedra, "Lindsey Graham Signals America's Next Move Against Iran," *The Daily Wire*, 2 January 2020, available at
https://www.dailywire.com/news/breaking-lindsey-graham-drops-hint-at-americas-next-move-against-iran.

obligation to defend America by killing this bastard."[235] Some analysts argued that Soleimani's killing was "a lawful act, wholly compatible with President Trump's responsibilities as commander-in-chief. Trump had no obligation to consult Congress before ordering the operation" because the action was "overt and narrowly defined in scope" and "that authorization isn't necessary where a credible near-term threat exists."[236] The Editorial Board of *The Wall Street Journal* also weighed in, arguing that critics of the president's action are "wrong on the law and Constitution" and that the long-standing prohibition on assassinations[237] "has never applied to terrorists." "Mr. Trump also has the power, as Commander in Chief, to use military force against anyone waging war against the U.S.," they argued.[238]

Former Obama Administration Secretary of Homeland Security Jeh Johnson argued that the War Powers Act "is outdated, plain and simple" and "should be repealed and replaced." He stated, "The intended executive/legislative balance is – in a word – broken," asserting, "The current

---

[235] Tal Axelrod, "Congress reacts to US assassination of Iranian general," *The Hill*, 2 January 2020, available at https://thehill.com/policy/defense/476612-congress-reacts-to-us-assassination-of-iranian-general.

[236] Tom Rogan, "Why Trump didn't need congressional approval to kill Qassim Soleimani," *Washington Examiner*, 3 January 2020, available at https://www.washingtonexaminer.com/opinion/why-trump-didnt-need-congressional-approval-to-kill-qassem-soleimani.

[237] The ban on assassinations is contained in Executive Order (E.O.) 12333, dating from 1981. A summary of E.O. 12333 and the context for its issuance can be found at "Assassination Ban and E.O. 12333: A Brief Summary," Congressional Research Service, CRS Report RS21037, 4 January 2002, available at https://www.everycrsreport.com/files/20020104_RS21037_b53d9101b d1e6e57b98fb3058e000663015f55cb.pdf.

[238] "Trump's Legal Authority," *The Wall Street Journal*, 3 January 2020, available at https://www.wsj.com/articles/trumps-legal-authority-11578095410.

scope of the executive's authority in this space is indeed the product of decades of 'unilateralist presidencies and submissive legislatures.' Essentially, Congress has abandoned this space, and the executive, in the national security real or perceived, has filled it.... Collectively, members of Congress no longer want to take a hard vote on whether to go to war if they can avoid it."[239]

Former Trump Administration National Security Advisor John Bolton declared the War Powers Act "unconstitutional," arguing, "It reflects a fundamental misunderstanding of how the Constitution allocated foreign affairs authority between the President and Congress. The Resolution should be repealed."[240] Most presidents have considered the War Powers Act unconstitutional but have notified Congress of major military actions more as a courtesy than as a legal requirement. The language of these notifications has been relatively uniform throughout multiple administrations, stating that notification is being made "consistent with" the War Powers Act rather than "pursuant to" the act, which could suggest a legal requirement to do so.[241] President Trump notified Congress of the airstrike that killed Soleimani, though his notification was classified.[242]

---

[239] Jeh Johnson, "War Powers: The Broken Balance Between the Branches," Speech before the American Constitution Society Symposium at the Georgetown University Law Center, 6 February 2020, available at https://www.lawfareblog.com/war-powers-broken-balance-between-branches.

[240] Justine Coleman, "Bolton says war powers resolution should be repealed," *The Hill*, 9 January 2020, available at https://thehill.com/homenews/administration/477498-bolton-says-war-powers-resolution-should-be-repealed.

[241] See "War Powers Act," *Encyclopædia Britannica*, available at https://www.britannica.com/topic/War-Powers-Act.

[242] Seung Min Kim, "The White House has formally notified Congress of the Soleimani strike," *The Washington Post*, 4 January 2020, available at https://www.washingtonpost.com/politics/the-white-house-has-

Subsequently, he tweeted, "These Media Posts will serve as notification to the United States Congress that should Iran strike any U.S. person or target, the United States will quickly & fully strike back, & perhaps in a disproportionate manner. Such legal notice is not required, but is given nevertheless!" The House Foreign Affairs Committee tweeted back, "This Media Post will serve as a reminder that war powers reside in the Congress under the United States Constitution. And that you should read the War Powers Act. And that you're not a dictator."[243]

Signing Statements

Tension between the executive and legislative branches is also evident in how the laws passed by Congress are to be interpreted and implemented. Although the Constitution directs the president to "take care that the laws be faithfully executed," there is often disagreement as to *how* the law should be executed. In recent years, the debate between what the Congress intended and how the executive branch interprets it has increasingly played out through the president's use of "signing statements."

Signing statements reflect the president's views on legislation signed into law. They generally describe the positive provisions contained in the legislation and how the legislation's enactment will benefit the American people.

---

formally-notified-congress-of-the-soleimani-
strike/2020/01/04/1cc60090-2f3f-11ea-be79-83e793dbcaef_story.html.

[243] Shawn Snow and Leo Shane III, "Trump says Tweet serves as 'notification' to Congress that U.S. may 'quickly & fully strike back' against Iran," *Military Times*, 5 January 2020, available at https://www.militarytimes.com/flashpoints/2020/01/05/trump-says-tweet-serves-as-notification-to-congress-that-us-may-quickly-fully-strike-back-against-
iran/?utm_source=Sailthru&utm_medium=email&utm_campaign=EBB%2001.06.20&utm_term=Editorial%20-%20Early%20Bird%20Brief.

However, presidents have come to use signing statements more frequently to identify those provisions in the bill they object to and to specify how they intend to implement them. Occasionally these statements suggest an interpretation of the law at variance with what its congressional supporters intended.

Unlike the law itself, the accompanying signing statements carry no legal weight and have no legal standing. They are neither authorized nor prohibited by anything in the Constitution, but have become general practice, nevertheless. President James Monroe was the first to issue signing statements, which at that time were mostly for ceremonial or political proclamations. Over time, however, they have become more substantive in nature.

President Ronald Reagan significantly expanded the use of signing statements, using them as a tool to assert his presidential authority. During his administration, he issued 250 signing statements, of which more than one-third expressed objections to particular provisions of the legislation he signed.[244] Nearly one-half of the signing statements issued by President George H.W. Bush raised legal or constitutional objections to the laws he signed. President Clinton issued 381 signing statements, yet only a modest percentage of these were critical of legislative provisions. Although President George W. Bush issued only 161 signing statements, 79 percent of those statements raised legal or constitutional objections to more than 1,000 specific provisions of law.[245]

---

[244] "Presidential Signing Statements: Constitutional and Institutional Implications," Congressional Research Service, CRS Report RL33667, 4 January 2012, p. 2, available at https://www.everycrsreport.com/files/20120104_RL33667_8e67dd21b 7737fb5a72093f92955fd92ad2bb91b.pdf.

[245] Ibid., pp.2-9.

In 2006, the American Bar Association (ABA) criticized President George W. Bush's actions, saying, "The President's constitutional duty is to enforce laws he has signed into being unless and until they are held unconstitutional by the Supreme Court or a subordinate tribunal. The Constitution is not what the President says it is."[246]   The ABA declared that signing statements "undermine the rule of law and our constitutional system of separation of powers."[247]   The Bush Administration's Office of Legal Counsel defended President Bush's use of signing statements by noting they "are indistinguishable from those issued by past Presidents" and that they are "an essential part of the constitutional dialogue between the Branches that has been a part of the etiquette of government since the early days of the Republic" and "an attempt to preserve the enduring balance between coordinate Branches of Government."[248]

Then-Senator Barack Obama called President Bush's use of signing statements a "clear abuse of power"[249] and pledged during his presidential campaign, "I will not use

---

[246] See American Bar Association Task Force on Presidential Signing Statements and the Separation of Powers Doctrine, August 2006, pp. 23-24, available at
https://balkin.blogspot.com/aba.signing.statments.report.pdf.

[247] American Bar Association Press Release, "Blue-Ribbon Task Force Finds President Bush's Signing Statements Undermine Separation of Powers," 24 July 2006, available at
https://web.archive.org/web/20120615163547/http://www.abanow.org/2006/07/blue-ribbon-task-force-finds-president-bushs-signing-statements-undermine-separation-of-powers/.

[248] John P. Elwood, "Statement Before the House Committee on the Judiciary," 31 January 2007, pp. 1-2, available at
https://www.justice.gov/sites/default/files/olc/opinions/2007/01/31/presidential-signing-stmt.pdf.

[249] Michael McConnell, "President Obama's Signing Statement on 'Czars,'" The Hoover Institution, 3 May 2011, available at
https://www.hoover.org/research/president-obamas-signing-statement-czars.

signing statements to nullify or undermine congressional instructions as enacted into law."[250]   President Obama issued his first signing statement on March 11, 2009, attached to an omnibus spending bill. As of January 2012, one-half of the signing statements issued by President Obama challenged the constitutionality of legal provisions he signed into law.[251]   In one signing statement on the National Defense Authorization Act (NDAA) for Fiscal Year 2013, he challenged more than 20 separate provisions of the law.[252]

In that particular NDAA signing statement, President Obama criticized provisions regarding the transfer of detainees at the U.S. detention facility at Guantanamo Bay, Cuba, stating, "In the event that the restrictions on the transfer of Guantanamo detainees in sections 1034 and 1035 operate in a manner that violates constitutional separation of powers principles, my Administration will implement them in a manner that avoids the constitutional conflict."[253] Similarly, in a signing statement on the fiscal year 2012 NDAA, President Obama stated, "Other provisions in this bill above could interfere with my constitutional foreign affairs powers... should any application of these provisions

---

[250] Charlie Savage, "Barack Obama's Q&A," *The Boston Globe*, 20 December 2007, available at
http://archive.boston.com/news/politics/2008/specials/CandidateQ A/ObamaQA/.

[251] Congressional Research Service, Report RL33667, op. cit., p. 10.

[252] "Statement by the President on H.R. 4310," 3 January 2013, available at https://obamawhitehouse.archives.gov/the-press-office/2013/01/03/statement-president-hr-4310.

[253] "Statement by the President on H.R. 3304," 26 December 2013, available at https://obamawhitehouse.archives.gov/the-press-office/2013/12/26/statement-president-hr-3304.

conflict with my constitutional authorities, I will treat the provisions as non-binding."[254]

While signing statements are not legally binding, the law is. Certainly, statements such as those above raise important constitutional questions and are another example of how the struggle between the executive and legislative branches for the privilege of directing American foreign policy plays out.

In response to controversies over the impact and legitimacy of signing statements, Sen. Arlen Specter (R-PA) introduced the "Presidential Signing Statements Act of 2006." The bill would have directed the courts to reject signing statements as lacking authority and would have instructed the Supreme Court to allow congressional lawsuits challenging their constitutionality.[255] Despite Sen. Specter's former chairmanship of the Senate Judiciary Committee, the bill died in committee.

Certainly, the balance of power between the executive and legislative branches waxes and wanes depending on the issue. The issue of war powers is a perennial topic of controversy on which the president and Congress struggle for primacy. Signing statements are also a tool in the tug of war between the branches of government. In the national security realm, much of this power struggle plays out in the annual ritual of crafting and negotiating the NDAA and the Defense Appropriations Act. These are the two bills that have the most impact on U.S. national security and which are the most significant tools Congress has at its disposal to influence the course of American national security policy.

---

[254] "Statement by the President on H.R. 1540," 31 December 2011, available at https://obamawhitehouse.archives.gov/the-press-office/2011/12/31/statement-president-hr-1540.

[255] S. 3731, "Presidential Signing Statements Act of 2006," available at https://www.congress.gov/bill/109th-congress/senate-bill/3731/text.

As a Professional Staff Member on the House Armed Services Committee, I had the opportunity to travel on various congressional delegations (CODELs) and staff trips (STAFFDELs).

These photos were taken during the mid- to late 1990s when I was on the HASC staff.

At the NATO Stabilization Force Headquarters in Sarajevo, Bosnia

Standing on the Great Wall of China

North of the Arctic Circle in Murmansk, Russia
with two SASC colleagues

At the Chornobyl nuclear reactor in Ukraine

*Inside the control room at the
Vladimir Ilych Lenin ("Chornobyl") Nuclear
Power Plant near the town of Prypiat, Ukraine*

*In Red Square with the Spassky Tower of the Kremlin
and St. Basil's Cathedral in the background*

Standing in front of the Russian "White House" in Moscow

On the flight deck of the USS America (CV-66)

*Aboard the Ohio-class ballistic missile submarine
USS Kentucky (SSBN-737)*

HASC Chairman Floyd D. Spence (R-SC) poses with a caricature of me that my wife had made

HASC staffers have fun celebrating my departure from the committee as I prepared for my first tour at the Pentagon

TOM DeLAY
TEXAS

H-107, The Capitol
Washington, DC 20515-6503
(202) 225-0197

One Hundred Fourth Congress
U.S. House of Representatives
Office of the Majority Whip

May 17, 1996

David Trachtenberg
National Security Committee
2117 A Rayburn HOB
Washington, DC 20515

Dear David:

I would like to thank you for having taken the time to brief legislative staff at this morning's Whip Briefing. Your expertise is an invaluable part of trying to keep Members of Congress informed of upcoming legislative activity.

I know you are very busy, and your assistance is appreciated. Please let me know if my office can ever assist you in any way. Once again, thank you.

Sincerely,

Tom DeLay

Tom DeLay
Majority Whip

HOUSE OF REPRESENTATIVES
WASHINGTON, D. C. 20515

SAXBY CHAMBLISS
EIGHTH DISTRICT
GEORGIA

23 February, 1998

David-
Thanks for helping to make our trip to Bosnia such a good one. Your professionalism is readily apparent + I am thankful for people like you working on the Hill. Let's do it again

Saxby

CURT WELDON
SEVENTH DISTRICT
PENNSYLVANIA

December 8, 1999

Mr. David Trachtenberg
House Armed Services Committee
2117 Rayburn House Office Building
Washington, D.C. 20515

Dear Trachto:

Thank you for all of your efforts in support of my recent CODEL to Russia. The success of this trip was in no small way due to your work on our behalf.

I look forward to continuing to work with you over the next year on the issue of crime and corruption in Russia. I think that this is one of the issues which will define our future relationship with Russia, and that now more than ever it is important to proactively engage the Duma. Working together, I know that we can enact positive changes to the legislative and judicial systems in Russia which will help the average Russian citizen.

Thank you again for all of your efforts to make this very important trip a success. I look forward to seeing you again soon, and hope that you have a wonderful holiday season.

Sincerely,

CURT WELDON
Member of Congress

CHAPTER SEVEN

MANAGING THE MILITARY AND THE MILITARY BUDGET

The Department of Defense (DoD) is the largest federal agency both in terms of size and fiscal resources. It comprises nearly two million men and women in uniform representing all of the military services and a civilian workforce numbering in the hundreds of thousands. With an annual budget in excess of $700 billion, DoD is considered the nation's largest employer with a presence and impact in every state of the Union, including military bases and installations and contractor facilities. The Pentagon is said to be the world's largest office building and is home to roughly 25,000 employees. Consequently, oversight of DoD and the nation's military apparatus is a major endeavor and one on which Congress can have the most impact on national security policy.

Congressional management of the nation's military and military budget follows a traditional cyclical pattern. That pattern is in evidence during the annual process of developing the National Defense Authorization Act and the Defense Appropriations Act. The NDAA and appropriations processes afford Congress the opportunity to weigh its national defense priorities against those of the administration and to make whatever adjustments and modifications it believes are necessary to ensure the national security.

The Preeminence of Strategy

On matters of national defense, practice does not always align with theory. Ideally, the amount we spend on defense should flow from the strategy we pursue, not vice versa; in reality, strategy often conforms to budget realities.

In theory, it is important to understand the threats to U.S. national security; determine a policy course for addressing those threats; develop a strategy that supports the preferred policy outcomes; decide on the programs necessary to execute the strategy; and then to ascertain the cost of implementing those programs. In the past, however, the approach taken has often stood this process on its head: first, by deciding how much DoD can reasonably afford to spend; then determining what programs should be given priority in a budget-constrained environment; and finally ascertaining the strategy that can be supported with the programs procured.

This disconnect between budgets and strategy has often been a source of congressional frustration and was most evident in congressional debates over the Quadrennial Defense Review (QDR)—a congressionally-mandated process whereby DoD would assess the nation's defense needs and develop a strategy for addressing those needs with appropriate programs and budgetary resources. The requirement for a QDR dates back to the NDAA for fiscal year 1997, which directed that:

> The Secretary of Defense shall every four years, ...conduct a comprehensive examination (to be known as a "quadrennial defense review") of the national defense strategy, force structure, force modernization plans, infrastructure, budget plan, and other elements of the defense program and policies of the United States with a view toward determining and expressing the defense strategy of

the United States and establishing a defense program for the next 20 years.[256]

The last QDR was released in 2014 and, as described by then-Secretary of Defense Chuck Hagel, outlined "the tough choices we are making in a period of fiscal austerity."[257] The QDR called for "rebalancing our defense efforts in a period of increasing fiscal constraint."[258] Congressional criticism of the QDR focused on concerns that the strategy was inappropriately "resource-constrained," while supporters of the document contended that it was simply "resource-informed." As HASC member Adam Smith (D-WA) commented at the time:

> There has been much criticism leveled at this, and prior, Quadrennial Defense Reviews. Members believe that the reviews are overly constrained by resources, that the reports do not fully meet the congressional intent, and that no QDR has really presented a 20 year strategy as required by law. To some extent, I believe some of these criticisms are unfair. All strategies, for example, are constrained by resources to some degree.[259]

---

[256] Department of Defense, Office of Public Affairs, "QDR 101: What You Should Know," available at https://dod.defense.gov/Portals/1/features/defenseReviews/QDR/QDR_101_FACT_SHEET_January_2010.pdf.

[257] Department of Defense *Quadrennial Defense Review 2014*, 4 March 2014, available at https://archive.defense.gov/pubs/2014_Quadrennial_Defense_Review.pdf.

[258] Ibid., p. iv.

[259] Ranking Member Adam Smith's Statement at QDR Hearing, 3 April 2014, available at https://armedservices.house.gov/2014/4/ranking-member-adam-smith-s-statement-at-qdr-hearing.

Opposition to the QDR, however, was decidedly bipartisan. The Obama Administration's former Under Secretary of Defense for Policy, Michèle Flournoy, stated, "the QDR has become a routinized, bottom-up staff exercise that includes hundreds of participants and consumes many thousands of man-hours, rather than a top-down leadership exercise that sets clear priorities, makes hard choices and allocates risk."[260] Then-SASC Chairman John McCain (R-AZ) noted that "The development of policy, strategy, and plans in the DoD has become paralyzed by an excessive pursuit of concurrence or consensus... what results too often seems to be watered-down, lowest common denominator thinking that is acceptable to all relevant stakeholders precisely because it is threatening to none of them."[261] And then-HASC Chairman Mac Thornberry (R-TX) commented that "in recent years, the Quadrennial Defense Review has been a slick, glossy publication that justifies how much money an administration wants to spend."[262]

As a result of these concerns, the requirement for a QDR was repealed in the NDAA for fiscal year 2017 and replaced with a requirement for DoD to produce a National Defense Strategy. The first such strategy was released by the Trump Administration in January 2018 and focused on addressing the reemergence of great-power competition with China and Russia. It contained three major lines of effort: building a more lethal force; strengthening alliances and developing

---

[260] Joe Gould, "QDR Dead in 2017 Defense Policy Bill," *Defense News*, 25 April 2016, available at https://www.defensenews.com/home/2016/04/25/qdr-dead-in-2017-defense-policy-bill/.

[261] Ibid.

[262] Council on Foreign Relations, "Mac Thornberry on the Budget, National Security, and Policy Reform," 24 February 2015, available at https://www.cfr.org/event/mac-thornberry-budget-national-security-and-policy-reform-0.

new partnerships; and reforming the department's business practices for greater performance and affordability.[263]

The Defense Budget in Context

There are two main categories of federal spending: **Mandatory** and **Discretionary**. **Mandatory spending** is spending on programs required by law, such as Medicare, Medicaid, Social Security, farm subsidies, food stamps, and child nutrition programs. Spending on these programs is determined by eligibility criteria. Mandatory spending programs are often referred to as entitlement programs, and the growth in spending on these programs has ballooned substantially over the years, increasing from roughly 18 percent of federal spending in 1940 to more than 63 percent by 2018.[264]

Discretionary spending is optional and reflects choices that can be made on an annual basis. These choices generally reflect the nation's priorities. For example, how much to spend on housing and education versus space exploration, infrastructure construction, or foreign aid is determined on an annual basis by Congress as it considers the administration's budget request against its own set of priorities.

The defense budget comprises the largest single portion—roughly one-half—of the federal government's discretionary spending. Spending on national defense is

---

[263] Although the National Defense Strategy is classified, an unclassified summary was released and is available at https://dod.defense.gov/Portals/1/Documents/pubs/2018-National-Defense-Strategy-Summary.pdf.

[264] See Jordan, et al., *American National Security*, op. cit., p. 197. Also see "Trends in Mandatory Spending: In Brief," Congressional Research Service, CRS Report R44641, 14 September 2018, p. 3, available at https://www.everycrsreport.com/files/20180914_R44641_1ec59b95e5c ae037b9fe0d04870bfe5ba156de4f.pdf.

more than just DoD, as it includes funding for the intelligence community, nuclear weapons programs administered by the DOE, various DHS programs, and other activities funded outside of DoD. The DoD budget consists of two parts: the "base" budget, which pays for most of the department's regular planned programs, and the "overseas contingency operations" or "OCO" budget, which funds unanticipated needs in support of unplanned activities like overseas conflicts.

Because of restrictions imposed by the Budget Control Act (BCA) of 2011, there is a limit to how much DoD can spend as part of its base budget without triggering "sequestration"—a mandatory reduction in spending resulting from exceeding the statutory budget caps imposed by the BCA.[265] Consequently, in recent years DoD has shifted some funds from its base budget to the OCO account in order to avoid exceeding the legal spending caps. This has been criticized by some in Congress as a form of budget "gimmickry." HASC Chairman Adam Smith (D-WA) and House Budget Committee Chairman John Yarmuth (D-KY) called it "a gimmick to prop up defense spending" and stated, "This is nothing more than a blatant attempt to make a mockery of the federal budget process, obscure the true cost of military operations, and severely shortchange other investments vital to our national and economic security."[266]

There is often confusion over military spending because of the different categories of spending involved, the different departments of government that invest in defense

---

[265] See "The Budget Control Act of 2011," Congressional Research Service, CRS Report R41965, 19 August 2011, available at https://www.everycrsreport.com/files/20110819_R41965_f3c12f0d946a 5cd140b30da7db871d97486d5143.pdf.

[266] Joe Gould, "Border wall casts long shadow over FY20 defense budget — and that's not all," *Defense News*, 1 March 2019, available at https://www.defensenews.com/congress/2019/03/01/trumps-border-wall-to-cast-long-shadow-over-fy20-defense-budgetand-thats-not-all/.

activities, and the difference between authorizations and appropriations. There is also a difference between the defense *budget* and actual defense *spending* — the former is a request submitted in accordance with a plan for spending while the latter is the actual amount of money spent. In other words, the defense budget represents the administration's request for how much money it believes is necessary for defense. The amount of defense spending may be more or less than the amount requested. Per Article I, Section 9 of the Constitution, the Congress has the final say.

Congressional Oversight of the Budget Process

Congressional management of the defense budget process has ebbed and flowed over the decades, with Congress generally not challenging the administration's defense budget requests aggressively until the post-Vietnam war era. Greater congressional assertiveness coincided with an increase in the number of congressional committees and subcommittees responsible for defense issues; an expansion in the number of congressional staffers; significant growth in the number of hearings; and an explosion in the size of the annual NDAA and the number of required reports to Congress.[267] This led to greater DoD concern about congressional "micromanagement" of defense programs.

---

[267] As former Secretary of Defense Donald H. Rumsfeld testified: "The last time I was Secretary of Defense, the 1977 defense authorization bill was 16-pages long — in the year 2001 it had grown to 534 pages." See Testimony of Donald H. Rumsfeld before the Senate Armed Services Committee, "Department of Defense Authorization for Appropriations for Fiscal Year 2004," 13 February 2003, p. 19, available at https://books.google.com/books?id=1BmqIszKgREC&pg=PA19&lpg= PA19&dq=congress+did+not+have+expertise+to+challenge+defense+p rograms+in+50s&source=bl&ots=pyrxCVEOIZ&sig=ACfU3U2wZ4VW- bttxiyHOuJTkP4zbazG9A&hl=en&sa=X&ved=2ahUKEwjAzePb3OXm AhWDVt8KHfsWAxAQ6AEwCXoECAsQAQ#v=onepage&q=congress

In 1974, Congress passed the "Congressional Budget and Impoundment Control Act" (a kluge of the "Congressional Budget Act of 1974" and the "Impoundment Control Act"), which governs the role of Congress in the budget process. Passage of the act (subsequently amended in 1985, 1990, and 1997) was spurred by Congress' desire to tighten control over the budgeting process after President Nixon "impounded" funds by refusing to spend money that the Congress had appropriated. The act removed the president's power of impoundment, first exercised by President Thomas Jefferson in 1803.[268] To avoid spending money appropriated by Congress, presidents are now required to propose "rescissions," which would revoke the requirement to spend appropriated funds, allowing Congress up to 45 days to approve such requests.[269]

President Trump's impeachment in 2019 was based, in part, on his temporary suspension of military assistance to Ukraine, which Congress had previously approved. Some of the president's critics argued that he had violated the Impoundment Control Act by withholding funds and failing to notify Congress. Senator Christopher Van Hollen (D-MD) asked the GAO to investigate, stating, "The withholding was illegal."[270] In a decision memo released in

---

[268] William Bradford Middlekauf, "Twisting the President's Arm: The Impoundment Control Act as a Tool for Enforcing the Principle of Appropriation Expenditure," *Yale Law Journal*, Volume 100, Issue 1, 1990, p. 211, available at https://digitalcommons.law.yale.edu/cgi/viewcontent.cgi?article=7306&context=ylj.

[269] See https://www.senate.gov/reference/glossary_term/rescission.htm.

[270] Melissa Lemieux, "Trump Violated Another Law, the Impoundment Control Act, by Withholding Ukraine Aid, Democratic Senator Van Hollen Says," *Newsweek*, 23 December 2019, available at

January 2020, the GAO concluded that the Impoundment Control Act had been violated, noting "Faithful execution of the law does not permit the President to substitute his own policy priorities for those that Congress has enacted into law."[271] The 300-page impeachment inquiry report produced by the House Permanent Select Committee on Intelligence also asserted that President Trump violated the Impoundment Control Act.[272]

For a brief period of time, the president was granted the ability to refuse to spend funds approved by Congress through Congress' adoption of the "Line-Item Veto Act of 1996." President Bill Clinton used the line-item veto 82 times before it was declared unconstitutional by a Federal District Court in a ruling upheld by the Supreme Court in 1998.[273]

The Congressional Budget Act also created the Congressional Budget Office (CBO), which serves as the congressional equivalent of OMB. CBO provides economic data to Congress in order to help with congressional oversight of the budget process. This is a reflection of the importance Congress attaches to its Article I, Section 9

---

https://www.newsweek.com/trump-violated-another-law-impoundment-control-act-withholding-ukraine-aid-democratic-senator-1478966.

[271] Thomas H. Armstrong, Government Accountability Office, "Office of Management and Budget-Withholding of Ukraine Security Assistance," Decision Memo B-331564, 16 January 2020, available at https://www.gao.gov/assets/710/703909.pdf.

[272] Report of the House Permanent Select Committee on Intelligence, Pursuant to H. Res. 660 in Consultation with the House Committee on Oversight and Reform and the House Committee on Foreign Affairs, *The Trump-Ukraine Impeachment Inquiry Report*, December 2019, available at https://intelligence.house.gov/uploadedfiles/20191203_-_full_report___hpsci_impeachment_inquiry_-_20191203.pdf.

[273] Robert Pear, "U.S. Judge Rules Line Item Veto Act Unconstitutional," *The New York Times*, 13 February 1998, available at https://www.nytimes.com/1998/02/13/us/us-judge-rules-line-item-veto-act-unconstitutional.html.

authorities and what James Madison referred to in *Federalist 58* as Congress' "power of the purse." The act also required that Congress pass a Budget Resolution each year, which reflects agreement between the House and Senate on the overall size and general composition of the federal budget. Notwithstanding Congress' failure to do so consistently in recent years, passage of a Budget Resolution is usually done by mid-April and breaks out funding levels for the government into 20 functional categories.[274] These agreed-upon allocations are then forwarded to each committee with jurisdiction over spending and serve as guidelines for the committees' subsequent budget actions.[275]

Congress is responsible for passing a dozen annual appropriations bills to fund the activities of the federal government. In recent years, this has proven to be easier said than done. Occasionally, some appropriations bills are passed on time while others are not. This can lead to a temporary shutdown of agency activities or passage of a Continuing Resolution (CR). Sometimes a number of appropriations bills funding multiple agencies are rolled

---

[274] For example, the functional budget category for national defense (including DoD and the defense-related programs of other federal departments and agencies) is labeled "050" and international affairs spending is classified under category "150." Within the "050" account, DoD-only spending is classified as a separate "051" subcategory. See Bill Heniff Jr., "Functional Categories of the Federal Budget," Congressional Research Service, CRS Report 98-280 GOV, 13 June 2003, available at https://www.everycrsreport.com/files/20030613_98-280_8473fe96e58a2f4b51c31f780d24c240ef9b8ed5.pdf. Also see House Committee on the Budget, "Focus on Function: An Introduction," 11 June 2018, available at https://budget.house.gov/sites/democrats.budget.house.gov/files/documents/Focus%20on%20Function%20Intro_1.pdf.

[275] Congress did not pass a Budget Resolution in fiscal year 2020, but rather used a procedural process known as "deeming" to establish budget allocation limits. See Committee for a Responsible Federal Budget, "Appropriations 101," 7 June 2019, available at https://www.crfb.org/papers/appropriations-101.

into one "omnibus" or "minibus" appropriations bill. In fiscal year 2020, Congress failed to pass the necessary appropriations bills on time and instead passed two CRs funding the government through December 20, 2019, when Congress completed its work and President Trump signed the final appropriations measures into law.[276]

Although the appropriations process has often been challenging, the authorization process also establishes funding levels. However, controversy has persisted over the legal standing of the authorization of funds to be appropriated. The Military Construction Act of 1959 provided that "No funds may be appropriated after December 31, 1960, to or for the use of any armed force of the United States for the procurement of aircraft, missiles, or naval vessels unless the appropriation of such funds has been authorized by legislation enacted after such date."[277] This established a clear role for the authorization committees and was a way of increasing Congress' control of the budget process. However, more recently, the need for a specific authorization before funds can be appropriated has been questioned, and the GAO stated that "The existence of a statute (organic legislation) imposing substantive functions upon an agency that require funding for their performance is itself sufficient legal authorization for the necessary appropriations."[278]

---

[276] Committee for a Responsible Federal Budget, "Appropriations Watch: FY 2020," 24 December 2019, available at http://www.crfb.org/blogs/appropriations-watch-fy-2020.

[277] Section 412(b) of Public Law 86-149, 10 August 1959, p. 322, available at https://uscode.house.gov/statutes/pl/86/149.pdf.

[278] "Authorization of Appropriations: Procedural and Legal Issues," CRS Report R42098, op. cit.

The DoD Budget Process

Few things are as complex and labyrinthine as the DoD budget process. Prior to World War II, the Army and Navy developed and submitted separate budgets to Congress. This changed with the creation of the Department of Defense by the National Security Act of 1947. Within DoD, the Office of the Secretary of Defense (OSD) centralized development of the budget using a process that came to be known as Planning, Programming, Budgeting, and Execution or PPBE (originally called Planning, Programming, and Budgeting System, or PPBS, and later PPBES). The PPBE process is the primary method for managing and allocating resources within DoD and setting program priorities.[279] (See Figures 2 and 3)

Then-Secretary of Defense Robert S. McNamara created the PPBS in 1961 as a way to give the Pentagon greater control over long-range defense planning. McNamara required each of the services to document its planning and programming needs over a five-year period. The process was used to develop a Five-Year Defense Program (also known as a Future Years Defense Program) or "FYDP" (pronounced "fiddip") that would help DoD plan and manage its resources more effectively and efficiently. The effort is defined as "a formal, systematic structure for making decisions on policy, strategy, and the development of forces and capabilities to accomplish anticipated missions."[280]

The process of developing a DoD budget is complicated and time-consuming. Military operators in the field identify their needs based on mission requirements and

---

[279] Brendan W. McGarry, "Defense Primer: Planning, Programming, Budgeting and Execution (PPBE) Process," *Congressional Research Service*, 27 January 2020, available at https://crsreports.congress.gov/product/pdf/IF/IF10429.

[280] Ibid.

submit their requests up through their chains of command. They are weighed by the individual services and combatant commanders and then go through OSD and the Joint Staff,

Figure 2. Key Documents and Products of the PPBE System (as of October 2017)[281]

Phase	DOD Lead	Key Documents
Planning	*USD(P)*	Inputs = strategy documents (e.g., National Security Strategy, Defense Strategy Review, National Military Strategy); Chairman's advice; formal or informal guidance from the President. Products: Defense Planning Guidance (OSD) & Fiscal Guidance to military departments and agencies (OMB) Next Steps: Departments and agencies develop and provide service Program Objective Memoranda (POMs)
Programming	*CAPE*	Inputs: POMs; Chairman's Program Assessment Products: SecDef Resource Management Decisions directed to the services; adjudication of all programming decisions; POMs adjusted
Budgeting	*USD(C)*	Inputs: Final adjusted POMs Products: Defense budget -- input to the Presidential Budget
Execution	*USD(C)*	Inputs: Defense Authorization and Appropriation Acts Products: Obligations; re-programming requests

---

[281] This chart appears in Tom Galvin (Ed.), Doug Waters, Lou Yuengert, Richard Meinhart, and Fred Gellert, *Defense Management – Primer for Senior Leaders, First Edition* (Department of Command, Leadership, and Management, School of Strategic Landpower, U.S. Army War College, Carlisle, PA, 2018), available at https://publications.armywarcollege.edu/pubs/3534.pdf. The DoD lead organizations listed are the Under Secretary of Defense (Policy), Cost Assessment and Program Evaluation (CAPE), and the Under Secretary of Defense (Comptroller).

Figure 3. The PPBE Process[282]

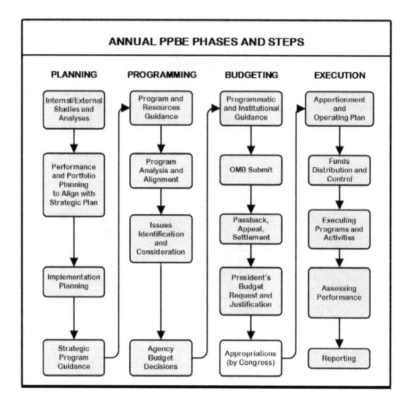

where they must be prioritized against competing requests and programs. All programs are grouped into various mission-oriented defense categories and subdivided into Program Elements (PEs). A PE specifies the resources applied to a program and is also referred to as a "line item." Identifying programs by their PE or line-item number

---

[282] This chart is extracted from Chapter 1 of the *National Aeronautics and Space Administration (NASA) Procedural Requirements* document NPR 9420.1A, 7 September 2016, available at https://nodis3.gsfc.nasa.gov/npg_img/N_PR_9420_001A_/N_PR_9420_001A__Chapter1.pdf.

makes it easy to follow where budget resources are being applied.[283]

Various defense documents also provide planning guidance used to prioritize programming and budget requests. Over the years, these documents have included the "Defense Planning Guidance" (formerly called "Defense Planning and Programming Guidance"), "Guidance for the Development of the Force," "Strategic Planning Guidance," "Joint Programming Guidance," and others, each of which is intended to provide guidance to each DoD component in preparing its respective "Program Objective Memorandum" or "POM." The POM is a tool for prioritizing and allocating resources for programs over a five-year period in support of military objectives. POM requirements are reviewed within OSD and adjusted as necessary to meet contemporary strategic requirements.[284]

Unfortunately, the DoD acquisition process is so complex it can take as long as two decades for a weapon system to develop from concept to procurement. Threats to national security, however, can change rapidly; consequently, so can requirements and the resource needs necessary to meet them. Technology also advances at a much faster speed than the DoD procurement process. This has been a source of great consternation not only within

---

[283] Brendan W. McGarry and Heidi M. Peters, "Defense Primer: Future Years Defense Program (FYDP)," Congressional Research Service, CRS Report IF10831, 28 January 2020, available at https://fas.org/sgp/crs/natsec/IF10831.pdf.

[284] For a more detailed explanation of the POM process and how it relates to other elements of the DoD budget process, see the Defense Acquisition University presentation, "Lunch and Learn: POM Development," 29 March 2017, available at https://www.dau.edu/Lists/Events/Attachments/8/03-29-2017%20LnL-POM%20Development_B.%20Melton.pdf. Also see AcqNotes, "PPBE Process: Program Objective Memorandum (POM)," 30 May 2018, available at http://acqnotes.com/acqnote/acquisitions/program-objective-memorandum-pom.

DoD itself but among members of Congress who have repeatedly sought to make the defense acquisition system more agile and responsive to current and future needs. The "Weapon Systems Acquisition Reform Act," passed by Congress and signed into law by President Obama in 2009, was a major reorganization of the defense acquisition process.[285] Yet despite the significant reforms it enabled, there remains substantial criticism over the length of time it takes to develop and procure modern military equipment and weaponry. In 2012, the Chairman of the Defense Business Board stated, "When you look at the thousands and thousands and thousands of pages of regulations that have crept in over the years, we say 'start over'," declaring, "If it was me, I'd take 'em all and put a match to it."[286] In 2015, then-SASC Chairman John McCain called the defense acquisition system "a clear and present danger to the national security of the United States."[287]

Despite general agreement on the need for improvement, congressional efforts to reform the defense acquisition system have not been universally hailed. Former Under Secretary of Defense for Acquisition, Technology and Logistics (AT&L), Frank Kendall, criticized provisions in the fiscal year 2017 NDAA as being "totally divorced from the reality of new product development," stating, "Acquisition improvement is going to come from

---

[285] Public Law 111-23, 22 May 2009, available at https://www.congress.gov/111/plaws/publ23/PLAW-111publ23.pdf.

[286] Sydney J. Freedberg Jr., "'Put A Match To It' And Scrap DoD's Buying Rules: Top Pentagon Advisor EXCLUSIVE," *Breaking Defense*, 30 August 2012, available at https://breakingdefense.com/2012/08/put-a-match-to-it-and-scrap-dods-buying-system-top-pentagon/.

[287] Senate Armed Services Committee Press Release, "Senate Armed Services Committee Completes Markup of National Defense Authorization Act for Fiscal Year 2016," 14 May 2015, available at https://www.armed-services.senate.gov/press-releases/senate-armed-services-committee-completes-markup-of-national-defense-authorization-act-for-fiscal-year-2016.

within [the department]. It is not going to be engineered by Hill staffers writing laws for us, it's going to be done by the people who are in the trenches every day...."[288] The FY 2017 NDAA also eliminated AT&L, dividing its functions into two separate organizations: the Under Secretary of Defense for Acquisition and Sustainment (A&S) and the Under Secretary of Defense for Research and Engineering (R&E), again demonstrating the power of Congress to work its will by making changes to DoD's organizational structure.

In any given year, DoD is actually working on three budgets simultaneously. First, the department is obligating, spending, and managing the funds Congress had appropriated for the current fiscal year. Second, DoD officials are working to explain and defend next year's budget request before congressional members and staff. And third, they are preparing and developing the subsequent year's budget request by using the PPBE and POM processes.

Because of the length of time it takes to see a program through to fruition, Congress often finds it difficult to cut or cancel programs after they are initially funded. Cutting the funding usually results in greater total costs and program delays (which often means fewer units procured). Terminating a program entirely, especially after millions (if not billions) of dollars have been invested, risks having it perceived as a colossal waste of taxpayer dollars and is likely to incur the wrath of contractors and defense industry supporters (i.e., constituents) who believe their program is absolutely essential to the nation's security. Many terminated programs are killed as a result of decisions taken by DoD, rather than Congress; however, Congress has

---

[288] Jared Serbu, "In final speech, DoD acquisition chief knocks congressional reforms as unhelpful," *Federal News Network,* 18 January 2017, available at https://federalnewsnetwork.com/defense/2017/01/final-speech-dod-acquisition-chief-knocks-congressional-reforms-unhelpful/.

successfully de-scoped or terminated some significant defense programs, to include President Reagan's Strategic Defense Initiative. The FY 2009 Weapon Systems Acquisition Reform Act required termination of defense programs that exceed certain cost parameters established by the "Nunn-McCurdy" Act, unless certified as necessary by the Secretary of Defense.[289]

Additional Complications

Various other nuances complicate the defense budget process and are often confusing to the general public. For example, not all defense dollars are equal. There are various "pots" of money that are available for obligation over different time periods, depending on the purpose for which they are to be used. Defense dollars fall into different categories—there is money for research, development, testing and evaluation (RDT&E); procurement; operations and maintenance (O&M); military construction (MILCON); and military personnel (MILPERS). O&M money generally pays for the costs of ongoing military operations and maintenance and is considered one-year money, i.e., the funds are available to be spent only in the fiscal year in which they are appropriated. However, RDT&E funds are available for obligation over a two-year period; this is because it generally takes time to research and develop new military capabilities. Procurement funds are available for three years, as most major buys of equipment happen in tranches over multiple years. And MILCON funding is

---

[289] The Act was sponsored by Sen. Sam Nunn (D-GA) and Rep. David McCurdy (D-OK). See Heidi M. Peters and Charles V. O'Connor, "The Nunn-McCurdy Act: Background, Analysis, and Issues for Congress," Congressional Research Service, CRS Report R41293, 12 May 2016, available at
https://www.everycrsreport.com/files/20160512_R41293_98924a507e8
ec5a0bfe6dac75c6c5dac3ad38b1f.pdf.

five-year money, as construction projects often take many years to complete.

Because (with the exception of O&M) not all appropriated funds must be spent in the year in which they are appropriated, it is not always easy for DoD budget officials or congressional staffers to know with certainty precisely how much money is needed in subsequent years to meet military requirements. The situation is complicated further if the process of obligating funds is disrupted as a result of delays in passing appropriations bills, the impact of CRs, or a government shutdown.

Additional complications arise when not all appropriated funds can be obligated or spent during the required time period. Unanticipated changes to plans or schedules can result in program slippages that make it more difficult to meet earlier expenditure timeframes. In certain cases, Congress reacts to the lack of timely execution in the current fiscal year by reducing the budget request for the subsequent year. This is not an uncommon occurrence.

Occasionally, DoD will ask Congress for a "reprogramming" action. Reprogramming is "the shifting of funds within an appropriation to purposes other than those contemplated at the time of appropriation."[290] A reprogramming of procurement funds may be needed if fewer units of one weapon system and more units of another are required. Reprograming actions must be approved by all four congressional defense committees— HASC, SASC, HAC, and SAC. Should even one committee disapprove, the funds may not be repurposed. Former Secretary of Defense Donald H. Rumsfeld highlighted the

---

[290] While "transfer authority" allows funds to be shifted between accounts, a reprogramming allows funds to be used for other activities within the same account. See Office of the General Counsel, Government Accountability Office, "Principles of Federal Appropriations Law, Chapter 2 – The Legal Framework," GAO Report GAO-16-464SP, Fourth Edition, 2016 Revision, p. 2-44, available at https://www.gao.gov/assets/680/675709.pdf.

difficulties this can cause when he testified to the SASC in 2004: "The Department of Defense spends an average of $42 million an hour – yet we are not allowed to move $15 million from one account to another without getting permission from 4-6 different congressional committees, a process that can take several months to complete."[291]

Of course, global events may require a rapid and unexpected reallocation of defense resources from one activity to another. In today's dynamic international security environment, it is difficult to predict where tomorrow's national security threats will emerge. As much of the defense budget supports programs that are necessarily responsive to world events beyond our capacity to control, long-term defense planning is fraught with uncertainty. U.S. military forces may be called upon to intervene rapidly and unexpectedly in areas of the world where threats to U.S. security emerge in unpredictable fashion. The wars in Afghanistan and Iraq, and the efforts to crush the ISIS caliphate in Syria, are notable examples. This is where emergency supplemental appropriations (or OCO funds) play a major role. Only the appropriations committees, however, formally approve an OCO request in cases where DoD asks for a supplemental appropriation to fund an unanticipated emergency requirement. The unstable nature of the international system makes supplemental budget requests a regular staple of the defense budgeting process. In the first five years after the terrorist attacks of September 11, 2001, Congress passed at least nine supplemental appropriations bills for military operations totaling more than $300 billion.[292]

---

[291] Testimony of Donald H. Rumsfeld before the Senate Armed Services Committee, "Department of Defense Authorization for Appropriations for Fiscal Year 2004," op. cit., p. 18.

[292] "Military Operations: Precedents for Funding Contingency Operations in Regular or in Supplemental Appropriations Bills," Congressional Research Service, CRS Report RS22455, 13 June 2006, p. 1, available at

Because of these complications, some have suggested moving to a biennial defense budgeting process. This was tried briefly in the past, but ultimately rejected.[293] Some in DoD objected to a biennial budget cycle because it locked the department into spending guidelines for two years; this was seen as unduly restrictive, especially during periods of great uncertainty and volatility in the international security environment. Some in Congress objected to the fact that authorizing the defense budget every two years would lessen their ability to use the process to set policy or attach favored amendments. And, since the term of House members is only two years, some might have only one "bite at the defense apple" during their term of office.

How the NDAA Is Organized

The annual NDAA is a complex document, usually exceeding 1,000 pages in length, written in "legalese," and often difficult to understand. It is organized according to "Titles," which are essentially chapters that correspond to the various "pots" of money discussed earlier. Title I deals with procurement and contains funding authorizations for

---

https://www.everycrsreport.com/files/20060613_RS22455_d99aa9b5be63f38c00159a4b2c1f9fe1d0de7abe.pdf.

[293] For example, the National Defense Authorization Act for Fiscal Years 1990 and 1991, and the National Defense Authorization Act for Fiscal Years 1992 and 1993, both signed into law by President Bill Clinton, each authorized military funding for a two-year period. However, in both cases the authorization of funding for the second year was "effective only with respect to appropriations made during the first session" of the One Hundred First (and One Hundred Second) Congresses." Consequently, two subsequent and separate NDAAs for Fiscal Years 1991 and 1993 were enacted. See Public Law 101-189, available at https://www.govinfo.gov/content/pkg/STATUTE-103/pdf/STATUTE-103-Pg1352.pdf and Public Law 102-190, available at https://www.govinfo.gov/content/pkg/STATUTE-105/pdf/STATUTE-105-Pg1290.pdf.

all weapons buys—everything from big ticket items like ships, planes, and tanks, to small line items like widgets. With some exceptions, whatever hardware the department seeks money to buy is generally found in Title I of the NDAA.   This also includes procurement of contract services, which account for more than one-half of the overall DoD budget. DoD takes thousands of contract actions each day and as of FY 2018, roughly $350 billion of the department's nearly $700 billion budget went to contracting services.[294]

Title II deals with RDT&E. Before a weapon or system can be bought it must be developed—sometimes from scratch.   As new technologies come along, they are researched, developed, tested, and evaluated using Title II funds. RDT&E funds are used to determine if a new system is safe, reliable, and effective before it is procured.

Title III provides operations and maintenance funding for the military. It pays to maintain equipment in working order and to fix equipment that breaks. Ongoing U.S. overseas contingency operations with a high operations tempo, such as deployments in the Middle East where the climate and operating environment can be harsh on materiel, increase the likelihood that equipment will break, wear out, or need to be replaced more frequently. O&M funding allows for this, including the purchase of spare parts.

Title IV funds the military personnel accounts. This includes the salaries of the active duty and reserve forces, as well as the benefits necessary to recruit and retain motivated, high-quality personnel in the All-Volunteer Force. An All-Volunteer Force is expensive, and the cost of paying for our men and women in uniform and providing

---

[294] See Government Accountability Office, "DoD Contract Management – High Risk Issue," available at
https://www.gao.gov/key_issues/dod_contract_management/issue_s ummary.

for their families comprises roughly a quarter of all DoD spending.[295]

Other Titles in the NDAA deal with acquisition policy (Title VIII), the organization of DoD (Title IX), matters relating to foreign nations (Title XII), strategic programs (Title XVI), and various DoE/NNSA activities (Title XXXI). The Nunn-Lugar Cooperative Threat Reduction program (discussed in greater detail in Chapter Twelve) is a separate Title in the NDAA (Title XIII). There may also be a classified annex to the NDAA.[296]

Timetables for Action: From Budget Submission, to Mark-Up, to Conference

The government operates on a fiscal year (FY) cycle that runs from October 1 through September 30. Therefore, when funds are appropriated for a certain fiscal year, such as FY 2020, they are available for obligation (i.e., to be put on contract) beginning on October 1 of the prior year (2019).

By law, the president must submit a budget for the upcoming fiscal year by the first Monday in February (though in practice this is occasionally delayed). Work on preparing the budget begins in the various agencies about 10 months before the president submits the budget to Congress (usually around the April timeframe, which is

---

[295] One estimate indicates that the costs of the All-Volunteer Force increased from $90 billion in 2001 to $170 billion in 2010. See Spencer Ackerman, "Gates (Delicately) Criticizes the All-Volunteer Military," *Wired*, 29 September 2010, available at https://www.wired.com/2010/09/gates-delicately-criticizes-the-all-volunteer-military/.

[296] For a summary of the organization of the NDAA, see Brendan W. McGarry and Valerie Heitshusen, "Defense Primer: Navigating the NDAA," Congressional Research Service, CRS Report IF10516, 29 January 2020, available at https://fas.org/sgp/crs/natsec/IF10516.pdf.

roughly 18 months before the start of the fiscal year).[297] After submitting the budget to Congress, the defense portion of the president's budget request is referred to the four main defense committees and subcommittees, the HASC, SASC, HAC-D, and SAC-D. At this point, the committees begin the process of reviewing the administration's budget request and determining what to support, what to reject, and what to modify.

The process starts with a series of "posture hearings," during which defense officials appear before the committees to explain and justify their budget request. The Secretary of Defense and Chairman of the Joint Chiefs of Staff are usually the first to testify, followed in turn by the service secretaries, service chiefs, and other officials, all the way to the individual program managers. These officials appear separately before the various House and Senate committees. At the same time, committee staffers are meeting with DoD officials and pouring over the thousands of pages of budget justification documents DoD submits to the Hill that provide details on and rationale for the department's various program budget requests. (See Figure 4)

This activity is designed to provide Congress with the necessary background information to allow the committees to make informed judgments about the president's budget request for DoD. By late spring (usually around May), the authorization committees (HASC and SASC) are ready to proceed with their respective "mark-ups" of the budget request. During the mark-up process the committees essentially rewrite the department's budget request to

---

[297] A summary of the budget process timetable can be found in Michelle D. Christensen, "The Executive Budget Process Timetable," Congressional Research Service, CRS Report RS20152, 5 December 2012, available at https://www.senate.gov/CRSpubs/eb724dfb-7318-4c33-9485-3de8ae76faab.pdf.

reflect committee priorities and provide guidance and direction to DoD on multiple policy issues.

The SASC conducts most of its mark-up process behind closed doors, ostensibly to protect any inadvertent discussion of classified information. However, the HASC has traditionally held its mark-up in open session, allowing members of the public to witness the proceedings. The individual subcommittees are the first to mark up their parts of the authorizing legislation, considering funding and legislative provisions in their respective areas of jurisdiction (e.g., strategic forces, personnel, readiness, etc.). The text of the bill is generally prepared by staff, working with the Office of Legislative Counsel, and based on the desires of the chairman and individual subcommittee and committee members. Members can propose amendments to the language during the formal mark-up session, which are debated and voted on. Once each subcommittee marks up its section of the bill, the subcommittee marks are reported to the full committee for further action.

Mark-up is often a tense time for staff, as it is the only time staffers sit at the witness table and respond to member questions about specific provisions in the bill. Members rely heavily on staff to explain the nuances and implications of the legislative provisions being discussed and debated, so detailed knowledge is critical. The HASC steps through each subcommittee mark methodically, then considers "full committee" issues that do not fall within the purview of the individual subcommittees. Unlike the SASC, the HASC traditionally conducts the full committee mark-up in one day, starting in the morning and going until completion, which often lasts into the wee hours of the following morning. What emerges at the end of the process is called the NDAA "Chairman's Mark," and reflects all of the legislative provisions agreed to in the subcommittees and the full committee. Unsurprisingly, many of the provisions are worked out in advance of the formal mark-up, through agreement between the majority and minority staffs. There are always major issues of political controversy that lead to spirited debates among the members; however, in general, the closer the staffs work together, the less painful the process of preparing the NDAA.

One major political controversy that occurred during the process of crafting the FY 1997 NDAA involved the intelligence community's assessment of missile threats to the United States. A National Intelligence Estimate (NIE) that some Republican members of Congress believed downplayed the ballistic missile threat to the United States, led Congress to establish a "Commission to Assess the Ballistic Missile Threat to the United States."[298]   The commission was chaired by former Secretary of Defense Donald H. Rumsfeld (who would later serve again as Secretary of Defense) and came to be known as the "Rumsfeld Commission."   Debate over the NIE ("NIE 95-19"), whose key findings had been declassified by the Clinton Administration, became politically charged.

As the staffer working this issue for the Republican chairman and majority at the time, I worked with my Democratic staff colleague to find common ground in support of the commission. However, Democrats on the committee saw this as an attack on the integrity of the intelligence community and an effort to generate support for a more robust missile defense posture than the Clinton Administration desired. The stalemate was broken only after we agreed to a compromise: in addition to establishing an independent commission, the NDAA directed the Director of Central Intelligence (DCI) to conduct an outside, independent review of NIE 95-19 to see if the intelligence community's assessment was "politicized."[299] The panel of

---

[298] Title XIII, Subtitle B of Public Law 104-201, 23 September 1996, available at https://www.congress.gov/104/plaws/publ201/PLAW-104publ201.pdf.

[299] Section 1311 of Public Law 104-201, Ibid.

independent experts was headed by former DCI Robert M. Gates and concluded that, although there had been methodological flaws in the NIE and it was "politically naïve," there was "no evidence of politicization."[300] By contrast, the Rumsfeld Commission concluded that emerging ballistic missile threats to the United States were "broader, more mature and evolving more rapidly than has been reported in estimates and reports by the Intelligence Community."[301] The commission's conclusions formed the basis for a more assertive congressional approach to U.S. missile defense policy.[302]

In the House, full committee mark-up of the NDAA is governed by rules that require all provisions of the bill to fall squarely within the jurisdiction of the HASC. Provisions that fall outside the HASC's exclusive jurisdiction subject the bill to a process called "sequential referral," meaning that the entire NDAA (not just those provisions that touch on the jurisdictions of other committees) must be referred to the other relevant committees for action. Therefore, the committee seeks to pass a "clean" bill that will not be subjected to sequential referral. The only exception is if the other committees with

---

[300] Statement of Robert M. Gates before the Senate Select Committee on Intelligence, 4 December 1996, pp. 15-16, available at https://books.google.com/books?id=CUpkTs-D0aMC&pg=PA14&lpg=PA14&dq=gates+nie+by+an+independent,+non-governmental+panel+of+individuals+with+appropriate+expertise+and+experience.&source=bl&ots=23PhxEGkWE&sig=ACfU3U2iez7qaA0cGJE4JjQutQZRMxuJPQ&hl=en&sa=X&ved=2ahUKEwjpqfuPyufmAhWFAZ0JHbT3AmAQ6AEwAHoECAgQAQ#v=onepage&q=gates%20nie%20by%20an%20independent%2C%20non-governmental%20panel%20of%20individuals%20with%20appropriate%20expertise%20and%20experience.&f=false.

[301] *Executive Summary of the Report of the Commission to Assess the Ballistic Missile Threat to the United States*, 15 July 1998, available at https://fas.org/irp/threat/bm-threat.htm.

[302] Additional details on this issue are included in Chapter Eleven.

jurisdiction over specific provisions in the NDAA submit a letter waiving their jurisdictional claims. Once the bill is passed in committee, it can be amended on the House floor, where provisions that were deemed unacceptable in committee mark-up can be debated, approved, and subsequently added to the NDAA.

As previously noted, the actual NDAA bill language is often difficult to understand because of the legal language used. References to modifications of obscure U.S. Code provisions or the insertion of words in subparagraphs of prior Public Laws often lack context unless the reader is aware of the underlying statutory language being modified. This is not always readily apparent when reading the legislative text of the NDAA.

To aid in understanding the committee's actions, the HASC and SASC release reports that accompany their respective versions of the NDAA. These narrative documents are intended to explain what the committee did and why. Occasionally, the committee will direct actions or require reports from the Secretary of Defense or other officials in the committee report language rather than the statutory NDAA bill language. This has long been a source of controversy between the Department of Defense and Congress, because committee report language does not carry the same weight as statutory language and is not legally binding. It only reflects the committee's views and, unlike the bill text itself, is not signed into law by the president. Nevertheless, DoD has traditionally tracked and responded to committee report language requests as though they were legally binding, because failing to do so would likely incur the committee's wrath and could lead to subsequent statutory restrictions that penalize the department by withholding funds for programs or otherwise constraining the department's flexibility to operate.

In recent years, the number of congressionally mandated reports to Congress has grown substantially. Some of these required reports are "legacy" reports where the requirement has been on the books for years, even though the original rationale for the report no longer exists, or the member or staffer who originally drafted the requirement is no longer on the Hill. One survey of all congressionally required government reports noted that the number had increased from 303 reports in 1928 to more than 4,000 in 2014. Rep. Mark R. Warner (D-VA) commented, "Remember the original movie 'Raiders of the Lost Ark,' where the ark got put away in that government storeroom? Probably next to the lost ark are all the reports that have never been reviewed."[303]

In an effort to reduce the number of congressionally mandated reports, the Obama Administration identified hundreds of reports that were "outdated or duplicative" and called for their elimination.[304] In 2010, then-Secretary of Defense Robert M. Gates required that all DoD reports to Congress include a cost estimate for producing the report on the title page.[305] This requirement has carried over to this day.[306]

---

[303] David Fahrenthold, "Unrequired Reading," *The Washington Post*, 3 May 2014, available at https://www.washingtonpost.com/sf/national/2014/05/03/unrequired-reading/?utm_term=.999ddc386723.

[304] Beth Cobert, "Calling on Congress to Eliminate Outdated and Duplicative Reporting Requirements," The White House, 25 June 2014, available at https://obamawhitehouse.archives.gov/blog/2014/06/25/calling-congress-eliminate-outdated-and-duplicative-reporting-requirements.

[305] Department of Defense, News Release, "Sec. Gates Announces Efficiencies Initiatives," 9 August 2010, available at https://archive.defense.gov/Releases/Release.aspx?ReleaseID=13782.

[306] For example, the department's June 2019 report to Congress on "Enhancing Security and Stability in Afghanistan" notes, "The estimated cost of this report for the Department of Defense is approximately $304,528 for the Fiscal Year 2019. This includes $17,000

Once committee mark-up is complete, the bill then goes to the chamber floor, where it is debated and amended according to the respective rules of the House or Senate. Because the House contains so many more members than the Senate, the House Rules Committee establishes rules for consideration of the NDAA on the House floor. Those rules identify which amendments are germane and in order for debate and the length of time allocated for debate on each. By contrast, Senate rules allow for a less structured and more open floor debate, with hundreds of amendments considered. Consequently, the House usually disposes of the NDAA in less time than the Senate, which can debate the bill for days or even weeks before voting on final passage.

During my time on the Hill, committee staff access to the floor was generally restricted with few exceptions (e.g., the Staff Director and General Counsel). When the NDAA was debated on the floor, staffers generally waited in their offices until a particular issue for which they had responsibility was debated, at which time they were called to the floor to answer any questions members might have. This was often referred to as a "hurry up and wait" process, as staffers were "on call" and could be summoned at a moment's notice.

---

in expenses and $304,511 in DoD labor." Available at
https://media.defense.gov/2019/Jul/12/2002156816/-1/-
1/1/ENHANCING-SECURITY-AND-STABILITY-IN-
AFGHANISTAN.PDF.

Figure 4. Extract from the Department of the Air Force FY 2021 RDT&E Budget Request[307]

UNCLASSIFIED

Department of the Air Force
FY 2021 President's Budget
Exhibit R-1 FY 2021 President's Budget
Total Obligational Authority
(Dollars in Thousands)

Appropriation: 3600F Research, Development, Test & Eval, AF

Line No	Program Element Number	Item	Act	FY 2021 Base	FY 2021 OCO for Base Requirements	FY 2021 OCO for Direct War and Enduring Costs	FY 2021 Total OCO	FY 2021 Total (Base + OCO)	S e c
174	0101126F	B-1B Squadrons	07	15,766				15,766	U
175	0101127F	B-2 Squadrons	07	187,399				187,399	U
176	0101213F	Minuteman Squadrons	07	116,569				116,569	U
177	0101316F	Worldwide Joint Strategic Communications	07	27,235				27,235	U
178	0101324F	Integrated Strategic Planning & Analysis Network	07	24,227				24,227	U
179	0101328F	ICBM Reentry Vehicles	07	112,753				112,753	U
181	0102110F	UH-1N Replacement Prog	07	44,464				44,464	U
182	0102326F	Region/Sector Operation Control Center Modernization Program	07	5,929				5,929	U
183	0102412F	North Warning System (NWS)	07	100				100	U
184	0205219F	MQ-9 UAV	07	162,080				162,080	U
185	0205671F	Joint Counter RCIED Electronic Warfare	07			4,080	4,080	4,080	U
186	0207131F	A-10 Squadrons	07	24,535				24,535	U
187	0207133F	F-16 Squadrons	07	223,437				223,437	U
188	0207134F	F-15E Squadrons	07	298,908				298,908	U
189	0207136F	Manned Destructive Suppression	07	14,960				14,960	U
190	0207138F	F-22A Squadrons	07	665,038				665,038	U
191	0207142F	F-35 Squadrons	07	132,229				132,229	U
192	0207146F	F-15EX	07	159,761				159,761	U
193	0207161F	Tactical AIM Missiles	07	19,417				19,417	U

UNCLASSIFIED

---

[307] This page is extracted from the thousands of pages of budget justification materials submitted to Congress by the Department of Defense detailing its FY 2021 budget request. It shows the Air Force request for Research, Development, Test, and Evaluation funds for specific projects, which are identified by their Program Element or "PE" number. Committee staff spend countless hours scouring the details of each line item, comparing the budget request to previous years' requests and prior congressionally allocated funding levels in an effort to understand DoD priorities and trends and to assist members in their oversight of DoD programs. Source: Office of the Under Secretary of Defense (Comptroller), "RDT&E PROGRAMS (R-1) - Department of Defense Budget Fiscal Year 2021," February 2020, available at https://comptroller.defense.gov/Portals/45/Documents/defbudget/fy2021/fy2021_r1.pdf.

Figure 5. Covers of the HASC and SASC Reports on the FY 2020 NDAA, and the Conference Report

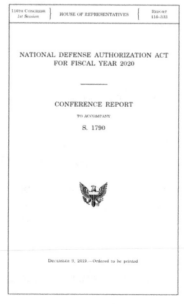

Of course, the amended versions of the House and Senate NDAA are different, reflecting the different priorities of the HASC and SASC and the members of each chamber. This means that before a final version of the bill can be presented to the president for signature (or veto), the competing versions must be reconciled in a House-Senate "conference" committee.   Conferees are chosen among HASC and SASC members, and the process of negotiating a compromise NDAA begins, usually in the summer. It is during conference that much of the serious "horse-trading" occurs, with many issues being resolved by the staffs of both committees.   Some of the most controversial issues, however, are elevated to the "Big Four" members – the Chairmen and Ranking Members of the HASC and SASC – who must decide which provisions in their respective bills to adopt or reject.

During my tenure on the HASC staff, conference meetings often took place in a room in the basement of the Capitol building where SASC and HASC conferees would work to resolve differences on the most contentious NDAA provisions that the staffs were unable to settle at their level. I recall one meeting where a highly controversial provision in the NDAA that I had been working on was discussed. The Senators present wished to address this issue early; however, the HASC members who could explain and advocate for the House position had been unavoidably detained elsewhere and were not present. Seizing the opportunity, the Senators pressed on with their arguments against the HASC provision. One Senator in particular railed against the provision and asked for an explanation of its rationale. As I was the only one in the room familiar with the issue, I began to engage with the Senator on the topic – something that rarely happens, as staffers do not debate members in conference meetings. Needless to say, my interventions were not well received by the Senator, who grew visibly annoyed at this turn of events. Despite my pitch for the House position, the Senate position prevailed.

The administration also seeks to influence the conference outcome by weighing in with a separate "Statement of Administration Policy" (SAP) on both the HASC and SASC versions of the NDAA. These SAPs identify what provisions in the respective bills the administration supports and opposes. Sometimes, a SAP will identify those provisions that, if included in the final conference package, are likely to prompt a presidential veto. This is a negotiating tool the administration uses to "limit damage" to its priorities by threatening an unpalatable action (i.e., a veto).[308]

Once conferees reach agreement on a compromise version of the bill, both the full House and Senate must revote on it, since the earlier versions approved by both chambers were different. This time, however, the agreed-to compromise language, submitted in a "conference report," is not subject to amendment on the chamber floor and is decided by a straight up or down vote. If the conference report is defeated, the bill is sent back to the conference committee for additional work. Once approved by both chambers, the bill then goes to the president for signature or veto. (See Figure 5)

The conference report also contains a "Statement of Managers" — an explanatory narrative describing which provisions of the House and Senate version of the NDAA were accepted or rejected by the conferees. This practice is similar to the committee reports issued by the HASC and SASC after their respective mark-ups and dates back to the

---

[308] Meghan M. Stuessy, "Statements of Administration Policy," Congressional Research Service, CRS Report R44539, 21 June 2016, available at https://www.everycrsreport.com/files/20160621_R44539_7e42b2e047c b7596ad245c7b35ae05c9037c4181.pdf.

reforms adopted by the Legislative Reorganization Act of 1946.

Ideally, the entire process is supposed to be completed before the start of the new fiscal year on October 1 but is often delayed by partisan political wrangling over controversial issues. The process is basically the same for consideration of the annual defense appropriations bill; however, because the appropriations bill focuses on spending amounts rather than policy guidance for DoD, it is often less encumbered by controversy and completed in less time than the NDAA. (See Figure 6, below)

Figure 6. A Simplified Version of the DoD Budget and Legislative Processes[309]

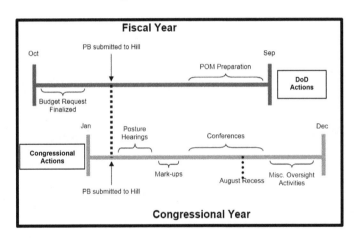

The NDAA process is the most significant way Congress exercises its legitimate oversight role of the military and the military budget. Yet other committees have jurisdiction over important national security issues that affect the U.S. military as well. This includes the House Foreign Affairs Committee; Senate Foreign Relations Committee; House Homeland Security Committee; Senate

---

[309] Chart prepared by author.

Homeland Security and Governmental Affairs Committee; House Oversight and Reform Committee; House Veterans' Affairs Committee; and Senate Veterans' Affairs Committee. It also includes the intelligence committees of Congress, which may not be as public in their activities as the armed services committees, but whose actions are arguably just as important and consequential to the nation's security.

CHAPTER EIGHT

CONGRESSIONAL OVERSIGHT OF THE INTELLIGENCE COMMUNITY AND WEAPONS OF MASS DESTRUCTION

Intelligence oversight has been one of the more controversial issues for Congress and one of the more important given the nation's post-9/11 focus on counterterrorism and the strong bipartisan support for limiting the proliferation of weapons of mass destruction and the technologies that can be used to develop them. The intelligence community budget is more than $80 billion, far less than the DoD budget, although more than 10 percent of the appropriations for intelligence activities are included in the defense budget.[310]

Intelligence spending is divided into two categories: The National Intelligence Program (NIP) and the Military Intelligence Program (MIP). The NIP includes spending that benefits multiple intelligence agencies while the MIP generally addresses the tactical and military requirements of the Department of Defense.

"Intelligence" in this context is defined as "the collection of information of military or political value."[311] The Central

---

[310] Office of the Director of National Intelligence, "U.S. Intelligence Community Budget," available at https://www.dni.gov/index.php/what-we-do/ic-budget. Also see Michael E. DeVine, "Intelligence Community Spending: Trends and Issues," Congressional Research Service, CRS Report R44381, 6 November 2019, available at https://www.everycrsreport.com/files/20191106_R44381_8e36b461d08d310ea0fab734e9f0574cd9680608.pdf.

[311] Oxford dictionary definition, available at https://www.lexico.com/definition/intelligence.

Intelligence Agency (CIA) defines intelligence simply as "the information our nation's leaders need to keep our country safe."[312] The ability to gather, analyze, and process ever expanding amounts of information is the job of intelligence community professionals.

Types of Intelligence

There are multiple types of intelligence that the intelligence community gathers and processes daily. Among the main categories are the following:

- Human Intelligence (HUMINT)
- Geospatial Intelligence (GEOINT)
- Measurement and Signature Intelligence (MASINT)
- Open Source Intelligence (OSINT)
- Signals Intelligence (SIGINT)
- Technical Intelligence (TECHINT)
- Financial Intelligence (FININT)

HUMINT is information gathered from human sources. It is often the most valuable type of intelligence because it can provide information on what people think, which is often unobtainable through technical means. GEOINT is gathered from satellite data or aerial photography. During the Cold War, U-2 aircraft overflights of the Soviet Union provided valuable geospatial intelligence, much like satellite surveillance now provides around the globe. Imagery intelligence (IMINT) is a form of GEOINT based on satellite or aerial photography. MASINT is used to describe the technical characteristics of various targets. OSINT is gathered from open source information. And SIGINT is

---

[312] See Central Intelligence Agency, "What is Intelligence?," 20 June 2008, available at https://www.cia.gov/news-information/featured-story-archive/2007-featured-story-archive/what-is-intelligence.html.

gathered from either communications intercepts (COMINT) or other forms of electronic emissions (ELINT). TECHINT refers to technical intelligence derived from an analysis of the equipment and weapons of other countries, while FININT is gathered from an analysis of the monetary transactions conducted by others.

Some analysts occasionally talk about "TRASHINT," which is the ability to gather unique intelligence information from rummaging through other people's discarded trash. This is not an official designation, however, and the basic point is that there many types of intelligence and many ways to acquire it.

The Intelligence Process and Congressional Oversight

The general difference between information and intelligence is that the latter is a refined and processed form of the former. Intelligence officials speak of the intelligence cycle as having multiple stages. The preliminary stage involves **Planning and Direction**, which is an effort to determine what needs to be done in order to meet established objectives. The **Collection** stage involves gathering as much information as possible from a variety of sources, both classified and unclassified. This may include any or all of the types of intelligence identified above. Once collected, the information goes through a **Processing** stage where it is collated into a report. The **Analysis and Production** stage is where intelligence analysts assess the relative value, meaning, and implications of the information in order to maximize its utility to policy makers. The final stage is **Dissemination**, where the intelligence is provided to policy makers and those with a need to know in order to inform their decision making.[313]

---

[313] Ibid.

The magnitude of the intelligence challenge, and the difficulty of ensuring effective congressional oversight of the intelligence community, is magnified by the fact that there are 16 separate intelligence agencies that fall under the authority of the Director of National Intelligence (DNI), a position that was created in 2004 as an outgrowth of the September 11, 2001 terrorist attacks. Of these 16 agencies, only the CIA is considered independent. Eight entities fall under DoD (the Defense Intelligence Agency (DIA), National Security Agency (NSA), National Geospatial-Intelligence Agency (NGA), National Reconnaissance Office (NRO), Army Intelligence, Navy Intelligence, Air Force Intelligence, and Marine Corps Intelligence). Two entities fall under the Department of Homeland Security (the DHS Office of Intelligence and Analysis and the U.S. Coast Guard). Two other entities fall under the Department of Justice (the Federal Bureau of Investigation (FBI) and the Drug Enforcement Agency (DEA)). And three others operate within other executive branch departments (the State Department, Department of Energy, and Department of the Treasury).

Because of the spread of intelligence agencies and functions throughout the U.S. government, congressional oversight of the intelligence community falls under the jurisdiction of multiple committees. The key committees of jurisdiction include the SSCI, HPSCI, SAC, and HAC, as well as the HASC and SASC authorizing committees. SSCI and HPSCI are the main oversight committees. These are select committees, the membership of which is appointed by the leadership of the Senate and House. House members are limited to six-year terms on the HPSCI, while Senators can serve on the SSCI for eight years. Both the SSCI and HPSCI are authorization committees and provide policy guidance to the intelligence community. Whereas the HPSCI is run under traditional House rules that specify a chairman and ranking (minority) member, the SSCI operates differently. To foster bipartisanship on such important national security issues, the ranking minority Senator is considered the vice chairman of the committee, with the authority to run the committee when the chairman is unavailable. The unusual arrangement is unique among congressional committees and is embodied in the SSCI's rules of procedure.[314]

After the creation of the CIA by the National Security Act of 1947, Congress generally took a hands-off approach to intelligence matters, deferring to the executive branch on many intelligence matters. In 1955, Sen. Mike Mansfield (D-MT) proposed legislation to create a Joint Committee on Central Intelligence. The bill was opposed by President Eisenhower, who declared that "this kind of a bill would be passed over my dead body."[315] In fact, the Senate voted it down by a greater than two-to-one margin.[316] The following year, Sen. Leverett Saltonstall (R-MA) stated that "it is not a question of reluctance on the part of the CIA officials to speak to us. Instead, it is a question of our reluctance, if you will, to seek information and knowledge

---

[314] Senate Select Committee on Intelligence, "Rules of Procedure," available at https://www.intelligence.senate.gov/about/rules-procedure.

[315] Cited in Arthur M. Schlesinger, *The Imperial Presidency*, (Houghton Mifflin Company, Boston and New York, 2004), p. 451, available at https://books.google.com/books?id=ZkxlY4S2iWYC&pg=PT481&lpg=PT481&dq=eisenhower+intelligence+committee+this+bill+would+be+passed+over+my+dead+body&source=bl&ots=Zu8B4qXYVE&sig=ACfU3U0NJzJybpA6RR9ukbqo6j-WfBUikA&hl=en&sa=X&ved=2ahUKEwigyN-ylujmAhUsTt8KHaEWAGwQ6AEwCXoECAoQAQ#v=onepage&q=eisenhower%20intelligence%20committee%20this%20bill%20would%20be%20passed%20over%20my%20dead%20body&f=false.

[316] Frederick M. Kaiser, "Legislative History of the Senate Select Committee on Intelligence," Congressional Research Service, 16 August 1978, pp. 2-3, available at https://fas.org/sgp/crs/intel/ssci-leghist.pdf.

on subjects which I personally, as a Member of Congress and as a citizen, would rather not have...."[317]

Congressional deference to the executive branch on intelligence matters changed dramatically after Congress began investigating various CIA activities, including assassination attempts against Cuban leader Fidel Castro and U.S. involvement in the overthrow of regimes in Iran and Guatemala. In 1975, the Senate established the Senate Select Committee to Study Governmental Operations with Respect to Intelligence Activities (the "Church Committee"), headed by Sen. Frank Church (D-ID). That same year in the House, a Select committee (the "Pike Committee") chaired by Rep. Otis G. Pike (D-NY) also investigated illicit CIA activities. As a result of these congressional investigations, the Senate formally created the SSCI in 1976, and the House created the HPSCI in 1977.[318]

Both the SSCI and HPSCI set policy on intelligence matters; assess the organization and structure of the intelligence community; establish limits of various intelligence activities and actions; authorize funding; and oversee and approve covert actions. They also play an important role in assessing arms control treaty verification capabilities. Because of the highly classified nature of the

---

[317] Comments of Sen. Leverett Saltonstall, *Congressional Record*, 9 April 1956, p. 5924, available at
https://books.google.com/books?id=rcxCVDdfLZEC&pg=PA5924&lpg=PA5924&dq=sen+saltonstall+reluctance+to+seek+information+on+matters&source=bl&ots=PkgBxuazPD&sig=ACfU3U2_-hVJPZO7pPM3W9UEqVt96x4LeA&hl=en&sa=X&ved=2ahUKEwiB2a-lk-jmAhUmwVkKHQKKDxMQ6AEwAXoECAwQAQ#v=onepage&q=sen%20saltonstall%20reluctance%20to%20seek%20information%20on%20matters&f=false.

[318] Central Intelligence Agency, "The CIA and Congress: The Creation of HPSCI," 30 April 2013, available at https://www.cia.gov/news-information/featured-story-archive/2011-featured-story-archive/cia-and-congress-hpsci.html.

intelligence work they oversee, most SSCI and HPSCI hearings are closed to the public and the number of legislative bills they pass is small.

Key Legislation

There have been several key pieces of intelligence-related legislation passed by Congress that have had an enduring effect on the operation of the intelligence community. For example, the 1974 Hughes-Ryan Amendment to the 1961 Foreign Assistance Act (named for its co-sponsors Sen. Harold E. Hughes (D-IA) and Rep. Leo Ryan (D-CA)) was passed in the wake of the Watergate scandal and concerns over a variety of CIA activities abroad. The legislation required the president, before spending any money on covert action activities, to issue a "finding" that said the activity was "important to the national security" and to report that finding to the appropriate congressional committees (numbering from six to eight at the time).[319]

In 1978, Congress passed the Foreign Intelligence and Surveillance Act (FISA), which allows for the physical and electronic surveillance of foreign terrorism suspects. The law also established the Foreign Intelligence and Surveillance Court, where government requests for warrants to eavesdrop on U.S. citizens are reviewed. This has been a highly controversial aspect of the law, which has been amended several times in an attempt to strike a balance between the need to protect the privacy of Americans and to allow for legitimate intelligence gathering on possible terrorist-related cases.

---

[319] James S. Van Wagenen, Central Intelligence Agency, "A Review of Congressional Oversight - Critics and Defenders," 27 June 2008, available at https://www.cia.gov/library/center-for-the-study-of-intelligence/csi-publications/csi-studies/studies/97unclass/wagenen.html.

The Intelligence Oversight Act of 1980 modified the Hughes-Ryan Amendment to the Foreign Assistance Act and reduced the requirement for the executive branch to report intelligence findings to only the HPSCI and SSCI.

The post-9/11 Intelligence Reform and Terrorism Prevention Act of 2004 created the position of DNI and established the National Counterterrorism Center, which has the mission of integrating U.S. counterterrorism (CT) activities "by fusing foreign and domestic CT information, providing terrorism analysis, sharing information with partners across the CT enterprise, and driving whole-of-government action to secure our national CT objectives."[320]

Among the more controversial pieces of legislation passed by Congress was the Uniting and Strengthening America by Providing Appropriate Tools Required to Intercept and Obstruct Terrorism Act of 2001, better known colloquially as the "PATRIOT Act." Signed into law by President George W. Bush, it dramatically reduced restrictions on the ability of U.S. law enforcement agencies to search telephone, email, medical, financial, and other records as part of an effort to ease foreign intelligence gathering within the United States. The act was set to expire in 2011, when President Obama extended three of its key provisions for four additional years: those involving "roving wiretaps"; surveillance of "lone wolves"; and the "bulk collection" of phone records (the so-called NSA "metadata" or "Section 215" program).

In the wake of the Edward Snowden leaks in 2013, Congress limited the metadata program in 2015 by passing the Uniting and Strengthening America by Fulfilling Rights and Ensuring Effective Discipline Over Monitoring Act of 2015 (the "USA FREEDOM Act"), but which also reauthorized some of the provisions in the original USA

---

[320] Office of the Director of National Intelligence, "The National Counterterrorism Center," Mission Statement, available at https://www.dni.gov/index.php/nctc-who-we-are/mission-vision.

PATRIOT Act.[321]   However, the provisions of this act, scheduled to sunset on December 15, 2019, were extended until March 15, 2020, and had not been renewed at the time of this writing.[322] Sen. Patrick Leahy (D-VT) and Sen. Mike Lee (R-UT) argued for a reauthorization of the restrictions in the USA FREEDOM Act, with Sen. Leahy declaring that it would strike an appropriate balance between the need to protect the privacy of Americans and the necessity of targeting terrorists.[323]

Even the act of signing a controversial bill into law can become politicized, as evidenced when some in Congress challenged President Obama's use of an autopen to sign the extension of the USA PATRIOT Act in 2011. In a letter to the president, Rep. Tom Graves (R-GA) quoted Article I,

---

[321] See Jake Laperruque, "It's Time to End the NSA's Metadata Collection Program," *Wired*, 3 April 2019, available at https://www.wired.com/story/wired-opinion-nsa-metadata-collection-program/. Also see Jennifer Steinhauer and Jonathan Weisman, "U.S. Surveillance in Place Since 9/11 Is Sharply Limited," *The New York Times*, 2 June 2015, available at https://www.nytimes.com/2015/06/03/us/politics/senate-surveillance-bill-passes-hurdle-but-showdown-looms.html.

[322] Robert Chesney, "Three FISA Authorities Sunset in December: Here's What You Need to Know," *Lawfare*, 16 January 2019, available at https://www.lawfareblog.com/three-fisa-authorities-sunset-december-heres-what-you-need-know. Also see Jake Laperruque, "What to Expect for the PATRIOT Act Reauthorization," Project on Government Oversight, 11 February 2020, available at https://www.pogo.org/analysis/2020/02/what-to-expect-for-the-patriot-act-reauthorization/ and Charlie Savage, "House Departs Without Vote to Extend Expired F.B.I. Spy Tools," *The New York Times*, 27 March 2020, available at https://www.nytimes.com/2020/03/27/us/politics/house-fisa-bill.html.

[323] Bob Kinzel and Matthew Smith, "Co-Sponsor Leahy Works To Renew USA Freedom Act Before Legislation Sunsets," Vermont Public Radio, 8 November 2019, available at https://www.vpr.org/post/co-sponsor-leahy-works-renew-usa-freedom-act-legislation-sunsets#stream/0.

Section 7 of the Constitution, which states: "Every Bill which shall have passed the House of Representatives and the Senate, shall, before it become a Law, be presented to the President of the United States; If he approve he shall sign it, but if not he shall return it..." Rep. Graves asked President Obama for confirmation that the bill "was presented to you prior to the autopen signing, as well as a detailed, written explanation of your Constitutional authority to assign a surrogate the responsibility of signing bills passed by Congress into law."[324]

This was apparently the first time a president had used an autopen to sign a bill into law, a practice President Obama continued to follow on multiple occasions. Indeed, a 2005 Bush Administration memorandum concluded that "the President need not personally perform the physical act of affixing his signature to a bill to sign it" and, therefore, "may sign a bill in this manner."[325]

Significant Intelligence Failures Related to WMD

Few national security issues are arguably more important than keeping weapons of mass destruction out of the hands of U.S. adversaries. Accurate and timely intelligence is indispensable to this effort, and Congress takes its oversight responsibilities in this area seriously. Nevertheless, there have been some notable intelligence failures involving

---

[324] Frank James, "Obama's Autopen 'Signing' Of Patriot Act Raises Eyebrows, Has Unlikely Ally," National Public Radio, 27 May 2011, available at https://www.npr.org/sections/itsallpolitics/2011/05/27/136724009/obamas-autopen-signing-of-patriot-act-raises-eyebrows-has-unlikely-ally.

[325] Memorandum from Howard C. Nielson, Jr., Deputy Assistant Attorney General, Office of Legal Counsel, Department of Justice, 7 July 2005, available at https://www.justice.gov/file/450876/download.

WMD that have led Congress to act in an attempt to strengthen the effectiveness of the intelligence community.

For example, in 1998, India conducted a series of underground nuclear tests, catching the U.S. intelligence community by surprise. This was followed within weeks by a series of nuclear tests conducted by Pakistan, raising the prospect of a nuclear war between these two nuclear nations. Then-Chairman of the SSCI, Sen. Richard Shelby (R-AL), declared, "It looks to me like this is a colossal failure of our intelligence-gathering system, perhaps the greatest failure in a decade.... We simply cannot and must not tolerate such failure on the part of the intelligence community."[326] Sen. Tom Harkin (D-IA) noted, "A thorough review needs to be made of the whole CIA operation."[327] Both the SSCI and HPSCI held hearings to determine the reasons for the intelligence failure and what could be done to prevent such failures in the future. Other committees of Congress did the same. In response to the nuclear tests, Congress passed several economic sanctions bills that allowed the president to waive sanctions against India and Pakistan as a tool to encourage nuclear restraint by both parties.[328] (The issue of sanctions is discussed in greater detail in Chapter Thirteen.)

The United States received another shock in 1998, when North Korea launched a three-stage Taepodong rocket in an attempt to place a satellite in orbit. While the satellite failed to achieve orbit, the intelligence community was surprised

---

[326] Robin Wright, "U.S. Intelligence Failed to Warn of India's Atom Tests," *Los Angeles Times*, 13 May 1998, available at https://www.latimes.com/archives/la-xpm-1998-may-13-mn-49267-story.html.

[327] Ibid.

[328] Jonathan Medalia, Dianne Rennack, et al., "India-Pakistan Nuclear Tests and U.S. Response," Congressional Research Service, CRS Report 98-570 F, 24 November 1998, pp. 34-36, available at https://www.everycrsreport.com/files/19981124_98-570_6ba82961282f5bb2b429282bbb444eeda17df798.pdf.

by the solid-fuel third stage, which was a major step forward in North Korea's efforts to develop the capability to launch a missile at intercontinental distances.[329] While the first stage of the rocket splashed down in the Sea of Japan, the second stage overflew Japan, traveling a distance of more than 1,300 kilometers.

North Korea's rocket launch followed on the heels of the release of the Rumsfeld Commission's report, which criticized the intelligence community's estimate in NIE 95-19 that "No country, other than the major declared nuclear powers, will develop or otherwise acquire a ballistic missile in the next 15 years that could threaten the contiguous 48 states or Canada." A GAO review of NIE 95-19 concluded that this key finding was "overstated" and that the intelligence estimate suffered from "analytic shortcomings."[330] North Korea's Taepodong launch, in conjunction with the Rumsfeld Commission and GAO reports, laid the groundwork for congressional support of a more robust missile defense posture for the United States.

In 2003, prior to the start of Operation Iraqi Freedom, then-Secretary of State Colin Powell told the UN Security Council that the United States had "solid intelligence" of an Iraqi WMD program. This was based, in part, on an October 2002 intelligence assessment that concluded Iraq "has maintained its chemical weapons effort, energized its missile program, and invested more heavily in biological

---

[329] Wisconsin Project on Nuclear Arms Control, "North Korea Missile Update – 1998," 1 November 1998, available at https://www.wisconsinproject.org/north-korea-missile-update-1998/.
[330] Statement of Richard Davis, Director, National Security Analysis, National Security and International Affairs Division, General Accounting Office, before the Senate Select Committee on Intelligence, "FOREIGN MISSILE THREATS – Analytic Soundness of National Intelligence Estimate 95-19," 4 December 1996, available at https://webcache.googleusercontent.com/search?q=cache:6JtcMMMTf 9AJ:https://www.hsdl.org/%3Fview%26did%3D440918+&cd=8&hl=en &ct=clnk&gl=us.

weapons." The assessment also concluded that Baghdad is "reconstituting its nuclear weapons program" and "could make a nuclear weapon within a year."[331] However, the George W. Bush Administration never found solid evidence of the nuclear weapons program that Saddam Hussein was thought to have reconstituted, causing President Bush to state that "The biggest regret of all the presidency (sic.) has to have been the intelligence failure in Iraq."[332] To this day, some in Congress cite this intelligence failure as a reason not to trust administration warnings about the WMD programs of other countries.

Congressional Actions

In an effort to exercise its legitimate oversight function on WMD matters, Congress has repeatedly sought to assert its right to force the administration to provide it with intelligence information on the WMD activities of other countries. One approach Congress took in the FY 1997 Intelligence Authorization Act was to require a recurring report to Congress on the acquisition by other countries of WMD technologies. The report, required to be submitted by the DNI, included information on "the acquisition by foreign countries during the preceding 6 months of dual-use and other technology useful for the development or production of weapons of mass destruction (including

---

[331] Director of Central Intelligence, *Iraq's Weapons of Mass Destruction Programs*, October 2002, p. 1, available at
https://www.cia.gov/library/reports/general-reports-1/iraq_wmd/Iraq_Oct_2002.pdf.

[332] Tabassum Zakaria, "Bush calls flawed Iraq intelligence biggest regret," Reuters, 1 December 2008, available at
https://www.reuters.com/article/us-bush1/bush-calls-flawed-iraq-intelligence-biggest-regret-idUSTRE4B071020081201.

nuclear weapons, chemical weapons, and biological weapons)...."[333]

These unclassified reports (known as "721 Reports" because they were required by Section 721 of the Act) were provided to Congress until the requirement was repealed in the FY 2013 Intelligence Authorization Act. As the SSCI noted in its report accompanying the FY 2013 Intelligence Authorization Act, this reporting requirement, along with several others, was revoked because it was "burdensome to the Intelligence Community when the information in the reports could be obtained through other means or was no longer considered relevant to current concerns."[334] Despite the repeal of this reporting requirement, a similar reporting requirement was contained in the FY 1998 NDAA[335] and subsequently amended in the FY 2013 NDAA to make the report an annual one covering the acquisition of WMD-related technologies by foreign countries during the previous 12-month period.[336]

Some critics have suggested that Congress has become too deferential to the executive branch regarding its oversight responsibility on this issue. The 9/11 Commission (formally the "National Commission on Terrorist Attacks Upon the United States") concluded in

---

[333] Section 721 of Public Law 104-293, 11 October 1996, available at https://www.congress.gov/104/plaws/publ293/PLAW-104publ293.pdf.

[334] See the report of the Senate Select Committee on Intelligence accompanying the Intelligence Authorization Act for Fiscal Year 2013, 30 July 2012, p. 5, available at https://www.congress.gov/congressional-report/112th-congress/senate-report/192/1?q=%7B%22search%22%3A%5B%22intelligence+authoriza tion+fiscal+year+2013%22%5D%7D&s=10&r=2.

[335] Section 234 of Public Law 105-85, 18 November 1997, available at https://www.congress.gov/105/plaws/publ85/PLAW-105publ85.pdf.

[336] Section 1065 of Public Law 112-239, 2 January 2013, available at https://www.congress.gov/112/plaws/publ239/PLAW-112publ239.pdf.

2004 that "Congress needs dramatic change… to strengthen oversight and focus accountability."[337] More recently, a 2016 CRS report recommended, "Congress may wish to consider requiring additional reporting from the executive branch on WMD proliferation because the number of unclassified reports to Congress on WMD-related issues has decreased considerably in recent years."[338] One analyst suggested the repeal of Section 721 in particular "does unfortunately eliminate a valued, unclassified source of data for academic researchers."[339]

At other times, Congress has been highly aggressive in its approach to intelligence oversight. For example, in 2014 the SSCI released a 700-plus page declassified (redacted) report on the George W. Bush Administration's detention and "enhanced interrogation" program during the Global War on Terror. The full classified report was 6,700 pages long and the committee voted to approve it along mostly partisan lines, with all Democrats voting in favor and all but

---

[337] *Final Report of the National Commission on Terrorist Attacks Upon the United States*, 2004, p. xvi, available at https://www.9-11commission.gov/report/911Report.pdf.

[338] Paul K. Kerr, Steven A. Hildreth, and Mary Beth D. Nikitin, "Iran-North Korea-Syria Ballistic Missile and Nuclear Cooperation," Congressional Research Service, CRS Report R43480, 14 July 2016, available at https://www.everycrsreport.com/files/20160714_R43480_dc75cb195fe8deeeda9abfabc15aaf4a2b1e9efc.pdf.

[339] Albert J. Mauroni, *Countering Weapons of Mass Destruction: Assessing the U.S. Government's Policy*, (Rowman & Littlefield, Lanham, Boulder, New York, and London, 2016), p. 104, available at https://books.google.com/books?id=pCQADQAAQBAJ&pg=PA103&lpg=PA103&dq=repeal+of+721+wmd+acquisition+report+a+mistake&source=bl&ots=YtLb_nrnvQ&sig=ACfU3U2QjYGcv6KxF3pIpySWiGnoKXXi_g&hl=en&sa=X&ved=2ahUKEwi6wZDQ2fHmAhUFjVkKHQy8CXsQ6AEwAHoECAoQAQ#v=onepage&q=repeal%20of%20721%20wmd%20acquisition%20report%20a%20mistake&f=false.

one Republican (Sen. Olympia Snowe (R-WA)) voting against release.[340]

In the process of preparing the report, SSCI staffers were given access to CIA computers, and the CIA later argued that staffers had inappropriately removed classified documents from the computers that were unrelated to the investigation. In response, the SSCI accused the CIA of improperly examining the computers used by the staffers to "spy" on their investigative activities. Then-CIA Director John Brennan issued an apology to the committee after the CIA Inspector General found that the Agency had "improperly accessed" information on the computers used by the SSCI staffers. The result was a strong downturn in the generally collegial relationship between the executive and legislative branches of government, with Sen. Dianne Feinstein (D-CA), then-Chairwoman of the SSCI, saying that the CIA's actions were unconstitutional and Sen. Rand Paul (R-KY) stating, "I think I perceive fear of an intelligence community drunk with power, unrepentant and uninclined to relinquish power."[341] Sen. Feinstein declared, "How this will be resolved will show whether the intelligence committee can be effective in monitoring and investigating our nation's intelligence activities or whether our work can be thwarted by those we oversee."[342]

---

[340] Report of the Senate Select Committee on Intelligence, "Committee Study of the Central Intelligence Agency's Detention and Interrogation Program," 9 December 2014, available at
https://www.intelligence.senate.gov/sites/default/files/publications/CRPT-113srpt288.pdf.

[341] Fred Fleitz, "CIA Director Brennan Should Resign," *National Review*, 4 August 2014, available at
https://www.nationalreview.com/2014/08/cia-director-brennan-should-resign-fred-fleitz/.

[342] Greg Miller and Adam Goldman, "Public feud between CIA, Senate panel follows years of tension over interrogation report," *The Washington Post*, 12 March 2014, available at
https://www.washingtonpost.com/world/national-security/public-feud-between-cia-senate-panel-follows-years-of-tension-over-

More recently, members of the HPSCI accused the National Security Agency (NSA) of withholding documents from Congress relevant to the impeachment proceedings against President Trump. Rep. Adam B. Schiff (D-CA), Chairman of the HPSCI, stated, "The NSA in particular is withholding what are potentially relevant documents to our oversight responsibilities on Ukraine, but also withholding documents potentially relevant that the Senators might want to see during the trial.... And there are signs that the CIA may be on the same tragic course." The administration responded by stating, "The intelligence community is committed to providing Congress with the information and intelligence it needs to carry out its critical oversight role."[343] This is yet another example of the tension that often exists between the executive and legislative branches of government.

Commission Recommendations

It is sometimes said that when Congress doesn't know what to do about an issue, it forms a commission. In matters of national security, Congress has formed multiple commissions since 2008, including the Congressional Commission on the Strategic Posture of the United States; Commission on the National Defense Strategy of the United States; National Security Commission on Artificial Intelligence; and Cyberspace Solarium Commission.[344] The

---

interrogation-report/2014/03/12/f0633d1c-aa1d-11e3-b61e-8051b8b52d06_story.html.

[343] David E. Sanger, "Struggle Between N.S.A. and Congress Over Ukraine Records Breaks Into Open," *The New York Times*, 19 January 2020, available at https://www.nytimes.com/2020/01/19/us/politics/nsa-ukraine-schiff.html.

[344] For a summary of the various commissions authorized by Congress since the late 1980s, see Jacob R. Straus and William T. Egar,

Commission to Assess the Threat to the United States from Electromagnetic Pulse (EMP) Attacks, established in 2000 (and which I supported as a consultant), produced multiple reports warning that the risk of an EMP attack should not be underestimated. As the Commission's Chairman, William R. Graham, testified, "After massive intelligence failures grossly underestimating North Korea's long-range missile capabilities, number of nuclear weapons, warhead miniaturization, and proximity to an H-Bomb, the biggest North Korean threat to the U.S. remains unacknowledged — nuclear EMP attack."[345]

There have been multiple bipartisan commissions established to review intelligence and national security matters, including the 1994 Commission on the Roles and Capabilities of the United States Intelligence Community and the aforementioned Rumsfeld Commission and 9/11 Commission. A number of these commissions were headed by former members of Congress and had relatively robust recommendations for strengthening congressional oversight of the intelligence community and preventing the emergence of WMD threats to the nation. Three in particular are worth mentioning here.

The 9/11 Commission was co-chaired by former Republican Governor of New Jersey Thomas H. Kean and former Representative Lee H. Hamilton (D-IN). The commission called upon Congress to restructure its oversight of the intelligence community in one of two ways: either 1) create a single committee in the House and Senate

---

"Congressional Commissions: Overview and Considerations for Congress," Congressional Research Service, CRS Report R40076, 22 November 2019, pp. 12-20, available at https://fas.org/sgp/crs/misc/R40076.pdf.

[345] Statement of William R. Graham and Peter V. Pry before the House Homeland Security Subcommittee on Oversight and Management Efficiency, 12 October 2017, p. 2, available at https://docs.house.gov/meetings/HM/HM09/20171012/106467/HH RG-115-HM09-Wstate-PryP-20171012.pdf.

with both authorization and appropriation authorities (a move that would be inconsistent with the way Congress generally operates); or 2) create a joint bicameral committee. The commission also recommended establishing an intelligence committee subcommittee "specifically dedicated to oversight, freed from the consuming responsibility of working on the budget."[346] It also recommended abolishing term limits for intelligence committee members and for shrinking their size.

Importantly, the commission concluded, "So long as oversight [of intelligence efforts] is governed by current congressional rules and resolutions, we believe the American people will not get the security they want and need. The United States needs a strong, stable, and capable congressional committee structure to give America's national intelligence agencies oversight, support, and leadership."[347]

In 2005, the "Commission on the Intelligence Capabilities of the United States Regarding Weapons of Mass Destruction," co-chaired by Republican U.S. Circuit Court Judge Laurence H. Silberman and former Senator Chuck S. Robb (D-VA), recommended that both the House and Senate create "focused oversight subcommittees, that the Congress create an intelligence appropriations subcommittee and reduce the Intelligence Community's reliance on supplemental funding, and that the Senate intelligence committee be given the same authority over joint military intelligence programs and tactical intelligence programs that the House intelligence committee now exercises."[348]

---

[346] *Final Report of the National Commission on Terrorist Attacks Upon the United States*, 2004, op. cit., p. 421.

[347] Ibid., p. 419.

[348] *Report of the Commission on the Intelligence Capabilities of the United States Regarding Weapons of Mass Destruction*, 31 March 2005, p. 20, available at https://fas.org/irp/offdocs/wmd_report.pdf.

These recommendations were not uniformly supported. Some believe that a separate intelligence appropriations subcommittee would be unwise, as most intelligence programs are defense programs and considering them separately from defense appropriations would make oversight more difficult. In addition, the budgeting processes for NIP and MIP programs are different, which could further complicate congressional oversight.[349]

The "Commission on the Prevention of WMD Proliferation and Terrorism," led by former Senators Bob Graham (D-FL) and Jim Talent (R-MO), concluded in 2008 that "it is more likely than not that a weapon of mass destruction will be used in a terrorist attack somewhere in the world by the end of 2013."[350] Although this stark prediction fortunately did not materialize, the commission argued that "U.S. policy and strategy… have not kept pace with the growing risks."[351]

The report also contained harsh words for Congress, calling congressional oversight of WMD issues "dysfunctional" and noting, "The existing committee structure does not allow for effective oversight of crosscutting national security threats, such as WMD proliferation and terrorism."[352] Further, the commission stated, "The current structure of congressional oversight of national security is a relic of the Cold War. It has not evolved in response to the changing nature of the threats

---

[349] See, for example, "Intelligence Spending and Appropriations: Issues for Congress," Congressional Research Service, Report R42061, 18 September 2013, available at https://www.everycrsreport.com/files/20130918_R42061_df58a8933d5 b6f22f5defbd1a57a07f2ba8567b0.pdf.

[350] *World at Risk - The Report of the Commission on the Prevention of WMD Proliferation and Terrorism,* (Vintage Books, Random House, New York and Toronto, 2008), p. xv, available at https://apps.dtic.mil/dtic/tr/fulltext/u2/a510559.pdf.

[351] Ibid., p. xvii.

[352] Ibid., p. xxv.

that the United States faces in the 21st century."[353] While noting the oversight reforms of the Legislative Reorganization Act of 1946, the commission argued that Congress has been more interested in "preserving institutional stovepipes and protecting jurisdictional turf. Congressional oversight has thus been hampered by the fact that national security priorities such as the federal government's efforts to prevent weapons of mass destruction proliferation transcend the antiquated jurisdiction of any single committee."[354]

In response to the multiple recommendations that emerged from various commissions, Congress took some actions to reform its oversight ability of the intelligence community. For example, the Senate removed term limits for members of the SSCI, allowing experienced Senators to serve longer. However, a move to create an intelligence subcommittee of the Senate Appropriations Committee was never enacted. The House created a Select Intelligence Oversight Panel on the Appropriations Committee in 2007. This was a "hybrid" panel comprised of both appropriations and intelligence committee members. However, the 112th Congress decided to eliminate this panel in 2011. Instead, the House decided to allow three appropriations committee members to participate in HPSCI hearings and briefings. In this manner, it was thought oversight and budgeting responsibilities could be more aligned. The House also reduced the size of the HPSCI.[355]

---

[353] Ibid., p. 87.

[354] Ibid.

[355] For an excellent discussion of the pros and cons of various proposals to reform congressional oversight of the intelligence community, see Michael E. DeVine, "Congressional Oversight of Intelligence: Background and Selected Options for Further Reform," Congressional Research Service, CRS Report R45421, 4 December 2018, available at https://crsreports.congress.gov/product/pdf/R/R45421.

As former 9/11 Commission Vice Chairman Lee Hamilton testified before the SSCI in 2007, "It is much easier for the Congress to reform the Executive Branch than it is to reform its own institutions."[356] This is likely to remain true for the foreseeable future.

---

[356] Hearing Before the Senate Select Committee on Intelligence, 13 November 2007, available at https://fas.org/irp/congress/2007_hr/oversight.html.

CHAPTER NINE

THE ROLE OF INTEREST GROUPS AND OTHER EXTERNAL ACTORS

As noted earlier, James Madison, writing in *Federalist 51*, was concerned that various "factions" in the new Republic could unite to impose their will on the minority. He favored a multiplicity of groups representing all aspects of society. This was the beginning of a move to ensure government is responsive to all its citizens, not just the majority; therefore, the more voices the better. In a sense, one could argue that the multiple factions Madison envisioned were the intellectual precursor to today's advocacy organizations, public and special interest groups, and lobbyists — all representing different aspects of society and all competing to have their particular interests addressed by the powers that be.

There are many kinds of interest groups seeking to curry favor with the government. This chapter will focus on four in particular: **lobbyists**, **defense contractors**, **think tanks**, and **non-governmental organizations** (NGOs). Although these external actors have different approaches and agendas, there are common threads that apply to each which allow them to maximize their effectiveness. Though described differently by various authors, there are four primary characteristics that make an interest group effective: 1) resources; 2) level of commitment; 3) representative legitimacy; and 4) information.[357]

---

[357] The categorization of these characteristics is taken primarily from Daniel McCool, "Subgovernments as Determinants of Political Viability," *Political Science Quarterly*, Vol. 105, No. 2 (Summer, 1990), pp. 269-293, available at https://www-jstor-org.proxy.missouristate.edu/stable/pdf/2151026.pdf?ab_segments=0%

Of course, one of the most important resources an interest group can possess is money. This can come from either the private or public sector and is used for multiple purposes, such as hiring employees, printing reports, and holding meetings or briefings in public locations. The more resources an interest group commands, the more effective it can be in conveying its message and achieving results.

The level of commitment a group or organization has is also central to its prospects for success. A shared commitment leads to a sense of common purpose and organizational cohesiveness.[358] Some interest groups have a greater sense of commitment than they do resources. Controversial issues that engender a strong degree of emotionalism can be useful organizing tools around which coalitions can unite to push forward an agenda. Climate change is one area that has seen an outpouring of activism. The #MeToo movement has also ballooned recently. The "Code Pink" organization is one group whose activism against war and what it perceives as U.S. "militarism" has disrupted congressional hearings and reflects a strong desire to get its voice heard in ways that don't require a lot of money or resources. It is one of more than two dozen organizations that have joined forces in a "People Over the Pentagon" campaign, calling for reductions in defense spending by "at least $200 billion annually" and sharing the view that the United States "should never go to war until such action has been authorized by Congress."[359] This level of commitment may not always succeed in obtaining the desired results, but it is usually effective in generating public attention for a particular cause.

2Fbasic_SYC-

4929%2Ftest&refreqid=search%3A714e13024f384faee76ce9e198576e33.

[358] Ibid., p. 288.

[359] See "People Over the Pentagon" agenda, available at https://peopleoverpentagon.org/the-agenda/.

"Representative legitimacy" is a term used to describe an organization that advocates on behalf of others.[360] In most cases, those groups that represent only a modest number of constituents will generally have less influence on policy matters than those that represent a vast number of people. For example, the American Automobile Association (AAA) and the American Association of Retired Persons (AARP) are nationwide organizations that advocate on behalf of millions of members. As such, they carry a greater degree of representative legitimacy than the local chapters of smaller organizations without extensive national footprints.

Finally, for an organization or interest group to be truly effective, it must be able to produce useful and credible information and analysis that is accessible to opinion makers and policy leaders.[361] Members of Congress rely heavily on such products from external groups and often cite this information in hearings and speeches to emphasize a point or advocate for a policy.

The experience of "consumer activist" Ralph Nader provides an example of how someone can combine the various elements discussed above into an effective campaign for influencing public policy. Nader's 1965 book, *Unsafe at Any Speed*, criticized automakers for producing unsafe cars and was instrumental in getting the government to tighten safety regulations governing the automotive industry. Indeed, the safety features in today's cars — from seat belts to airbags — are a direct result of changes in the industry that were spearheaded by the efforts of Ralph Nader and the hundreds of young activists inspired by him and who came to be known as "Nader's Raiders." In 1971, Nader founded the organization "Public Citizen," which focused its activities on exposing examples of government

---

[360] Daniel McCool, "Subgovernments as Determinants of Political Viability," op. cit., pp. 288-289.

[361] Ibid., p. 289.

corruption.[362] Nader's work led to the creation of dozens of grassroots public interest research groups (PIRGs) that sought to bring about political change through direct advocacy campaigns. Nader himself became an opponent of nuclear power and ran unsuccessfully for president in 1972, 1992, 1996, 2000, 2004, and 2008. His prominence in the public eye even led to an appearance on "Sesame Street" in 1988, in which he participated in a song explaining that "a consumer advocate is a person in your neighborhood."[363]

Lobbyists

In the American political system, the term "lobbyist" has assumed a decidedly negative connotation and has come to be associated in the public domain with some of the more egregious scandals of influence peddling and law breaking that are often highlighted as indicative of a corrupt political process. Yet this was not always the case. Indeed, at one time lobbying was viewed as an honorable profession and a way of exercising the constitutional right of citizens "to petition the Government for a redress of grievances."[364]

The term "lobbying" itself is often misunderstood and mischaracterized as something unseemly or pernicious. In fact, it simply refers to a process whereby a person or group seeks to influence the decisions of legislators or other

---

[362] Today, "Public Citizen" is a vocal critic of DoD spending, arguing that "an abhorrently bloated Pentagon budget is stupid, shameful and cruel." See Statement of Robert Weissman, "Pentagon Budget Remains Bloated, Proposed Cuts to Social Programs Are Shameful," *Public Citizen*, 10 February 2020, available at https://www.citizen.org/news/pentagon-budget-remains-bloated-proposed-cuts-to-social-programs-are-shameful/.

[363] Video available at https://dandelionsalad.wordpress.com/2008/04/10/ralph-nader-on-sesame-street-1988-video/.

[364] See the First Amendment in the Bill of Rights to the Constitution, available at https://constitutionus.com/.

government officials in support of (or opposition to) a particular cause or piece of legislation. Although there is debate over the origin of the term, it is sometimes assumed to have originated from the actions of various British groups who approached Members of Parliament in the lobbies of the House of Commons. In the United States, President Ulysses S. Grant is thought to have coined the term "lobbyists" after repeatedly being solicited for personal favors by people in the lobby of the Willard Hotel in Washington, D.C.[365]

Those who support the role of lobbyists in the American political system argue that it is a manifestation of each citizen's right to participate in the legislative process and, therefore, is a legitimate expression of the fundamental rights and duties of every American citizen. In 1956, then-Senator John F. Kennedy (D-MA) described his support for lobbyists this way:

> Lobbyists are in many cases expert technicians and capable of explaining complex and difficult subjects in a clear, understandable fashion. They engage in personal discussions with Members of Congress in which they can explain in detail the reasons for positions they advocate.... Because our congressional representation is based on geographical boundaries, the lobbyists who speak for the various economic, commercial, and other functional interests of this country serve a very useful purpose and have assumed an important role in the legislative process.[366]

---

[365] See "Where Does the Term Lobbyist Come From?," *Political Lobbying*, available at https://political-lobbying.co.uk/where-does-the-term-lobbyist-come-from/.

[366] Senator John F. Kennedy, "To Keep the Lobbyist Within Bounds," *The New York Times Magazine*, February 19, 1956. — *Congressional Record*,

In a nation of more than 325 million people, it is simply not possible for many who live outside our nation's capital to travel to Washington, D.C. to meet with influential decision makers in Congress or elsewhere. Therefore, individuals often seek to be part of a larger group that will advocate on behalf of their interests. Any person can join an organization that lobbies on their behalf. In fact, many Americans today are members of lobbying groups, though they may not actually know it.

For example, the American Automobile Association has more than 50 million dues-paying members nationwide. Most members call on AAA when they have a flat tire or a dead car battery. But the annual dues paid by members also fund the organization's lobbying efforts on behalf of motorists coast to coast. According to its website, AAA's Public and Government Affairs office is "a vocal advocate seeking to protect and improve the rights and safety of motorists and travelers" by engaging in "meaningful and effective public advocacy."[367] This includes lobbying Congress.

One issue that has garnered the attention of AAA is the move to legalize marijuana. A 2017 bill in Maryland to decriminalize the possession and use of marijuana was strongly opposed by an AAA Public and Government Affairs official who stated, "A vote to legalize the recreational use of marijuana in Maryland is also a vote for more injury and death on our roadways."[368] AAA also

---

March 2, 1956, Vol. 102, pp. 3802–3, cited in Bartleby.com, available at https://www.bartleby.com/73/1128.html.

[367] See https://midatlantic.aaa.com/public-affairs/government.

[368] Statement of John B. Townsend II, Manager of Public and Government Affairs at AAA Mid-Atlantic, cited in "It's Do or Die on Sine Die – Maryland Legislators Wrap Up 2017 General Assembly," 10 April 2017, available at https://midatlantic.aaa.com/public-affairs/press-release/?Id=edb53c38-1734-4e86-94dd-c979d714d01a.

tracks and reports on the status of other legislative actions at the state and national levels.

The American Association of Retired Persons has a membership of more than 35 million people over the age of 50 and lobbies on behalf of senior citizens, for whom access to affordable health care is a significant issue. AARP has been a strong advocate for the Affordable Care Act (ACA, or "Obamacare"), calling a 2018 federal court decision that ruled the ACA "unconstitutional" a "profound blow to millions of Americans" and vowing to fight the ruling in Congress and in the judicial system.[369]

Many other military and professional organizations and associations that charge membership dues also have a lobbying arm that seeks to influence the passage of legislation in Congress. Often, Americans join these organizations because of the benefits they provide, without realizing that some of their dues go to lobbying efforts that their individual members may or may not support. Some organizations are "501(c)(3)" organizations, Internal Revenue Service (IRS) designations that classify them as tax-exempt. For IRS purposes, a 501(c)(3) organization is one that is commonly referred to as a "charitable organization," and includes religious, educational, scientific, and public safety institutions. Importantly, there are limitations on the extent of political and lobbying activities a 501(c)(3) organization can conduct.[370]

Organizations like the Air Force Association, Navy League, National Guard Association, and the Association of the U.S. Army all have interests in particular legislative

---

[369] Statement of AARP Executive Vice President and Chief Advocacy and Engagement Officer Nancy LeaMond, cited in Dena Bunis, "AARP Vows to Fight ACA Court Decision," 17 December 2018, available at https://www.aarp.org/politics-society/advocacy/info-2018/aca-texas-court-ruling.html?intcmp=AE-POL-ADV-FFYH-BB-C1.

[370] A description of these limitations may be found at https://www.irs.gov/charities-non-profits/lobbying.

proposals and outcomes that affect their members, and all seek to influence those outcomes on behalf of their membership.

Some lobbyists are extremely effective, and their effectiveness is enhanced by a detailed knowledge of the legislative process and access to key decision makers whose support is required to achieve a successful outcome. Individual lobbyists represent trade associations, law firms, and other types of institutions. Some even represent foreign interests and governments (which is sometimes viewed as going beyond what the Founders had in mind). In the national security field, lobbying can be a lucrative pursuit, if the lobbyist understands when, where, and how to influence congressional decision making on defense issues.[371]

The telecommunications industry conducts a huge lobbying effort and has been engaged in a range of issues involving cellphones, including whether they should be allowed to be used on airplanes and what radiation limits are acceptable. The National Education Association (NEA) is the nation's largest teachers' union and engages in major lobbying efforts on behalf of educators nationwide. From 2009-2010, its Wisconsin affiliate spent $2.5 million on lobbying efforts—more than any political entity in the state—and played a major role in seeking to derail Wisconsin Governor Scott Walker's educational reform efforts.[372]

The American Farm Bureau Federation is the country's largest agricultural organization and has had a major impact on U.S. foreign policy on many agriculture-related

---

[371] For a detailed primer on how to lobby effectively on national defense issues, see Matthew R. Kambrod, *Lobbying for Defense – An Insider's View*, (Naval Institute Press, Annapolis, MD, 2007).

[372] Alix, "Wisconsin NEA Affiliate In the National Spotlight," 16 August 2011, available at https://www.aaeteachers.org/index.php/blog/512-wisconsin-nea-affiliate-in-the-national-spotlight.

issues. The Bureau notes that "Having a voice — a seat at the table and an impact on policy — is critical. Beginning at the grassroots level and involving Farm Bureau members' advocacy efforts across the country, all of agriculture speaks with one voice through the American Farm Bureau Federation."[373]

One of the Farm Bureau's most notable successes occurred during the debate over whether to grant China "Most Favored Nation" trading status (later referred to as "permanent normal trade relations"). Because China was the sixth largest market for U.S. agricultural products, billions of dollars of exports were at stake. The Farm Bureau played a large role in getting China approved for favored trade status in 1980, but the Tiananmen massacre in 1989 caused a rupture in U.S.-China relations and led to legislative efforts to deny China the benefits of loosened trade restrictions with the United States. Despite some congressional opposition, President Clinton signed legislation in 2000 granting permanent normal trade relations to China.[374]

Those who view lobbyists with disdain often see lobbying as unduly influencing the democratic process. Some believe it is unethical or immoral, playing a corrupting influence on politics. Even the American League of Lobbyists changed its name to the "Association for Government Relations Professionals" out of concern that the term "lobbying" carried a negative connotation in the public domain.[375] Prior to the 1980s, few Congressmen

---

[373] See https://www.fb.org/about/overview.

[374] Matt Smith, "Clinton signs China trade bill, CNN, 10 October 2000, available at https://www.cnn.com/2000/ALLPOLITICS/stories/10/10/clinton.pntr/.

[375] Holly Yeager, "Lobbyists' lobbying group wants a new name — one that doesn't mention lobbying," *The Washington Post*, 15 October 2013, available at https://www.washingtonpost.com/politics/lobbyists-lobbying-group-wants-a-new-name--one-that-doesnt-mention-

became lobbyists, as the profession was seen as tainted and unworthy of a former lawmaker. Over time, however, the number of former members of Congress who became lobbyists grew substantially. Since 1998, almost one-half of former members have become lobbyists. By one count, nearly 450 former members of Congress now serve as lobbyists on the payroll of companies or "special interest" groups.[376] In January 2020, former California Senator Barbara Boxer announced she was joining a major Washington lobbying firm.[377]

As noted earlier, part of the negative perception of lobbyists is the result of various scandals that have taken place involving systematic abuse, including the payment of bribes to members of Congress in exchange for favors. The Jack Abramoff scandal is often cited as the poster child for such abuses. In 2006, Abramoff, an American businessman and lobbyist, pleaded guilty to bribing public officials and to hiring former congressional staffers to lobby their former bosses in violation of federal rules. He received a jail sentence for his actions.

In response to incidents like this, numerous reform acts have been passed to tighten the rules and regulations on lobbying. These include the Ethics Reform Act of 1989, which tightened post-government employment restrictions on former executive and legislative branch employees; the

---

lobbying/2013/10/15/b410022c-2c42-11e3-97a3-
ff2758228523_story.html. The group later shut down as a result of a contract dispute. See Megan R. Wilson, "Trade group for lobbyists closing down," *The Hill*, 19 April 2016, available at
https://thehill.com/business-a-lobbying/business-a-lobbying/276897-trade-group-for-lobbyists-closing-down.

[376] See "Former Members," Center for Responsive Politics, available at https://www.opensecrets.org/revolving/top.php?display=Z.

[377] Jill Cowen, "Why Barbara Boxer Joined a Lobbying Firm," *The New York Times*, 17 January 2020, available at
https://www.nytimes.com/2020/01/17/us/barbara-boxer-lobbying-firm.html.

Lobbying Disclosure Act of 1995 (subsequently amended in 1998), which required lobbyists to register with Congress and to report annually on their activities; the Lobbying Transparency and Accountability Act of 2006, which tightened reporting requirements on lobbyists; and the Honest Leadership and Open Government Act of 2007, which was intended to reform lobbying and ethics rules by slowing the "revolving door" between government and the private sector, but which some criticized as ineffective.[378] Even the FY 2018 NDAA contained a provision to strengthen the constraints on lobbying by certain former Defense Department officials.[379] Other bills have been introduced to tighten lobbying restrictions even further but were never enacted.

The day after President Obama took office in 2009, he signed two Executive Orders and three memoranda imposing a lobbyist gift ban and a two-year "revolving door" ban on members of his administration.[380] Shortly after his inauguration, President Trump signed an Executive Order banning executive branch officials from lobbying for up to five years.[381] (This E.O. codified and strengthened a Code of Ethical Conduct, which Presidential

---

[378] Isaac Arnsdorf, "The lobbying reform that enriched Congress," *Politico*, 3 July 2016, available at
https://www.politico.com/story/2016/06/the-lobbying-reform-that-enriched-congress-224849.

[379] Section 1045 of Public Law 115-91, the National Defense Authorization Act for Fiscal Year 2018, 12 December 2017, available at https://www.congress.gov/115/plaws/publ91/PLAW-115publ91.pdf.

[380] See, for example, Executive Order 13490, "Ethics Commitments by Executive Branch Personnel," 21 January 2009, available at
https://www.govinfo.gov/content/pkg/DCPD-200900004/pdf/DCPD-200900004.pdf.

[381] Executive Order 13770, "Ethics Commitments by Executive Branch Appointees," 28 January 2017, available at
https://www2.oge.gov/web/oge.nsf/0/A43C4DBAB9EC4DC7852580 BC006FBA83/$FILE/Exec%20Order%2013770.pdf.

Transition Team members—including myself—signed prior to President Trump's inauguration.)[382]

In short, those who support the role of lobbying and lobbyists argue that it allows implementation of the constitutional right of citizens to petition their government; it is a fundamental and essential aspect of the legislative process; it ensures the views and opinions of citizens are considered before a bill is enacted; it gives voice to individual constituents; and it ensures the principles of democracy are sustained.[383] Those who oppose lobbying argue it promotes narrow agendas that favor some and not all; it creates incentives for legislators to "sell" their votes; it places self-interest above national interest; and it is the antithesis of representative democracy because the will of some trumps the will of many. These competing views continue to inform the debate today.

Defense Contractors

Defense contractors include the nation's major aerospace firms and companies with significant investments in the DoD marketplace. This includes Boeing, Lockheed Martin, Northrop Grumman, Raytheon, General Dynamics, and hundreds of other large and small enterprises that support

---

[382] The text of the President-Elect's Transition Team "Code of Ethical Conduct" is available at
https://www.wsj.com/public/resources/documents/ethicscode.pdf.

[383] Audrae Erickson, "Lobbying Congress: A Key Way U.S. Citizens Impact Foreign Policy," *U.S. Foreign Policy Agenda*, U.S. Department of State (Volume 5, Number 1, March 2000), pp. 45-47, available at
https://books.google.com/books?id=_VLyf1MeEvUC&pg=PA4&lpg=PA4&dq=audrae+erickson+lobbying+congress+key+way+citizens&source=bl&ots=stu6umNayS&sig=ACfU3U1T0loP78jvpI381c3JBAU-IdHaqg&hl=en&sa=X&ved=2ahUKEwi-joPavPfmAhUNT98KHSDZCVcQ6AEwAHoECAsQAQ#v=onepage&q=audrae%20erickson%20lobbying%20congress%20key%20way%20citizens&f=false.

the Department of Defense. Because of the size of the DoD budget and the cost of major weapons systems (some costing billions of dollars per unit), defense contractors are thought to play an outsized role in congressional lobbying efforts.

According to one source, the cost of lobbying by defense firms in 2019 totaled nearly $85 million and involved the efforts of 660 lobbyists.[384] In 2019, Lockheed Martin filed a report, per the requirements of the Lobbying Disclosure Act of 1995, indicating that the company spent more than $3 million on lobbying in the fourth quarter of 2018 alone on issues relating to numerous pieces of legislation; these included the John S. McCain National Defense Authorization Act for Fiscal Year 2019; the Consolidated Appropriations Act for 2019; and the Department of State, Foreign Operations, and Related Programs Appropriations Act for 2019.[385] In 2019, Boeing outspent all other defense contractors on lobbying, expending $13.8 million on its efforts. Northrop Grumman spent $13.3 million. Rounding out the top five were Lockheed Martin at $12.9 million, United Technologies at $12.7 million, and General Dynamics at $10.2 million.[386]

Despite these significant numbers, the defense industry is not even close to being the largest spender on lobbying

---

[384] See "Defense: Lobbying, 2019," Center for Responsive Politics, available at
https://www.opensecrets.org/industries/lobbying.php?ind=D.
[385] Lockheed Martin's lobbying report is a matter of public record and is available at
https://www.lockheedmartin.com/content/dam/lockheed-martin/eo/documents/governance/Lobbying-Report-4th-Quarter-2018.pdf.
[386] David Brown, "Boeing Tops Defense Firms in 2019 Lobbying," *Politico Morning Defense*, 24 January 2020, available at
https://www.politico.com/newsletters/morning-defense/2020/01/24/house-democrats-have-a-new-plan-of-attack-on-trumps-war-powers-784598.

efforts. In fact, defense lobbying comprises only a small fraction—roughly three percent—of overall industry lobbying expenditures. According to statistics, the top lobbying industry in 2018 was the pharmaceutical and health products industry, spending more than $280 million. They were followed by the insurance industry ($158 million); electronics industry ($146 million); business associations ($142 million); the oil and gas industry ($125 million); electric utilities ($122 million); and the real estate industry ($117 million). The defense aerospace industry barely cracked the top 20 list at number 20.[387]

It is certainly true that some of the largest contracts industry has with the federal government are in the defense sector. After an intense and controversial competition for a DoD contract to build the next generation of Air Force tanker aircraft valued at $35 billion, Boeing's KC-767 proposal was chosen as the winner. Another competition pitted Pratt & Whitney, a United Technologies company, against a General Electric/Rolls Royce consortium for an engine contract for the F-35 Joint Strike Fighter. Some of the efforts of competitors played out in the local media with companies placing full-page newspaper ads touting their product's superiority over their competitors.[388]

Think Tanks

The term "think tank" is generally applied to organizations that do not lobby but that seek to influence public policy through various research and educational efforts. Think

---

[387] "Top lobbying industries in the United States in 2018, by total lobbying spending," *Statista*, available at https://www.statista.com/statistics/257364/top-lobbying-industries-in-the-us/.

[388] See, for example, Pratt & Whitney's "F135 Engine Blog," at https://f135engine.blogspot.com/2010/?m=0 for examples of some newspaper advertisements.

tanks are numerous, especially in the national capital region; can be private or government-funded; include federally funded research and development centers (or FFRDCs); and espouse views and policies that can be liberal, conservative, or libertarian. Examples of well-established think tanks that focus on foreign policy and national security concerns include the Carnegie Endowment for International Peace, founded in 1910; the Council on Foreign Relations, established in 1921; and the RAND Corporation, which was created after World War II to serve as a source of independent thinking for the U.S. government and is located in Santa Monica, California to symbolically demonstrate its "independence" from the "inside the Beltway" world of Washington, D.C.

Numerous think tanks that focus on defense and national security issues exist in the Washington, D.C. area. Some of the better-known ones are the Institute for Defense Analyses; Center for Naval Analyses; Atlantic Council; Arms Control Association; U.S. Institute of Peace (publicly funded); Brookings Institution; Center for Strategic and International Studies; American Enterprise Institute; and the Heritage Foundation. Each has its own views; some hire scholars and experts with differing views. Some are considered partisan outlets while others are viewed as nonpartisan. Some think tanks educate, others advocate, and some do both. Many are 501(c)(3) organizations and, as such, are limited in what they can do to influence congressional actions.

Sometimes, however, an organization's analysts may advocate for legislative action although the organization itself is prohibited from doing so. For example, a 2019 report by the Heritage Foundation cited "57 recommendations for Congress on how to continue the crucial rebuilding of the U.S. military through the 2020 NDAA." However, the report contained the disclaimer: "Nothing written here is to be construed as necessarily reflecting the views of The Heritage Foundation or as an attempt to aid or hinder the passage of any bill before Congress."[389]

Many think tank experts go on to serve in government, and many come from government. For example, former Secretary of State Madeleine Albright became the head of the Center for National Policy, and former Under Secretary of Defense for Policy Michèle Flournoy established the Center for a New American Security. Critics sometimes disapprove of what they perceive as a "revolving door" between government and the private sector but others hold a more charitable view of the relationship. Think tanks are seen by some as a useful way to help grow the country's future leaders, shape American security policies, and educate decision makers and the general public on matters that affect U.S. national security.[390]

Non-Governmental Organizations

Non-governmental organizations (NGOs) are non-profit, voluntary, independent citizen groups that are organized on a local, national, or international level for a common purpose, usually to advance a social or political cause.

---

[389] Frederico Bartels, editor, "The Role of the 2020 National Defense Authorization Act (NDAA) in Rebuilding the U.S. Military," The Heritage Foundation, Special Report No. 208, 6 February 2019, available at https://www.heritage.org/sites/default/files/2019-02/SR208_0.pdf.

[390] Robert E. Hunter, "Think Tanks: Helping to Shape U.S. Foreign and Security Policy," *U.S. Foreign Policy Agenda*, U.S. Department of State (Volume 5, Number 1, March 2000), pp. 33-36, available at https://books.google.com/books?id=_VLyf1MeEvUC&pg=PA4&lpg=PA4&dq=audrae+erickson+lobbying+congress+key+way+citizens&source=bl&ots=stu6umNayS&sig=ACfU3U1T0loP78jvpI381c3JBAU-IdHaqg&hl=en&sa=X&ved=2ahUKEwi-joPavPfmAhUNT98KHSDZCVcQ6AEwAHoECAsQAQ#v=onepage&q=audrae%20erickson%20lobbying%20congress%20key%20way%20citizens&f=false.

Ralph Nader's Public Citizen NGO, referenced above, is a good example of how NGOs can successfully influence government policy.

There are more than one million NGOs operating in the United States representing various cultural, religious, environmental, social, and business organizations. Many are organized around social agendas that include a focus on human rights; rule of law; civic education; a free press; political parties; or government accountability. Some examples of well-known NGOs include the Big Brother/Big Sister organizations, the Boy Scouts and Girl Scouts, Goodwill, the Salvation Army, and the Young Men's (and Young Women's) Christian Association (YMCA/YWCA).

Many NGOs work closely with government and the government often solicits the views of NGOs on important policy matters. One of my responsibilities during my last tour at the Pentagon was serving as DoD's senior civilian coordinator for mitigating civilian casualties during military operations abroad — a position mandated in law by Section 936 of the FY 2019 NDAA.[391] In this capacity I met personally with representatives of the NGO community concerned with civilian casualty avoidance and solicited their views as part of an effort to develop formal DoD guidance on this issue. Former Secretary of Defense James Mattis also previously met with various NGO representatives on this issue. Doing so was a way of communicating not only the department's interest in the topic but the seriousness with which senior-level DoD

---

[391] Section 936 of Public Law 115-232 required the Under Secretary of Defense for Policy to designate "a senior civilian official of the Department of Defense within the Office of the Secretary of Defense at or above the level of Assistant Secretary of Defense to develop, coordinate, and oversee compliance with the policy of the Department relating to civilian casualties resulting from United States military operations." See Public Law 115-232, 13 August 2018, available at https://www.congress.gov/115/plaws/publ232/PLAW-115publ232.pdf.

officials took this responsibility. The fact that Congress mandated in law that DoD designate a senior official to assume this role clearly indicated the importance Congress attached to this issue.

Some international NGOs can have a huge influence on the domestic U.S. policy debate, even if the U.S. government does not support their ultimate objectives. One notable example involved the International Campaign to Ban Landmines, a coalition of organizations created in 1992 in support of a cause championed by Princess Diana, and which was awarded the Nobel Peace Prize in 1997. Various NGOs led the way toward advocating for a global ban on the use of landmines, including the International Committee of the Red Cross (ICRC), whose doctors in the 1980s dealt with a growing number of individuals who had been maimed or had lost limbs as a result of the use of landmines in conflicts around the globe. The ICRC was joined by other organizations, including Human Rights Watch, Physicians for Human Rights, and the Vietnam Veterans of America Foundation in calling for a global ban on anti-personnel landmines. Eventually, the movement expanded to include more than 1,300 NGOs in approximately 100 countries.[392]

In part due to the work of the campaign, the Ottawa Convention (formally known as the "Convention on the Prohibition of the Use, Stockpiling, Production and Transfer of Anti-Personnel Mines and on their Destruction") was crafted, leading to an extensive debate in Congress over whether the United States should accede to the treaty (to

---

[392] See "About Us," International Campaign to Ban Landmines, available at http://www.icbl.org/en-gb/about-us.aspx. Also see "NGOs and the International Campaign to Ban Landmines," Global Policy Forum, available at https://www.globalpolicy.org/ngos-and-the-international-campaign-to-ban-landmines.html.

date, it has not).[393] Unsurprisingly, the campaign was critical of the Trump Administration's revision to U.S. landmine policy, which would provide greater flexibility to combatant commanders regarding the use of anti-personnel landmines, calling it "a step backwards."[394] Senator Patrick J. Leahy (D-VT) was also critical, saying, "The Congress must be consulted before any decision that would reverse the gains we have made toward ending the carnage caused by landmines."[395]

In the area of nuclear weapons policy, the International Campaign to Abolish Nuclear Weapons (ICAN) received the 2017 Nobel Peace Prize for its "ground-breaking efforts to achieve a treaty-based prohibition of such weapons."[396] Some 80 countries have signed the UN-sponsored Treaty on the Prohibition of Nuclear Weapons; however, not a single nuclear weapons state (or country that enjoys the formal security protections of a nuclear weapons state) has signed on to the treaty. In April 2019, Representatives James P. McGovern (D-MA) and Earl F. Blumenauer (D-OR) introduced a resolution (H. Res. 302) supporting the treaty, which was referred to the House Foreign Affairs and Armed Services Committees and has not been acted on

---

[393] The debate in the HASC on this issue is briefly referenced in Chapter One.

[394] Press Release, "US Policy Reversal At Odds With Global Mine Ban Consensus," International Campaign to Ban Landmines, 3 February 2020, available at http://www.icbl.org/en-gb/news-and-events/news/2020/us-policy-reversal-at-odds-with-global-mine-ban-consensus.aspx.

[395] "Statement On Reports That The Trump Administration Plans To Roll Back Limits On U.S. Production And Use Of Anti-Personnel Landmines," 30 January 2020, available at https://www.leahy.senate.gov/press/statement-on-reports_that-the-trump-administration-plans-to-roll-back-limits-on-us--production-and-use-of-anti-personnel-landmines.

[396] See "ICAN receives 2017 Nobel Peace Prize," International Campaign to Abolish Nuclear Weapons, available at https://www.icanw.org/nobel_prize.

since.[397]   In light of the Trump Administration's 2018 *Nuclear Posture Review* (which I worked on during my last Pentagon tour) and the policies and programmatic decisions that have emerged from it, nuclear weapons issues remain controversial in some quarters on Capitol Hill.

There are other examples that highlight the role NGOs seek to play in shaping U.S. national security policy.[398] Along with lobbyists, defense contractors, and think tanks, these external groups can have a significant influence on U.S. national security decision making, including efforts to prevent the proliferation of weapons of mass destruction.

---

[397] The text and status of H. Res. 302 is available at https://www.congress.gov/bill/116th-congress/house-resolution/302/text.

[398] For example, more than 40 organizations joined together to urge the Senate to support Sen. Tim Kaine's war powers resolution (S.J. Res. 68) that would prevent the president from using force against Iran without prior congressional authorization (referenced in Chapter Six). See open letter to Senators, 11 February 2020, available at https://winwithoutwar.org/wp-content/uploads/2020/02/02.11.2020_S.J.Res_.68-NGO-letter.pdf.

CHAPTER TEN

CONGRESS' IMPACT ON WEAPONS OF MASS DESTRUCTION NONPROLIFERATION REGIMES

Over the decades, Congress has passed a great deal of legislation establishing, modifying, and enabling U.S. nonproliferation policy. In some cases, Congress took the initiative in passing laws to stem the proliferation of WMD and associated technologies; in other cases, Congress responded to executive branch actions. In the area of WMD proliferation, Congress has been criticized by some for abdicating its oversight role and by others for seeking to "micromanage" nonproliferation policy. Several examples highlight the difficulties Congress has faced in this realm.

123 Agreements

The Atomic Energy Act of 1954 established the legal authority for the United States to cooperate with other countries in the military and commercial development of nuclear energy sources. Section 123 of the act requires the administration to submit to Congress a nonproliferation assessment statement (NPAS) in connection with any proposed U.S. nuclear cooperation agreement with another country (these are "Executive Agreements" as discussed in Chapter Five). Today, the United States has nearly two dozen so-called "123 agreements" with other countries and entities, including friendly countries like Japan and Australia; not-so-friendly countries like Russia and China; and international consortia like the European Atomic

Energy Community (EURATOM).[399] An NPAS must demonstrate that the 123 agreement meets nine specific nonproliferation criteria dealing with safeguards, physical security of sites, transfer and retransfer of material, and other requirements.[400] Congress has 90 days to review the agreement and can only act to block it from taking effect by passing a Joint Resolution. If Congress takes no action within the specified timeframe, the agreement automatically becomes law.

Some 123 agreements have been highly controversial, with nonproliferation advocates in Congress questioning the value of nuclear cooperation with Russia or China, the need for nuclear power by countries with large supplies of fossil fuel energy, the effectiveness of nonproliferation safeguards, or the reliability of partner nations to abide by their obligations not to divert civilian nuclear technology to military purposes. Some members of Congress have also called for Congress to reverse the current approach that allows 123 agreements to take effect unless Congress objects by passing legislation that would prohibit 123 agreements from entering into force. Recently, a bipartisan group of Senators and Representatives introduced a resolution seeking to ensure that any 123 agreement signed with Saudi

---

[399] National Nuclear Security Administration, "123 Agreements for Peaceful Cooperation," available at
https://www.energy.gov/nnsa/123-agreements-peaceful-cooperation. The Trump Administration is also seeking to conclude a 123 agreement with Saudi Arabia, despite strong opposition in some congressional quarters.

[400] See Paul K. Kerr and Mary Beth D. Nikitin, "Nuclear Cooperation with Other Countries: A Primer," Congressional Research Service, CRS Report RS22937, 15 April 2019, available at
https://www.everycrsreport.com/files/20190415_RS22937_c03e63b38a 1c8f81a5a14f65f7029cfb25832d5a.pdf.

Arabia is affirmatively approved by Congress before taking effect.[401]

In 2008, President George W. Bush signed a 123 agreement with India. Although Congress did not act to block the agreement, concerns were expressed that Congress did not thoroughly review it to ensure it complied with an earlier piece of legislation—the "Henry Hyde United States-India Peaceful Atomic Energy Cooperation Act of 2006." That act allowed the United States to sell India technology useful for the generation of civil nuclear power but committed India to undertake a number of nonproliferation measures, including agreeing to international inspections, refraining from testing nuclear weapons, and strengthening its export control system. Indeed, President Bush saw some aspects of Congress' actions as intruding on his constitutional authority. In signing the 2006 act, the president stated, "My approval of the Act does not constitute my adoption of the statements of policy as U.S. foreign policy. Given the Constitution's commitment to the presidency of the authority to conduct the Nation's foreign affairs, the executive branch shall construe such policy statements as advisory."[402]

---

[401] Sen. Marco Rubio (R-FL) Press Release, "Rubio, Markey, Sherman, & Messer Introduce Bipartisan, Bicameral Legislation to Thwart Saudi Arabia's Nuclear Weapons Ambitions," 19 December 2018, available at https://www.rubio.senate.gov/public/index.cfm/2018/12/rubio-markey-sherman-messer-introduce-bipartisan-bicameral-legislation-to-thwart-saudi-arabia-s-nuclear-weapons-ambitions.

[402] George W. Bush, "Statement on Signing the Henry J. Hyde United States-India Peaceful Atomic Energy Cooperation Act of 2006," 18 December 2006, available at https://books.google.com/books?id=y27F8Gy0bqsC&pg=PA2221&lpg=PA2221&dq=Given+the+Constitution%27s+commitment+to+the+authority+of+the+presidency+to+conduct+the+nation%27s+foreign+affairs,+the+executive+branch+shall+construe+such+policy+statements+as+advisory&source=bl&ots=foD49zvYTH&sig=ACfU3U13INBg8qX9s2cujyCNk8QJNRSptg&hl=en&sa=X&ved=2ahUKEwj_h6yL9vnmAhWym-

In 2008, President Bush submitted a 123 agreement with Russia to Congress; however, he did so with fewer than the requisite 90 consecutive days in session and later withdrew it after Russia's invasion of Georgia. Some in Congress criticized the agreement with Russia, especially since Moscow had been assisting Iran in the construction of its nuclear reactor at Bushehr. Reps. Edward Markey (D-MA), Howard Berman (D-CA), and Ileana Ros-Lehtinen (R-FL) introduced multiple Joint Resolutions of disapproval, none of which were adopted.[403] President Obama resubmitted the agreement to Congress in 2010 and, without Congress generating enough votes in opposition, it entered into force the following year. Subsequent to a 2008 Memorandum of Understanding signed by the Bush Administration, the Obama Administration in 2009 concluded a 123 agreement with the United Arab Emirates (UAE), which nonproliferation advocates hailed as the "gold standard" for 123 agreements because the UAE agreed not to enrich uranium or reprocess plutonium for weapons purposes.[404]

Nonproliferation advocates have occasionally accused Congress of failing to devote sufficient attention to this issue and of not holding the executive branch accountable to laws regarding safeguards for peaceful nuclear programs. The 123 agreement with Turkey entered into force without Congress ever holding a hearing on it. Under the 1954 Atomic Energy Act, Congress required the

---

AKHZFRDn0Q6AEwCnoECAYQAQ#v=onepage&q=hyde%20act&f=false.

[403] Mary Beth Nikitin, "U.S.-Russian Civilian Nuclear Cooperation Agreement: Issues for Congress," Congressional Research Service, CRS Report RL34655, 11 January 2011, available at https://www.everycrsreport.com/files/20110111_RL34655_80f090ac61e30f7dd08d6121f4e8d0852b8b51de.pdf.

[404] Nuclear Threat Initiative, "UAE Promotes Nonproliferation 'Gold Standard' for Nuclear Energy Programs," 19 April 2012, available at https://www.nti.org/gsn/article/uae-promotes-nonproliferation-gold-standard-nuclear-energy/.

executive branch to ensure that inspections of other countries' nuclear programs carried out under the auspices of the International Atomic Energy Agency (IAEA) could provide "timely warning" of any diversion of nuclear materials from peaceful to military purposes. However, the definition of what constitutes "timely warning" is unclear in the legislation and Congress has never sought to clarify it. As a result, some have accused Congress of failing to hold the executive branch accountable.

Similarly, Title V of the 1978 Nuclear Nonproliferation Act requires the executive branch to conduct "general and country-specific" assessments of the energy sources of developing countries to determine whether their quest for nuclear power is necessary. The Commission on the Prevention of WMD Proliferation and Terrorism ("Graham-Talent Commission") concluded that these assessments have generally not been done and Congress has not challenged the administration's failure to do them.

Nonproliferation Regimes

Notwithstanding concerns over the extent and effectiveness of congressional oversight of U.S. nonproliferation policy, Congress has been generally supportive of U.S. nonproliferation efforts. There are multiple WMD nonproliferation regimes in effect that govern U.S. policy with respect to nuclear, chemical, and biological weapons, as well as missile technology. Although often hailed as successful by nonproliferation experts, all of them suffer from two common shortcomings: a lack of universality, and a lack of effective compliance and enforcement mechanisms. In other words, multilateral agreements and regimes established to restrict the proliferation of dangerous weapons technologies are only truly effective if all parties of concern adhere to their restrictions and if there are uniformly accepted and enforceable penalties for noncompliance. Unfortunately, this has never been the case and is not the case today.

In the nuclear realm, several regimes seek to prevent the spread of nuclear weapons and technologies to potentially dangerous actors. Perhaps the most notable is the 1968 Nuclear Nonproliferation Treaty (NPT). The NPT, which entered into force in 1970 and has more than 180 signatories, is considered among the more successful agreements in preventing nuclear proliferation. The treaty is not without its critics, however, some of whom argue that it is relatively toothless, as most signatories have no desire or intention to develop or acquire nuclear weapons in the first place, and that states of greatest proliferation concern, like North Korea, remain outside the treaty's strictures. In fact, North Korea was a signatory to the NPT but suspended its obligations for 89 days in 1993 until the Clinton Administration's "Agreed Framework" was negotiated. However, North Korea formally withdrew in 2003 after giving only one day's notice instead of the treaty's 90-day notification requirement, arguing that it had previously provided 89 days of notice in 1993.[405] Other states not a party to the NPT include India and Pakistan—both of whom developed nuclear arsenals—and Israel.[406]

In 1971, the Nuclear Exporters Committee (the "Zangger Committee") was formed by a handful of NPT states parties seeking to clarify some of the provisions in the NPT and to strengthen control over the export and re-export

---

[405] See George Bunn and John B. Rhinelander, "NPT Withdrawal: Time for the Security Council to Step In," *Arms Control Today*, May 2005, available at https://www.armscontrol.org/act/2005-05/features/npt-withdrawal-time-security-council-step.

[406] See, for example, The Center for Arms Control and Non-Proliferation, "Fact Sheet: Nuclear Non-Proliferation Treaty (NPT)," 14 April 2017, available at https://armscontrolcenter.org/fact-sheet-nuclear-non-proliferation-treaty-npt/. An official list of current States Parties to the NPT can be found at http://disarmament.un.org/treaties/t/npt.

of nuclear materials that could be used to create nuclear weapons. It has since expanded to 39 members, including the five major nuclear weapons states (the United States, UK, France, Russia, and China). The Zangger Committee developed a "trigger list" of equipment and materials, the export of which to non-nuclear weapon states would trigger IAEA safeguards. Yet the group is considered "informal" and its decisions are not legally binding on its members.[407]

There are three primary international regimes that govern the proliferation of chemical and biological weapons. These are the Chemical Weapons Convention (CWC), Biological Weapons Convention (BWC), and the Australia Group.

The BWC (formally called the "Convention on the Prohibition of the Development, Production and Stockpiling of Bacteriological (Biological) and Toxin Weapons and on their Destruction") dates to 1972 and entered into force in 1975. There are more than 180 states parties to the convention, which prohibits the use of biological agents for offensive weapons purposes but allows for defensive research "for peaceful purposes."[408] Like the NPT, however, there is no enforcement mechanism to ensure compliance.

The Australia Group (so named because of Australia's lead role in organizing the effort in 1985) is also an "informal" arrangement of more than 40 countries that seek to harmonize their national export control regimes in order to prevent the proliferation of chemical and biological

---

[407] Information on the Zangger Committee can be found at http://zanggercommittee.org/.

[408] United Nations Office for Disarmament Affairs, "Convention on the Prohibition of the Development, Production and Stockpiling of Bacteriological (Biological) and Toxin Weapons and on Their Destruction," available at http://disarmament.un.org/treaties/t/bwc.

weapons.[409]   Because of the non-binding nature of the group, it does not have the authority to sanction countries that acquire chemical or biological weapons or to penalize those members of the group who fail to abide by its agreed-upon controls.

The CWC (formally called the "The Convention on the Prohibition of the Development, Production, Stockpiling and Use of Chemical Weapons and on their Destruction") entered into force in 1997 and prohibits the development, production, stockpiling, transfer, and use of chemical weapons.   It also requires the destruction of existing chemical weapon arsenals. The CWC contains a verification regime that allows for "challenge inspections" to ensure compliance, but, as with the other WMD nonproliferation regimes, lacks an effective enforcement mechanism.[410] The use of chemical weapons by certain states parties to the Convention (e.g., Syria) testifies to the shortcomings in the CWC's enforcement regime.

Just as important as restrictions on the development of weapons of mass destruction are constraints on the means to deliver them. This includes missile technology that can be used to deliver WMD to targets thousands of miles away. The missile nonproliferation regime is centered on the 1987 Missile Technology Control Regime (MTCR). The MTCR is not a treaty, but an "informal political understanding" among 35 states that have agreed "to limit the risks of proliferation of weapons of mass destruction (WMD) by controlling exports of goods and technologies that could make a contribution to delivery systems (other than

---

[409] Information on the Australia Group can be found at https://australiagroup.net/en/index.html.

[410] See Organization for the Prohibition of Chemical Weapons, "Chemical Weapons Convention," available at https://www.opcw.org/chemical-weapons-convention.

manned aircraft) for such weapons."[411] Each member of the MTCR administers its export guidelines independently; the decision to export or transfer missile systems or technologies is a national one left up to individual governments; however, there is a "presumption of denial" regarding the transfer of critical technologies.

The MTCR includes "Category I" items — considered to be the most sensitive and restricted — and "Category II" items, which are less sensitive and dual-use in nature, but still governed by a strong presumption of denial regarding their export.   Category I items include rockets and unmanned aerial vehicles (UAVs) "capable of delivering a payload of at least 500 kg to a range of at least 300 km," as well as their related subsystems and technology.[412] UAVs were added in 1992 because of their perceived similarity to cruise missiles. A 2012 GAO study found that, despite the growth in the number of countries possessing UAV systems since 2005, "the U.S. government has determined that selected transfers of UAV technology support its national security interests by providing allies with key capabilities and by helping retain a strong industrial base for UAV production."[413] Similarly, a 2018 RAND study concluded "UAVs are valuable assets in achieving a variety of strategic, operational, and tactical objectives, including ISR missions and kinetic-strike operations.... we conclude that it is more beneficial to allow than prevent the sales of category I UAVs to allies and partners."[414] The United

---

[411] See "Missile Technology Control Regime Frequently Asked Questions," available at https://mtcr.info/frequently-asked-questions-faqs/.

[412] Ibid.

[413] Government Accountability Office, "Agencies Could Improve Information Sharing and End-Use Monitoring on Unmanned Aerial Vehicle Exports," Report GAO-12-536, July 2012, available at https://www.gao.gov/assets/600/593131.pdf.

[414] RAND Corporation, *Assessment of the Proliferation of Certain Remotely Piloted Aircraft Systems - Response to Section 1276 of the National Defense*

States sought to remove intelligence, surveillance, and reconnaissance (ISR) UAVs from the Category I list in 2007 because of their importance to coalition military operations but not all MTCR participants agreed. Category II items include components, equipment, material, and technology that can be used for the manufacture of Category I items.

MTCR participants have occasionally overlooked the strong presumption of denial with respect to the transfer of missiles and UAVs to partner countries. In 1998, France sold the "Storm Shadow" cruise missile to the United Arab Emirates despite U.S. objections that the sale violated MTCR guidelines on range and payload. Subsequently, the United States successfully pressed to revise MTCR guidelines on range in 2002 and, in 2006, the UK announced its intent to sell the Storm Shadow to Saudi Arabia to accommodate the kingdom's desire for a longer-range strike capability. The Obama Administration did not object to the sale.[415] More recently, Saudi Arabia used the Storm Shadow to attack Iranian-supported Houthi rebels and targets in Yemen.[416]

Some nonproliferation analysts argue that what they believe is the selective application of MTCR guidelines has opened the door for other countries to sell cruise missiles as well. For example, Russia has worked with India to develop a cruise missile called "Brahmos," which has a range just

---

Authorization Act for Fiscal Year 2017, Report RR-2369-JS, 2018, pp. 33-34, available at
https://www.rand.org/content/dam/rand/pubs/research_reports/R R2300/RR2369/RAND_RR2369.pdf.

[415] Jeffrey Lewis, "Storm Shadow, Saudi & the MTCR," Arms Control Wonk, 31 May 2011, available at
https://www.armscontrolwonk.com/archive/204051/saudi-arabia-storm-shadow-the-mtcr/.

[416] Andrew Chuter, "UK-Supplied Precision Weapons Prove Popular in Saudi-Led Yemen Campaign," *DefenseNews*, 17 October 2016, available at https://www.defensenews.com/global/2016/10/17/uk-supplied-precision-weapons-prove-popular-in-saudi-led-yemen-campaign/.

under the MTCR guidelines but can be modified to exceed them. Other countries in Africa, Asia, and the Middle East are also interested in UAV systems that can be adapted to carry weapons.

In 2012, in response to the Republic of Korea's request to counter a growing North Korean threat, the Obama Administration allowed improvements to some of the South's ballistic missiles, extending their range from less than 300 km. to 800 km. Critics contended that these improvements would not only extend the missiles' range to reach parts of China and Japan but would also undercut the restrictions in the MTCR.[417] The Obama Administration also notified Congress in 2012 of its intent to sell the "Global Hawk" UAV system to the Republic of Korea, despite an acknowledgement several years earlier by former Secretary of Defense Robert Gates that such a sale would raise MTCR issues.[418]

Despite apparent inconsistencies in its application, the MTCR has generally been seen as successful in slowing missile transfers and the acquisition by other states of critical missile technology. Neither North Korea nor China are members of the MTCR; however, China agreed to abide by some of the original MTCR guidelines.

---

[417] See Daniel Pinkston, "The New South Korean Missile Guidelines and Future Prospects for Regional Stability," International Crisis Group, 25 October 2012, available at https://www.crisisgroup.org/asia/north-east-asia/korean-peninsula/new-south-korean-missile-guidelines-and-future-prospects-regional-stability. Also see Bruce Klingner, "U.S. Should Allow South Korea to Extend Its Missile Range," The Heritage Foundation *Issue Brief*, 23 March 2012, available at https://www.heritage.org/asia/report/us-should-allow-south-korea-extend-its-missile-range.

[418] Jim Wolf, "U.S. moves to sell advanced spy drones to South Korea," Reuters, 25 December 2012, available at https://www.reuters.com/article/usa-korea-drones/u-s-moves-to-sell-advanced-spy-drones-to-south-korea-idINDEE8BO05620121225.

Congressional Involvement: A Mixed Bag

Congress' record of involvement in nonproliferation issues has been decidedly mixed. While some in Congress have taken a keen interest in the issue, the ability of the legislative branch to shape U.S. policy in this area has been constrained by the fact that many of these nonproliferation agreements are not treaties but rather voluntary, non-binding arrangements between like-minded parties. Also, as noted above, 123 agreements are executive agreements that do not require congressional approval to enter into force. Nevertheless, Congress has repeatedly sought to influence U.S. nonproliferation policy by proposing legislation to strengthen U.S. rules related to the export of sensitive technologies and seeking to constrain the executive branch's freedom of action in areas where Congress believes it deserves a greater say.

Historically, congressional debates over U.S. nonproliferation policy have pitted those who favor loosening export restrictions on American manufacturers to improve U.S. competitiveness in the global marketplace against those who argue that export controls should be tightened for national security reasons in the face of the rapid expansion of scientific know-how and the increasing ubiquity of WMD technologies. There have also been disagreements between those who prefer to grant the president greater autonomy in determining U.S. export policy and those who seek a greater role for Congress.

In recent years, concerns over nuclear and WMD proliferation have captured the attention of both the executive and legislative branches of government. There have been multiple documents released by various administrations outlining U.S. strategy for countering WMD and dealing with biological weapons hazards.[419]

---

[419] See, for example, the White House "National Strategy to Combat Weapons of Mass Destruction," December 2002, available at

Congressional involvement in nuclear nonproliferation matters has focused on issues relating to the Nunn-Lugar Cooperative Threat Reduction (CTR) program; North Korea's nuclear weapons development; Syria's chemical weapons use; Iran's nuclear ambitions; and the proliferation activities of Russia and China. The Congress has also been concerned with the future of the NPT, including the IAEA safeguards and inspections regime, as well as the impact of the U.S. nuclear modernization program on U.S. nonproliferation goals and objectives and the long-term viability of the NPT.

On chemical and biological weapons issues, Congress has focused on strengthening export controls and on overseeing CWC implementation. In particular, congressional interest in CWC implementation has focused on the U.S. inability to meet the chemical weapons elimination deadlines established by the treaty. Under the CWC, chemical weapons stockpiles were to be completely destroyed by 2007; this deadline was extended to 2012, but neither the United States nor Russia — the two countries with the largest declared stockpiles of chemical weapons — has been able to meet the revised deadline. Various NDAAs have required reports to Congress on options for accelerating destruction of the U.S. stockpile, which may extend beyond 2023. The FY 2013 NDAA, for example, required a semi-annual report to Congress "describing the Department's progress toward destruction of the U.S.

---

https://fas.org/irp/offdocs/nspd/nspd-wmd.pdf; the "Department of Defense Strategy for Countering Weapons of Mass Destruction," June 2014, available at
https://archive.defense.gov/pubs/DoD_Strategy_for_Countering_We apons_of_Mass_Destruction_dated_June_2014.pdf; and the White House "National Biodefense Strategy," 2018, available at
https://www.whitehouse.gov/wp-content/uploads/2018/09/National-Biodefense-Strategy.pdf.

stockpile of lethal chemical agents and munitions."[420]   The FY 2019 NDAA also accused Russia of violating the CWC for its 2018 nerve agent attack on Sergei and Yulia Skripal in Salisbury, England and its support of the Assad regime's use of chemical weapons in Syria.[421]

U.S. Export Control Regimes

The transfer of missiles and missile technology is primarily governed by the Arms Export Control Act (AECA) and the International Trade in Arms Regulations (ITAR). The 1976 AECA grants the president the statutory authority to control the export of defense articles and services. Under Executive Order 11958, signed by President Gerald R. Ford in 1977, the president delegated this authority to the Secretary of State.[422] The AECA requires that individuals who engage in the illicit trade of missile technology be sanctioned; however, it does not apply to transfers of technology that take place among MTCR adherents. The ITAR is a series of regulations implementing the AECA. Missiles and missile technology are generally considered munitions items. They are identified on the U.S. Munitions List (USML) and their export must be licensed by the

---

[420] Office of the Under Secretary of Defense for Acquisition, Technology and Logistics, "Department of Defense Chemical Demilitarization Program Semi-Annual Report to Congress," March 2014, p. 1, available at https://www.peoacwa.army.mil/wp-content/uploads/Report_Semi-Annual_to_Congress_Mar14.pdf.

[421] House Armed Services Committee, "Fiscal Year 2019 National Defense Authorization Act Conference Report Summary," available at https://armedservices.house.gov/_cache/files/9/b/9b3cf12c-53e2-4fe4-adbf-0068c519a22e/7FD759C5E1792048C39FA198641F1A5F.final-summary-of-the-fy-19-ndaa-conference-report-dem.pdf.

[422] Executive Order 11958, "Administration of Arms Export Controls," 18 January 1977, available at https://www.archives.gov/federal-register/codification/executive-order/11958.html.

government. All USML items are licensed by the State Department.

The export of sensitive dual-use items (those with both civilian and military applications) was governed by the Export Administration Act (EAA) of 1979, until its initial expiration in 1989. Since then, the act has been incrementally reauthorized; however, its authorities were mostly extended through the president's invocation of the International Emergency Economic Powers Act (IEEPA) until passage of the Exports Controls Act of 2018.[423]

While serving as a PSM on the HASC staff, I was involved in a major congressional effort to rewrite the EAA in a way that ensured an appropriate balance between the economic competitiveness interests of private industry and the demands of national security. This effort involved numerous congressional committees on the House and Senate side, including the House Armed Services Committee, House International Relations Committee, and Senate Banking, Housing, and Urban Affairs Committee (the Senate Banking Committee had primary jurisdiction over export control issues). After many months of negotiation at the staff level, a bill to reauthorize the EAA was presented to the members; however, lack of agreement between Republicans and Democrats in both chambers spelled ultimate doom for the effort.

Other congressional efforts to shape U.S. export control policy were more fruitful. The FY 1990 and 1991 NDAA included a provision requiring the Secretary of Defense to report to Congress on MTCR enforcement.[424] More

---

[423] "The Export Administration Act: Evolution, Provisions, and Debate," Congressional Research Service, CRS Report RL31832, 26 April 2010, available at
https://www.everycrsreport.com/files/20100426_RL31832_5a0e630089
3e1c7a05bb5a4e670619e4b6a0622d.pdf.

[424] Section 1639 of Public Law 101-189, 29 November 1989, available at
https://www.govinfo.gov/content/pkg/STATUTE-
103/pdf/STATUTE-103-Pg1352.pdf.

recently, the John S. McCain NDAA for Fiscal Year 2019 contained an entire title dealing with export controls (Title XVII) and various other provisions, including a provision on DoD participation in the dual-use export license application review process (Section 1073) and a statement of policy that U.S. export controls would be used "only after full consideration of the impact on the economy of the United States and only to the extent necessary."[425]

Like most such laws involving the imposition of sanctions on export control violators, the president may waive sanctions in the interest of national security by providing a statement of justification to Congress. The FY 1990 and 1991 NDAA amended the AECA to require the president to impose sanctions on those who trade illicitly in controlled missile technology to countries that do not adhere to MTCR guidelines. Under this provision, the United States sanctioned entities in Russia, North Korea, South Africa, India, Iran, Egypt, and Syria. Yet, the president retained the right to waive sanctions if doing so was determined to be in the national security interest.

Issue Leaders

One of the most prominent advocates of congressional involvement in WMD nonproliferation activities has been Sen. Edward J. Markey (D-MA). In 1997, then-Rep. Markey co-founded the Congressional Bipartisan Task Force on Nonproliferation. In 2012, Markey co-authored an opinion piece with former U.S. Ambassador to the UN and Under Secretary of State for Arms Control and International Security John Bolton (who later became President Trump's National Security Advisor) accusing the Obama

---

[425] Public Law 115-232, 13 August 2018, available at https://www.congress.gov/115/plaws/publ232/PLAW-115publ232.pdf.

Administration of abandoning its earlier support to include a "gold standard" provision in every 123 agreement that would prohibit enrichment or reprocessing activities because of the risk of diversion to military purposes. They wrote that the Obama Administration "is now poised to send this 'gold standard' to the trash heap" by taking a "'case-by-case' approach." "This may expedite the profitability of such agreements for the nuclear industry," they wrote, "but will do so at the expense of US and world security…. [The] likely result of jettisoning the 'gold standard' will be throwing open the doors to the spread of nuclear weapons."[426] They also criticized the inability of Congress to affirmatively approve 123 agreements, noting, "It is a strange approach indeed to national security to require Congressional approval for agreements involving cars, yarn, and peaches but not for those concerning nuclear matters."[427]

In an attempt to rectify this situation, Reps. Howard Berman (D-CA) and Ileana Ros-Lehtinen (R-FL) repeatedly introduced legislation to add the "gold standard" to the nine criteria that all 123 agreements must meet and to require an affirmative vote by Congress for 123 agreements to take effect. Like most legislative bills, their efforts failed. In 2011, the House Foreign Affairs Committee unanimously passed an amendment to the 1954 Atomic Energy Act that would codify the "gold standard," but it was opposed by the Obama Administration and also died.[428]

---

[426] John Bolton and Edward J. Markey, "How an Obama shift helps unstable regimes get nuclear weapons," *The Christian Science Monitor*, 10 February 2012, available at https://www.csmonitor.com/Commentary/Opinion/2012/0210/How-an-Obama-shift-helps-unstable-regimes-get-nuclear-weapons.

[427] Ibid.

[428] Fred McGoldrick and Duyeon Kim, "Decision Time: U.S.-South Korea Peaceful Nuclear Cooperation," Korea Economic Institute of America, *Academic Paper Series*, 13 March 2013, available at

In the years since, Congress has continued to weigh in on nonproliferation issues. In the 112th Congress alone, a search for "nonproliferation" legislation turned up nearly 150 bills or resolutions. All but nine of these died in committee; those that became Public Laws were generally part of larger bills like the NDAA or Intelligence Authorization Act. Individual bills focusing exclusively on nonproliferation issues had a tendency to go nowhere.[429]

---

http://www.keia.org/sites/default/files/publications/aps_march_201 3_mcgoldrick-kim_-_final.pdf.

[429] A good inventory of congressional nonproliferation actions through 2012 can be found in Mary Beth Nikitin, Paul K. Kerr, and Steven A. Hildreth, "Proliferation Control Regimes: Background and Status," Congressional Research Service, CRS Report RL31559, 25 October 2012, available at https://fas.org/sgp/crs/nuke/RL31559.pdf.

CHAPTER ELEVEN

CASE STUDIES ON THE PROLIFERATION SECURITY INITIATIVE, PROJECT BIOSHIELD, AND MISSILE DEFENSE

Several WMD-related case studies demonstrate that Congress has been at times highly deferential to the executive branch and at other times quite assertive in its attempts to shape U.S. policy on critical national security issues involving WMD. In some cases, the Congress has worked collaboratively with the executive branch to develop nonproliferation strategies and programs while in other cases the relationship between the two branches of government has been contentious.

One example of Congress' deferential approach is the Proliferation Security Initiative, or "PSI." This was an executive branch initiative that enjoyed strong bipartisan congressional support. The impetus for the initiative was the interception by the U.S. and Spanish navies in 2002 of a North Korean ship, the *So San*, in the Arabian Sea. The United States had been monitoring the vessel's course since it departed North Korea and believed it was transporting SCUD missiles; the destination turned out to be Yemen. Yemen was considered a haven for terrorists and some bin Laden operatives from Yemen were involved in the attack on the *USS Cole* in Aden harbor in 2000. The *So San* was operating as a "stateless" vessel and under international law it was subject to interdiction on the high seas.[430]

---

[430] This account of the *So San* interdiction is taken primarily from a monograph on the origins of the Proliferation Security Initiative published by the National Defense University's Center for the Study of Weapons of Mass Destruction. See Susan J. Koch, "Proliferation Security Initiative: Origins and Evolution." Center for the Study of

The United States and Spain had been cooperating in counter-terrorism activities at sea and the United States asked Spain to interdict the ship when it transited into an area patrolled by a Combined Task Force under Spanish command. Initially Spanish forces, followed by U.S. forces, boarded the ship and conducted a search. Although the ship's manifest indicated the cargo was cement, hidden underneath were 15 SCUD missiles, 15 warheads, and chemicals for missile propellant.

The government of Yemen initially denied it was the intended recipient of the shipment; however, after the interdiction became public, Yemen insisted that the shipment be allowed to continue. After two days of stalemate and high-level discussions, the United States, which saw Yemen as an important ally in the George W. Bush Administration's Global War on Terror, allowed the *So San* to resume its transit. In releasing the ship, White House Press Secretary Ari Fleischer stated, "There is no provision under international law prohibiting Yemen from accepting delivery of missiles from North Korea. While there is authority to stop and search, in this instance there is no clear authority to seize the shipment of Scud missiles from North Korea to Yemen. And therefore, the merchant vessel is being released."[431]

At the time, I was serving in the Pentagon as the Principal Deputy Assistant Secretary of Defense for International Security Policy, and I recall vividly the concern on the part of senior DoD officials over the inability to seize and hold the *So San*. Indeed, the president was also upset with the outcome and sought to avoid a similar situation in the future. The release of the *So San* was

---

Weapons of Mass Destruction, Occasional Paper, No. 9 (National Defense University Press, Washington, D.C., June 2012), available at https://ndupress.ndu.edu/Portals/97/Documents/Publications/Occasional%20Papers/09_Proliferation%20Security%20Initiative.pdf.

[431] Ibid., p. 2.

especially embarrassing in light of the fact that it occurred on the same day the Bush Administration released its *National Strategy to Combat Weapons of Mass Destruction*, which declared, "Effective interdiction is a critical part of the U.S. strategy to combat WMD and their delivery means. We must enhance the capabilities of our military, intelligence, technical, and law enforcement communities to prevent the movement of WMD materials, technology, and expertise to hostile states and terrorist organizations."[432]

As a result of this debacle, the Bush Administration undertook a comprehensive review of lessons learned, establishing an interagency working group to address ways governments could cooperate in such matters in the future. The group developed a framework of principles for interdiction that subsequently became the genesis of the Proliferation Security Initiative (PSI), which President Bush announced publicly in Poland in 2003. Ten U.S. allies were initially invited to participate, and the list of participants subsequently grew to more than 100. Countries endorsing the PSI "Statement of Interdiction Principles" agreed on a coordinated approach to hinder the spread of WMD and their associated delivery systems.[433]

Bipartisan support for PSI carried over from the Bush to the Obama Administration. In his 2009 Prague speech, President Obama expressed his support for PSI and called for steps to make it a "durable" international institution.[434] Since then, more than 60 interdiction exercises have

---

[432] Ibid., p. 5. Also see The White House, *National Strategy to Combat Weapons of Mass Destruction*, December 2002, p. 2, available at https://fas.org/irp/offdocs/nspd/nspd-wmd.pdf.

[433] Department of State, "About the Proliferation Security Initiative," available at https://www.state.gov/about-the-proliferation-security-initiative/.

[434] The White House, "Remarks By President Barack Obama In Prague As Delivered," 5 April 2009, available at https://obamawhitehouse.archives.gov/the-press-office/remarks-president-barack-obama-prague-delivered.

occurred.[435]   Most of these activities are unpublicized, though some have proven to be highly significant. For example, in 2003 the *BBC China* was interdicted carrying centrifuge components to Libya. The interdiction led to the unraveling of the A.Q. Khan proliferation network and is also credited with helping convince Libyan leader Col. Muammar Gadhafi to abandon his WMD programs.[436]

Despite the large number of countries that have agreed to participate in PSI, the program is not universally supported. China, Iran, and North Korea asserted that PSI violates international law, which guarantees the right of "innocent passage" through territorial seas. The UN Convention on the Law of the Sea allows ships "carrying nuclear or other inherently dangerous or noxious substances" the right of innocent passage; consequently, these countries view PSI as a form of international "piracy."[437]

Congress' Role in PSI

Because PSI is a voluntary agreement among countries and not a treaty, it is difficult for Congress to track and measure its success.   Nevertheless, notwithstanding Congress' generally strong support for the program, Congress has

---

[435] See "Proliferation Security Initiative Activities 2003-2018," May 2018, available at https://www.psi-online.info/blob/2077946/8afab8b0504e57157359d87a6a5b6a22/activities-data.pdf.

[436] Robin Wright, "Ship Incident May Have Swayed Libya," *The Washington Post*, 1 January 2004, available at https://www.washingtonpost.com/archive/politics/2004/01/01/ship-incident-may-have-swayed-libya/69244c5f-c895-4ec5-87bc-e17d34bffbe8/.

[437] See Wolff Heintschel von Heinegg, "The Proliferation Security Initiative: Security vs. Freedom of Navigation?," *International Law Studies*, Vol. 81, pp. 55-76, available at https://digital-commons.usnwc.edu/cgi/viewcontent.cgi?article=1246&context=ils.

sought to obtain greater information on PSI and to strengthen its effectiveness through several legislative actions. Early on, several members of Congress introduced the "Missile Threat Reduction Act of 2003," which stated "it should be the policy of the United States to promote the creation of new international mechanisms that would, in all future circumstances, allow the peace-loving and law-abiding nations of the world the authority to interdict and prevent the transfer" of missiles.[438] The bill was referred to the House International Relations Committee, but went nowhere. The "Implementing Recommendations of the 9/11 Commission Act of 2007" required submission to Congress of an annual joint DoD-State Department report that included details on PSI plans over the next three years. The act also called on the president to "expand and strengthen" PSI in various ways.[439]

Congressional supporters of PSI have introduced various other pieces of legislation, even though they did not always become law. For example, in 2009, Rep. Ileana Ros-Lehtinen (R-FL) introduced H. Res. 604 recognizing "the vital role of the Proliferation Security Initiative in preventing the spread of weapons of mass destruction."[440] She also sponsored a bill (H.R. 375) praising PSI for having "repeatedly demonstrated its effectiveness in preventing the proliferation of weapons of mass destruction."[441] Other

---

[438] H.R. 1875, 30 April 2003, available at https://www.govinfo.gov/content/pkg/BILLS-108hr1875ih/pdf/BILLS-108hr1875ih.pdf.

[439] Section 1821 of Public Law 110-53, 3 August 2007, available at https://www.govinfo.gov/content/pkg/PLAW-110publ53/pdf/PLAW-110publ53.pdf.

[440] H. Res. 604, 26 June 2009, available at https://www.congress.gov/bill/111th-congress/house-resolution/604/text.

[441] See Section 206 of H.R. 375, "Western Hemisphere Counterterrorism and Nonproliferation Act of 2009," available at

bills, including the FY 2013 Foreign Relations Authorizations Act and the FY 2017 Department of State, Foreign Operations, and Related Programs Appropriations Act, also contain provisions expressing congressional support for PSI.[442]

While PSI has enjoyed strong bipartisan congressional support since its creation in 2003, there has been some congressional criticism. Most of this has focused on ways to strengthen the program, increase its membership, and improve transparency. As former Sen. Richard Lugar (R-IN) stated, "PSI is an excellent step forward, but what is lacking is a coordinated effort to improve the capabilities of our foreign partners so that they can play a larger detection and interdiction role."[443] Nevertheless, this is one area where Congress has generally deferred to and supported the activities of the administration on a bipartisan basis.

Project BioShield

In his 2003 State of the Union address, President George W. Bush called upon Congress to support a new initiative to defend the nation against the threat of biological warfare, stating:

> I ask you tonight to add to our future security with a major research and production effort to guard our people against bioterrorism, called Project Bioshield. The budget I send you will propose almost $6 billion

---

https://www.congress.gov/bill/111th-congress/house-bill/375/text#toc-HA74DD3F3AC4E4650A2C282DAC6337BE0.

[442] Mary Beth Nikitin, "Proliferation Security Initiative (PSI)," Congressional Research Service, CRS Report RL34327, 9 August 2018, p. 10, available at https://www.everycrsreport.com/files/20180809_RL34327_c3f7ed5d3e 93cd2a2263ccf008c96a66567c36f6.pdf.

[443] Ibid., pp. 7-8.

to quickly make available effective vaccines and treatments against agents like anthrax, botulinum toxin, ebola and plague. We must assume that our enemies would use these diseases as weapons, and we must act before the dangers are upon us.[444]

The Congress was quick to react to the president's call. Sen. Judd Gregg (R-NH) introduced the "Project BioShield Act of 2004," which passed both the Senate and House nearly unanimously (only two House members voted against) and which President Bush signed into law in July 2004.[445]

The Act provided nearly $6 billion to buy vaccines in the event of a terrorist biological attack; but, what made this significant is that the Congress authorized appropriations to procure appropriate countermeasures through 2013. This "multiyear advance appropriation" was an uncommon funding mechanism and demonstrated the importance that Congress attached to this issue.[446]

Over the 10-year period, the United States spent a total of nearly $50 billion to counter biological weapons threats — more than $3 billion of which was spent by the Department of Health and Human Services (HHS), the key agency responsible for implementing Project BioShield. After the

---

[444] Text of President Bush's 2003 State of the Union Address, 28 January 2003, available at https://www.washingtonpost.com/wp-srv/onpolitics/transcripts/bushtext_012803.html.

[445] The text of Public Law 108-276 is available at https://www.congress.gov/108/plaws/publ276/PLAW-108publ276.pdf.

[446] Upon the expiration of the advance appropriation authorization, the project returned to the more traditional method of being funded on an annual basis. See "The Project BioShield Act: Issues for the 113th Congress," *Congressional Research Service*, CRS Report R43607, 18 June 2014, available at https://www.everycrsreport.com/files/20140618_R43607_340dcec7036 99dd545dfa87ff7c0fdcd7b3b71fe.pdf.

original 10-year advance appropriation expired, the "Pandemic and All-Hazards Preparedness Reauthorization Act of 2013" reauthorized the program through FY 2018.[447]

Similar to Congress' reaction to PSI, efforts to protect the nation against biological threats, including through Project BioShield, have met with strong bipartisan congressional support. In 2006, the Congress created the position of Assistant Secretary for Preparedness and Response within HHS to deal with public health emergencies.[448] In the Clinton and George W. Bush Administrations, the National Security Council or Homeland Security Council staff included a Special Assistant to the President for Biodefense. Some members of Congress called on the Obama Administration to re-establish this position. For example, Rep. Bennie G. Thompson (D-MS) called on President Obama to appoint a Special Assistant to the President for Biodefense "to coordinate Federal efforts on all biothreats confronting the nation. This approach has received bipartisan support through both legislative and oversight efforts," he stated.[449] In 2014, Rep. Bill Pascrell (D-NJ) introduced a bill that would have mandated this position in law and established its specific responsibilities. Although the bill was not adopted, the Trump Administration subsequently created the position of Special Assistant to the President and Senior Director for Weapons of Mass Destruction and Biodefense within the NSC staff. In addition, the Trump Administration issued its National Biodefense Strategy in 2018, declaring, "The use of biological weapons or their proliferation by state or non-

---

[447] Ibid.

[448] See Section 102 of Public Law 109-417, 19 December 2006, available at https://www.govinfo.gov/content/pkg/PLAW-109publ417/pdf/PLAW-109publ417.pdf.

[449] "Thompson Statement on Ebola Czar Appointment," 17 October 2014, available at https://homeland.house.gov/news/press-releases/thompson-statement-ebola-czar-appointment.

state actors presents a significant challenge to our national security, our population, our agriculture, and the environment" and noting, "Preventing acquisition of dangerous pathogens, equipment, and expertise for nefarious purposes, and maintaining the capability to rapidly control outbreaks in the event of a biological attack, are strategic interests of the United States."[450]

Though generally supportive of Project BioShield, Congress has questioned its implementation and some of the contracting procedures used. The GAO issued two reports on the program, in 2007 and 2009, calling for several improvements in the procurement and management of stockpiled vaccines to deal with biological threats.[451] Nevertheless, congressional interest and support for national preparedness against biological threats continues.

The declaration by President Trump in March 2020 of a national emergency to combat the coronavirus (COVID-19) pandemic and the debate in Congress on measures to mitigate its economic and health impacts provide a contemporary example not only of the seriousness of these kinds of unseen threats to human health but of the need for "whole of society" approaches to combatting them. Unfortunately, the current crisis has again demonstrated the highly partisan political atmosphere in Washington,

---

[450] The White House, *National Biodefense Strategy*, 2018, p. 2, available at https://www.whitehouse.gov/wp-content/uploads/2018/09/National-Biodefense-Strategy.pdf.

[451] Government Accountability Office, "Project BioShield – Actions Needed to Avoid Repeating Past Problems with Procuring New Anthrax Vaccine and Managing the Stockpile of Licensed Vaccine," Report GAO-08-88, October 2007, available at https://www.gao.gov/assets/270/268295.pdf. Also see Government Accountability Office, "Project BioShield - HHS Can Improve Agency Internal Controls for Its New Contracting Authorities," Report GAO-09-820, July 2009, available at https://www.gao.gov/new.items/d09820.pdf.

D.C. and exposed further rifts between the executive and legislative branches of government.

The Missile Defense Seesaw

One WMD-related area where the Congress and the administration have frequently been at loggerheads involves missile defense. The idea behind missile defense is to deter adversaries from attacking the United States or its allies with ballistic missiles that can carry nuclear, biological, or chemical warheads, or to defend against such attacks should they occur. The notion of missile defenses that can protect the entire United States has been controversial since President Reagan unveiled his "Strategic Defense Initiative" (SDI) program in a speech to the nation in March 1983.[452]

Arguments over missile defense have centered on whether such defenses were stabilizing or destabilizing to the strategic balance with the Soviet Union; their technological feasibility and cost; the timeframe whereby ballistic missile threats to the United States might emerge; and the appropriate balance between National Missile Defense (NMD), which would defend the U.S. homeland against long-range missile attack, and Theater Missile Defense (TMD), which would protect deployed U.S. military forces and allies from more numerous shorter-range missile threats.

After President Reagan's SDI speech, in which he stated his desire to render nuclear weapons "impotent and obsolete," the administration pressed for the development of an extensive architecture of ground-, sea-, air-, and space-based defense systems, including a constellation of space-

---

[452] Ronald Reagan, "Address to the Nation on Defense and National Security," 23 March 1983, available at http://www.atomicarchive.com/Docs/Missile/Starwars.shtml.

based interceptors (later dubbed "Brilliant Pebbles" in the George H.W. Bush Administration) designed to intercept ballistic missiles in various flight stages after launch.

Critics of the administration's plan considered it an impractical and unachievable "astrodome" defense. It was derisively referred to by Sen. Edward Kennedy (D-MA) as "Star Wars." Opponents also challenged it on the grounds that constructing a nationwide defense against ballistic missiles would directly violate the 1972 U.S.-Soviet Anti-Ballistic Missile (ABM) Treaty. In particular, Article V of the treaty states, "Each Party undertakes not to develop, test, or deploy ABM systems or components which are sea-based, air-based, space-based, or mobile land-based," while Article II defines ABM systems as those "currently consisting of" certain missiles, launchers, and radars.[453]

In 1985, after conducting a legal review led by the State Department, the administration announced a "broad interpretation" of the ABM Treaty that would allow the development and testing of space-based missile defense interceptors and systems, based on a contention that "Agreed Statement D" in the treaty restricted the Article V prohibition only to then-existing technology. Agreed Statement D declared that "the Parties agree that in the event ABM systems based on other physical principles... are created in the future, specific limitations on such systems and their components would be subject to discussion...."[454] ABM Treaty supporters, however, argued this interpretation would violate the letter and intent of the treaty.

Over the next two years, debate over the issue heated up. Sen. Sam Nunn (D-GA) warned there would be a

---

[453] "Treaty Between the United States of America and the Union of Soviet Socialist Republics on the Limitation of Anti-Ballistic Missile Systems," 26 May 1972, available at https://media.nti.org/documents/abm_treaty.pdf.

[454] Ibid.

"constitutional crisis of profound dimensions" if the administration unilaterally insisted on a broad interpretation of the treaty, threatening congressional retaliation by making deep cuts in the missile defense budget.[455] Congress held hearings on the issue, with Sen. Carl Levin (D-MI) accusing the administration of "providing Congress with an incomplete and misleading analysis" of the ABM Treaty, calling it "a fabrication."[456]

In a series of three speeches given on the Senate floor over a three-day period, Sen. Nunn laid out the case against the Reagan Administration's broad interpretation of the ABM Treaty. He challenged the administration's analysis as "woefully inadequate" and "fundamentally flawed," arguing that the meaning of the treaty is determined by the treaty's text, the negotiating record, and the Senate ratification debate.[457] Nunn argued that a comprehensive review of each of these elements demonstrated that the administration's contention that the treaty allowed the deployment of space-based missile interceptors was wrong.[458]

---

[455] Michael R. Gordon, "Reagan Is Warned By Senator Nunn Over ABM Treaty," *The New York Times*, 7 February 1987, available at https://www.nytimes.com/1987/02/07/us/reagan-is-warned-by-senator-nunn-over-abm-treaty.html.

[456] Carl Levin, "Administration wrong on ABM Treaty," *Bulletin of the Atomic Scientists*, Vol. 4, No. 6, April 1987, pp. 30-33, available at https://books.google.com/books?id=qQYAAAAMBAJ&pg=PA30&dq=levin+providing+congress+with+an+incomplete+and+misleading+analysis+fabrication&hl=en&sa=X&ved=2ahUKEwj3ou_I14XnAhVku1kKHS8pAvwQ6AEwAHoECAIQAg#v=onepage&q&f=false.

[457] Paul Houston, "ABM Review Wrong on All Counts, Nunn Says," *Los Angeles Times*, 14 March 1987, available at https://www.latimes.com/archives/la-xpm-1987-03-14-mn-9628-story.html.

[458] "Congress Reinforces Strings on Strategic Defense Initiative (SDI) Program," *CQ Almanac 1987*, 43rd Edition, pp. 195-210, available at https://library.cqpress.com/cqalmanac/document.php?id=cqal87-1144713#H2_2.

Sen. Nunn's view of the ABM Treaty was not shared by his fellow Democrat, Sen. Ernest F. "Fritz" Hollings (D-SC). Sen. Hollings argued:

> ...despite the crystal-clear text of the treaty and the equally unambiguous testimony of the treaty's drafters, Sen. Nunn seeks to shackle the United States to his new "narrow" interpretation. Shamefully, he threatens to use his muscle as Armed Services Committee chairman to gut future SDI funding.... This is wrong. In effect, he seeks to ratify a new treaty by a majority vote of the Senate instead of the constitutional two-thirds. He further corrupts the Constitution by inviting House participation in this new "ratification process."[459]

Sen. Hollings, who voted for the ABM Treaty in 1972, was in the minority on this issue. Although the Reagan Administration insisted the broad interpretation of the treaty was correct, it agreed as a matter of policy to continue developing missile defenses under a narrow interpretation of the treaty. In the struggle over the future course and direction of U.S. missile defense policy, congressional opponents of the administration's plan had clearly gained the upper hand. The outcome of this debate affected the later trajectory of U.S. missile defense efforts with an enduring impact to this day, as space-based missile defenses have never been built or deployed.

Although the ABM Treaty prohibited a nationwide missile defense of the U.S. homeland, defending against shorter-range missiles that could be launched against U.S. forces abroad or American allies was not prohibited and

---

[459] Ernest F. Hollings, "Fighting Over the ABM Treaty," *The Washington Post*, 29 September 1987, available at https://www.washingtonpost.com/archive/opinions/1987/09/29/fighting-over-the-abm-treaty/f9facf99-7030-48bc-ba78-cd8d4ccdaf94/.

proved to be less controversial in Congress. During the Gulf War in 1991, an Iraqi SCUD missile struck a barracks in Saudi Arabia killing 27 American military personnel. In the wake of this attack, and Iraqi SCUD missile attacks on Israel, Congress passed the "Missile Defense Act of 1991," which directed the Secretary of Defense to "aggressively pursue the development of advanced theater missile defense systems."[460]

While theater missile defenses remained relatively non-controversial in Congress, the issue of national missile defenses to protect the homeland continued to generate partisan debate and disagreement. This issue flared up again in 1995 after Republicans took control of the Congress, with many supporting a more aggressive missile defense posture than that favored by the Clinton Administration. The FY 1996 NDAA contained provisions (for which I had some responsibility at the time) strongly supporting development of a national missile defense capability to protect the United States against ballistic missile threats from countries like North Korea. These provisions led President Clinton to veto the bill. In his veto message to Congress, the president stated:

> ...the bill requires deployment by 2003 of a costly missile defense system able to defend all 50 States from a long-range missile threat that our Intelligence Community does not foresee in the coming decade. By forcing such an unwarranted deployment decision now, the bill would waste tens of billions of dollars and force us to commit prematurely to a specific technological option. It would also likely

---

[460] The Missile Defense Act of 1991 was incorporated into the *National Defense Authorization Act for Fiscal Years 1992 and 1993*, Public Law 102-190, 5 December 1991, available at https://www.govinfo.gov/content/pkg/STATUTE-105/pdf/STATUTE-105-Pg1290.pdf.

require a multiple-site architecture that cannot be accommodated within the terms of the existing ABM Treaty. By setting U.S. policy on a collision course with the ABM Treaty, the bill would jeopardize continued Russian implementation of the START I Treaty as well as Russian ratification of START II—two treaties that will significantly lower the threat to U.S. national security, reducing the number of U.S. and Russian strategic nuclear warheads by two-thirds from Cold War levels.[461]

The veto did not sit well with many congressional Republicans, who argued the administration was underestimating the ballistic missile threat to the United States posed by rogue regimes. The president's reference in his veto message to "a long-range missile threat that our Intelligence Community does not foresee in the coming decade" reflected the judgment of National Intelligence Estimate (NIE) 95-19, which concluded "No country, other than the major declared nuclear powers, will develop or otherwise acquire a ballistic missile in the next 15 years that would threaten the contiguous 48 states and Canada."[462]

The NIE's key findings were released in an unclassified letter to Sens. Carl Levin (D-MI) and Dale Bumpers (D-AR), leading to suggestions that the NIE was "politicized" to downplay the missile threat and undermine support for national missile defense. Consequently, the Congress took

---

[461] "Message from the President of the United States Transmitting His Veto of H.R. 1530, the 'National Defense Authorization Act for Fiscal Year 1996,'" 3 January 1996, available at https://www.govinfo.gov/content/pkg/CDOC-104hdoc155/pdf/CDOC-104hdoc155.pdf.

[462] See Craig Cerniello, "Rumsfeld Panel Releases Report on Missile Threat to U.S.," *Arms Control Today*, June 1998, available at https://www.armscontrol.org/act/1998-06/press-releases/rumsfeld-panel-releases-report-missile-threat-us. This issue is also briefly discussed in Chapters Seven and Eight.

several actions in the final, enacted version of the NDAA. Specifically, it required a GAO report on NIE 95-19; authorized an intelligence community "Team B" review of NIE 95-19 to ascertain if there was politicization of intelligence; and established an independent, outside commission to assess ballistic missile threats to the United States (which came to be known as the "Rumsfeld Commission").[463]

The GAO report concluded, "The wording of NIE 95-19's main judgment implies a 100-percent level of certainty that the predicted outcome will hold true during the next 15 years. However, the caveats and intelligence gaps noted in the NIE do not support this level of certainty."[464] The GAO also identified a number of methodological flaws in the NIE.

As noted in Chapter Seven, Republicans and Democrats on the HASC were at odds over whether to establish an independent commission to assess ballistic missile threats to the United States; however a compromise was reached that allowed the commission to be created, and authorized an intelligence community internal review of NIE 95-19 to evaluate the charge of "politicization." The CIA's "Team B" panel of experts, headed by former Director of Central Intelligence Robert Gates, concluded:

> The panel found no evidence of politicization and is completely satisfied that the analysts' views were based on the evidence before them and their substantive analysis. There was no breach of the integrity of the intelligence process. Beyond this, the panel believes that unsubstantiated allegations challenging the integrity of Intelligence Community

---

[463] Public Law 104-201, op. cit.

[464] General Accounting Office, "FOREIGN MISSILE THREATS Analytic Soundness of Certain National Intelligence Estimates," Report GAO/NSIAD-96-225, August 1996, p. 4, available at https://www.gao.gov/assets/230/223183.pdf.

analysts by those who simply disagree with their conclusions, including by Members of Congress, are irresponsible. Intelligence forecasts do not represent revealed truth, and it should be possible to disagree with them without attacking the character and integrity of those who prepared them, or the integrity of the intelligence process itself.[465]

However, "Team B" did find "presentational and analytical problems" with the estimate, as well as "some very important weaknesses and deficiencies in the analytical approach," including "the failure to address adequately the motives and objectives of governments developing missile programs." The NIE, Gates noted, also "did not give nearly enough attention to the potential for missiles launched from within several hundred miles of U.S. territory" and failed to ask "a critical question: What if our potential adversaries pursue approaches, technical or otherwise, unexpected by the Intelligence Community?" The Team B assessment also noted that "the possibility of a threat from missiles of less than intercontinental range warrants more attention than given in the Estimate" and concluded "the Estimate, in our view, too easily dismisses missile scenarios alternative to an indigenously developed and launched intercontinental ballistic missile by countries hostile to the United States...."[466]

The bipartisan Rumsfeld Commission unanimously concluded, "Concerted efforts by a number of overtly or potentially hostile nations to acquire ballistic missiles with biological or nuclear payloads pose a growing threat to the United States, its deployed forces and its friends and allies." It noted that with external help, "...they would be able to inflict major destruction on the U.S. within about five years

---

[465] Statement of Robert M. Gates before the Senate Select Committee on Intelligence, 4 December 1996, op. cit.
[466] Ibid.

of a decision to acquire such a capability" and that "the U.S. might not be aware that such a decision had been made." Further, the commission concluded, "The threat to the U.S. posed by these emerging capabilities is broader, more mature and evolving more rapidly than has been reported in estimates and reports by the Intelligence Community," noting, "The Intelligence Community's ability to provide timely and accurate estimates of ballistic missile threats to the U.S. is eroding" and that the "warning times the U.S. can expect of new, threatening ballistic missile deployments are being reduced."[467]

The Rumsfeld Commission released its report in July 1998; only weeks later (as noted in Chapter Eight), North Korea launched a three-stage rocket that overflew Japan. The rocket's unexpected solid-fuel third stage also added fuel to the arguments of congressional advocates of a stronger missile defense posture, who saw North Korea's action as confirmation of the Rumsfeld Commission's conclusions.

The Rumsfeld Commission was successful in large measure because the Congress narrowly limited its charter in the NDAA to assessing the ballistic missile threat to the United States and not to opining on missile defense issues. Had its charter been broader in scope to include missile defense policy recommendations, it is unlikely the bipartisan commissioners would have arrived at unanimous conclusions. Nevertheless, congressional missile defense proponents were able to use the Rumsfeld Commission's findings to advocate on behalf of a more robust U.S. missile defense posture.

The conclusions of the Rumsfeld Commission helped generate support for a more aggressive congressional stance on missile defense. The following year, Congress overwhelmingly passed the "National Missile Defense Act

---

[467] *Executive Summary of the Report of the Commission to Assess the Ballistic Missile Threat to the United States*, 15 July 1998, op. cit.

of 1999" with huge, bipartisan, veto-proof majorities in both chambers (345-71 in the House and 97-3 in the Senate). Faced with this overwhelming expression of congressional support for a national missile defense system, President Clinton signed the act, which declared, "It is the policy of the United States to deploy as soon as is technologically possible an effective National Missile Defense system capable of defending the territory of the United States against limited ballistic missile attack...."[468] Congressional supporters of missile defense hailed this as a major victory. The act again demonstrated Congress' ability to set U.S. policy on important national security issues.

Despite this success, the United States was still bound by the constraints of the ABM Treaty. Yet, the demise of the Soviet Union and the growth of missile threats made the treaty seem to some like a Cold War anachronism whose time had passed. In 2001, President George W. Bush announced his decision to withdraw the United States from the treaty and to proceed with the deployment of an initial missile defense capability to protect the country from rogue regime missile threats. In announcing his decision, the president stated:

> The 1972 ABM Treaty was signed by the United States and the Soviet Union at a much different time, in a vastly different world. One of the signatories, the Soviet Union, no longer exists. And neither does the hostility that once led both our countries to keep thousands of nuclear weapons on hair-trigger alert, pointed at each other.... Today, as the events of September the 11th made all too clear, the greatest threats to both our countries come not from each other, or other big powers in the world, but from

---

[468] Public Law 106-38, 22 July 1999, available at
https://www.congress.gov/106/plaws/publ38/PLAW-106publ38.pdf.

terrorists who strike without warning, or rogue states who seek weapons of mass destruction.[469]

Some congressional Democrats were critical of the decision, calling it misguided and poorly timed. Sen. Majority Leader Tom Daschle (D-SD) said the decision "poses some serious questions regarding our relationship with our allies, with Russia and with China, that we're going to have to consider very, very carefully." He indicated it could "rupture our relations with key countries and governments around the world" and could lead to future arms races.[470]   Then-Senate Foreign Committee Chairman Joseph Biden (D-DE) admonished the White House, saying the president's decision would lead to an arms buildup, not only in Russia but in India and Pakistan as well. He called the president's priorities "out of whack," saying the administration should be more concerned about WMD-armed terrorists than long-range ballistic missile threats from other countries. "September 11 indicated our country is vulnerable," Biden said, but added, "The thing we remain the least vulnerable to is an ICBM attack from another nation."[471]   Russian President Vladimir Putin reacted to the U.S. decision by calling it "mistaken," but added, "I can say with full confidence that the decision made by the President of the United States does not pose a threat to the national security of the Russian Federation."[472]

---

[469] Remarks by President George W. Bush, 13 December 2001, available at https://www.armscontrol.org/act/2002-01/us-withdrawal-abm-treaty-president-bush%E2%80%99s-remarks-us-diplomatic-notes.

[470] Manuel Perez-Rivas, "U.S. quits ABM treaty," CNN, 14 December 2001, available at https://www.cnn.com/2001/ALLPOLITICS/12/13/rec.bush.abm/.

[471] Ibid.

[472] Statement by Russian President Vladimir Putin, 13 December 2001, available at https://www.acq.osd.mil/tc/abm/ABM-PutinDec13.htm.

Despite significant pockets of congressional opposition, President Bush's decision to withdraw the United States from the ABM Treaty went into effect in 2002, in accordance with the treaty's Article XV provisions. After 30 years, the United States was no longer bound by the treaty's constraints.

Congressional Challenges

While some members of Congress questioned the merits of withdrawing from the ABM Treaty, others engaged on the legal issues surrounding withdrawal. As noted in Chapter Five, while Article II, Section 2 of the Constitution grants the president the power to make treaties with the advice and consent of the Senate, it is silent regarding the power to withdraw from them. This has led to various challenges to the constitutionality of a president unilaterally withdrawing from a treaty to which the Senate had consented.

In 1979, President Carter unilaterally withdrew the United States from the 1955 Mutual Defense Treaty with Taiwan and recognized the People's Republic of China as the official government of China. In response, more than two dozen Senators, led by Sen. Barry Goldwater (R-AZ), sued the president, arguing that if a two-thirds vote in the Senate is required to approve a treaty, a two-thirds vote should be required to revoke one. The case went all the way to the U.S. Supreme Court, which dismissed the lawsuit. The Senate, nevertheless, by a vote of 59-35, adopted a non-binding resolution sponsored by Sen. Harry F. Byrd, Jr. (I-VA) stating, "It is the sense of the Senate that approval of the United States Senate is required to terminate any mutual defense treaty between the United States and another nation."[473] However, as the resolution was non-binding it did not carry the force of law.

In the case of President Bush's withdrawal from the ABM Treaty, former Senator Russell Feingold (D-WI) commented that "only a few members of Congress protested; Congress as a whole failed to insist on a vote." He noted that a lawsuit filed by several members of the House "was rejected by the courts, because Congress had failed adequately to assert its powers and because the judge ruled 'issues concerning treaties are largely political questions best left to the political branches of the government, not the courts, for resolution.'"[474]

As one legal analyst has noted, "today it is widely (although not uniformly) accepted that presidents have a unilateral power of treaty termination." He attributes this to "a long accretion of executive branch claims and practice in the face of congressional inaction."[475] Clearly, the balance of power between the executive and legislative branches regarding international agreements weighs heavily in favor of the Executive.

---

[473] Bernard Gwertzman, "Senate Rebukes Carter Over Ending of Taiwan Pact," *The New York Times*, 7 June 1979, available at https://www.nytimes.com/1979/06/07/archives/senate-rebukes-carter-over-ending-of-taiwan-pact-vote-on-amendment.html.

[474] Russell Feingold, "Donald Trump can unilaterally withdraw from treaties because Congress abdicated responsibility," NBC *Think*, 7 May 2018, available at https://www.nbcnews.com/think/opinion/donald-trump-can-unilaterally-withdraw-treaties-because-congress-abdicated-responsibility-ncna870866.

[475] Curtis A. Bradley, "Treaty Termination and Historical Gloss," *Texas Law Review*, Vol. 92, 2014, p. 773, available at https://scholarship.law.duke.edu/cgi/viewcontent.cgi?article=5803&context=faculty_scholarship.

CHAPTER TWELVE

CASE STUDY ON THE COOPERATIVE THREAT REDUCTION PROGRAM

One of the more interesting examples of how Congress sought to influence the direction of U.S. national security policy in the area of weapons of mass destruction is the debate over the "Nunn-Lugar" Cooperative Threat Reduction program, or "CTR," mentioned briefly in Chapter One. This particular issue is one for which I had responsibility while working as a HASC PSM and provides a good example of how Congress can wield its power to shape U.S. policy in ways that may diverge from the administration's preferred course. It also illustrates the dynamic between the House and Senate; the execution of Congress' oversight role; the tools Congress can deploy to facilitate its desired outcomes; and the role that staffers play in helping to implement committee priorities.

The CTR program was an outgrowth of the collapse of the Soviet Union at the end of 1991 and concerns that Soviet nuclear and other WMD materials might fall into the wrong hands. The issue of "loose nukes" was a nightmare scenario that U.S. officials sought to contain by seeking ways to restore positive control over the nuclear materials of a state that no longer existed and that could no longer guarantee their security. Sen. Sam Nunn (D-GA) and Sen. Richard Lugar (R-IN) championed an effort whereby DoD would fund a variety of programs to transport, store, secure, dismantle, and eliminate former Soviet nuclear weapons. They proposed the "Soviet Nuclear Threat Reduction Act of

1991," which was enacted in 1992.[476] Originally conceived as an "emergency" program to deal with nuclear weapons and materials in the Soviet "successor entities" of Russia, Ukraine, Kazakhstan, and Belarus, it later expanded in size, scope, and geographic reach to include other types of WMD beyond the former Soviet states and, on occasion, non-WMD systems.

Though in retrospect, the CTR program is now generally viewed as a nonproliferation success, the program got off to a rocky start. Several CTR projects proved highly controversial in Congress, including efforts to dismantle, store, and eliminate nuclear materials in Russia; refocus former Soviet biological weapons scientists toward peaceful pursuits; build a chemical weapons destruction facility; and convert Russian plutonium-producing nuclear reactors. Although the SASC was generally supportive of the initiative taken by the former chairmen of the Senate Armed Services and Foreign Relations Committees, the most significant criticism of the program originated in the HASC (then named the House Committee on National Security), with Committee Chairman Rep. Floyd D. Spence (R-SC) and other members taking a skeptical view and questioning whether DoD money should be used to fund these activities in light of what was seen as other more pressing defense priorities.

Part of the criticism was based on a perception of the Clinton Administration as weak on defense and more willing to spend scarce defense dollars on "foreign assistance" programs instead of on needed U.S. defense capabilities. Some of the opposition was rooted in a latent post-Cold War distrust of Russia as a reliable partner (the "Cooperative" Threat Reduction effort, obviously, had to be carried out "cooperatively"). These concerns manifested themselves in various ways, causing consternation within

---

[476] Public Law 102-228, 12 December 1991, available at https://www.congress.gov/bill/102nd-congress/house-bill/3807/text.

both the Clinton Administration and among some Senators on the SASC who supported the original initiative of their Senate colleagues, Sens. Nunn and Lugar, and they led to major disagreements that carried over into the annual NDAA process.

The annual NDAA authorizes funding for the CTR program in a separate title (usually Title XIII), where the funding authorizations are broken out by project. Initially, DoD had a great deal of flexibility to move funds from one CTR account to another, but the Congress later restricted this in order to maintain greater oversight and control of where the Defense Department was spending its CTR money. This was one of the main concerns of HASC members, along with concerns that the focus of the CTR program was becoming increasingly diffuse; that Russia should be contributing more of its own money to the program; that the program had no end point and appeared to be an institutionalized program in perpetuity; and that this was not a "core" DoD mission. Importantly, some members objected to the fact that the United States would be paying to dismantle old, obsolete Russian nuclear weapons, freeing up resources for Moscow to spend on building new, more sophisticated weapons. Thus, some saw CTR as "subsidizing" the Russian nuclear modernization program.[477]

Russian Nuclear Weapons Elimination

DoD officials were forward leaning in justifying the CTR program by highlighting the number of Russian strategic nuclear weapons they argued the program had helped eliminate. By 2013, the department asserted that, as a result

---

[477] Many of these arguments are reflected in various HASC committee reports accompanying the annual NDAAs. I have attempted to summarize them briefly here.

of CTR funding, more than 13,000 former Soviet nuclear warheads had been deactivated; more than 1,400 ICBMs had been destroyed and over 800 ICBM silos eliminated; more than 900 sea-launched ballistic missiles and over 700 of their launchers had been eliminated; and more than 230 bombers had been removed from accountability. DoD also noted that CTR funding had helped seal nearly 200 nuclear test tunnels and had destroyed nearly 40,000 metric tons of chemical weapons. Thanks to the Nunn-Lugar CTR program, DoD contended that Belarus, Ukraine, and Kazakhstan were now "nuclear weapons free."[478]

Congress was generally supportive of these efforts; however, despite Russia's economic downturn following the breakup of the Soviet Union, some members wanted Russia to absorb a greater share of the cost. For example, in its report accompanying the FY 1998 NDAA, the HASC noted that a provision in its version of the bill would prohibit the expenditure of funds for certain elimination activities until after the president certifies to Congress "that the Russians have agreed to share the cost of these elimination activities" and the Secretary of Defense submits a report describing "the specific cost-sharing arrangements that have been agreed to with Russia."[479]

Congressional concerns over whether the CTR program was subsidizing Russian nuclear modernization were heightened when Russian First Vice Premier Yuri Maslyukov stated:

---

[478] See Defense Threat Reduction Agency and U.S. Strategic Command Center for Combatting WMD, "Nunn-Lugar CTR Scorecard," 13 March 2013, available at http://www.thelugarcenter.org/assets/htmldocuments/20130301_FY1 3_CTR-Scorecard_Slides_Mar13.pdf.

[479] *Report of the House Committee on National Security on H.R. 1119, the National Defense Authorization Act for Fiscal Year 1998*, 16 June 1997, p. 414, available at https://www.congress.gov/105/crpt/hrpt132/CRPT-105hrpt132.pdf.

...the funding of arms elimination under Nunn-Lugar [CTR] is now comparable with our annual expenditure on modernizing the strategic nuclear forces.... since the present missiles will anyhow have to be dismantled, the absence of the Nunn-Lugar program will compel Russia to take for these purposes the money currently planned for the deployment of new missile complexes, since there is simply nowhere to obtain any more money.[480]

Maslyukov's statement was seen as confirmation that U.S. taxpayer dollars were indirectly enabling improvements to Russian strategic military forces, as CTR funds used to dismantle older Russian weapons systems allowed Russia to pay for newer ones — a tradeoff that was not viewed positively by some members.

Fissile Material Storage

Another controversial project was the building of the Mayak storage facility in Russia to house excess Russian "weapons-grade" fissile material and warhead components. The project was originally intended to store material taken from dismantled nuclear warheads ("weapons-origin" material); however, the United States and Russia were unable to agree on the quantity and type of fissile material to be stored there. Further, Russia

---

[480] Cited in *Report of the House Committee on Armed Services on H.R. 1401, the National Defense Authorization Act for Fiscal Year 2000*, 24 May 1999, p. 413, available at
https://books.google.com/books?id=vy67irJ5VEEC&pg=PA413&lpg=
PA413&dq=maslyukov+funding+of+arms+elimination+since+the+pres
ent+missiles&source=bl&ots=7QJ3IW5ZCf&sig=ACfU3U17R2JAUtboh
_TaKtiMzJUOCEuMsA&hl=en&sa=X&ved=2ahUKEwiP9Z-
Pz4bnAhUJZd8KHc1sBm8Q6AEwAHoECAkQAQ#v=onepage&q=mas
lyukov%20funding%20of%20arms%20elimination%20since%20the%20p
resent%20missiles&f=false.

objected to a U.S. proposal for strict inspection procedures to verify the facility was being used for its intended purpose and that materials stored there would not be used to build new nuclear weapons. Because of these issues, the HASC fenced funding for the project pending a satisfactory resolution of the disputes.

In addition, DoD indicated that it would pay one-half of the cost of building the Mayak facility, with the other half to be paid for by Russia. However, given its economic situation, Russia reneged on its commitment to pay for half of the construction costs, leaving DoD to foot nearly the entire bill. I recall receiving a briefing from DoD officials noting the change in funding arrangements — a change that DoD had agreed to, but that had not been explained to the committee in advance. The lack of congressional consultation on this issue did not sit well with members who were skeptical of the project to begin with, especially in light of general concerns over cost-sharing.

Other issues developed with the project that led the HASC to impose a cap on funding. These included schedule delays; increased cost estimates; a reduction in the planned size and storage capacity of the facility; continuing uncertainty over Russia's commitment to fund its share of the costs; bureaucratic delays in receiving congressionally mandated DoD reports; and the lack of transparency and verification agreements with Russia. The committee requested that the GAO look into the project.

As the investigative arm of Congress, the GAO is often used as a tool to provide more details and analyses on issues of concern. In this case, the committee asked GAO to assess the cost and schedule implications of the project and whether it would meet U.S. national security objectives. The GAO report was critical, noting that the cost to the United States of building the facility had risen from $275 million to $413 million and "could ultimately increase to almost $1.3 billion."[481] Because of the concerns noted above, the GAO concluded, "The United States cannot ensure it will achieve the full range of its Mayak national security objectives."[482]   The GAO's critical assessment fueled additional oversight efforts by the HASC to ensure that DoD funding was being used appropriately; that Russia would adhere to the obligations it assumed to support the project; and that the necessary transparency agreements would be put in place to guarantee the Mayak facility would accomplish its intended national security objectives.

After more than a decade, the storage facility was finally completed at the end of 2003, but did not begin storing fissile materials until several years later.[483]

Biological Weapons Proliferation Prevention

During the Cold War, the Soviet Union possessed the largest and most sophisticated covert biological weapons program in the world. The sheer magnitude of the program was exposed by Ken Alibek, a biological warfare expert who ran the Soviet program until his defection to the West in 1992.[484]

---

[481] General Accounting Office, "WEAPONS OF MASS DESTRUCTION - Effort to Reduce Russian Arsenals May Cost More, Achieve Less Than Planned," Report GAO/NSIAD-99-76, April 1999, p. 2, available at https://www.gao.gov/archive/1999/ns99076.pdf.

[482] Ibid., p. 8.

[483] Pavel Podvig, Consolidating Fissile Materials in Russia's Nuclear Complex, International Panel on Fissile Materials, Research Report No. 7, May 2009, p. 10, available at http://fissilematerials.org/library/rr07.pdf.

[484] In 1999, Ken Alibek published a book detailing the Soviet Union's extensive biological weapons effort. See *Biohazard – The Chilling True Story of the Largest Covert Biological Weapons Program in the World-Told from the Inside by the Man Who Ran It*, (Random House, New York, 1999), available at https://www.nlm.nih.gov/nichsr/esmallpox/biohazard_alibek.pdf.

After the dissolution of the Soviet Union, the Soviet biological weapons apparatus ceased much of its activity and concern grew that former Soviet biological weapons scientists, researchers, and experts would seek gainful employment outside the former Soviet Union, perhaps by selling and proliferating their knowledge and capabilities to potential U.S. adversaries and states of concern. The prospect of this "brain drain" was alarming to many in the West, including officials in the U.S. Department of Defense, who sought to use CTR funding to redirect former Soviet biological weapons experts to peaceful research pursuits.

The CTR Biological Weapons Proliferation Prevention program was supported by many members of Congress; yet some members of the HASC objected strenuously to using DoD funds for this purpose. On one of my visits to Moscow as a HASC staffer I was introduced by a DoD official to one of the biological weapons experts whose research was now being funded by the CTR program. Over slices of pizza in a Moscow restaurant, he sought to impress upon me the value of this effort and the importance of maintaining the relationship between DoD and the former Soviet biological weapons community. Nevertheless, the HASC continued to raise questions about the value of this effort, focusing on concerns over the lack of Russia's transparency regarding the magnitude and extent of its biological weapons programs; a perception that DoD was spending resources to create a "jobs program" for Russians who would work on civilian projects of little utility to DoD; apprehension over whether the scientists whose work was being funded by DoD could hold the United States "hostage" by threatening to sell their expertise to potentially hostile regimes if the United States stopped paying them; and concern that the program would continue in perpetuity, perpetuating a knowledge base and skill set among former Soviet scientists that might make them more attractive targets for foreign recruitment.

Again, the HASC turned to the GAO to investigate the potential risks associated with the Biological Weapons Proliferation Prevention program. In its 2000 report, the GAO concluded, "Former Soviet biological weapons institutes continue to pose serious threats to U.S. national security," noting that peaceful research on biological agents "is difficult to distinguish from offensive [biological weapons] research because of the inherent dual-use nature of biotechnology."[485] The GAO also found that "expanding the program will pose certain risks to the United States. The key risks include sustaining Russia's existing biological weapons infrastructure, maintaining or advancing Russian scientists' skills to develop offensive biological weapons, and the potential misuse of U.S. assistance to fund offensive research."[486]

This GAO report was also cited in the HASC's mark-up of the FY 2001 NDAA, where the committee noted it "continues to support efforts directed toward reducing the risk of biological weapons proliferation, but continues to have concerns regarding the overall approach taken by the Department of Defense to addressing those risks."[487] On the other hand, the SASC generally did not share the HASC's concerns, and in its mark-up of the FY 2003 NDAA, directed the Secretaries of Defense and Energy to establish a pilot program whereby U.S. and former Soviet biological and chemical weapons experts would participate in an exchange program in each other's countries. The SASC noted, "The committee believes that there are significant, mutual, civil-

---

[485] General Accounting Office, "BIOLOGICAL WEAPONS - Effort to Reduce Former Soviet Threat Offers Benefits, Poses New Risks," Report GAO/NSIAD-00-138, April 2000, pp. 7, 9, available at https://www.gao.gov/new.items/ns00138.pdf.

[486] Ibid. p. 6.

[487] *Report of the House Committee on Armed Services on H.R. 4205, the Floyd D. Spence National Defense Authorization Act for Fiscal Year 2001,* 12 May 2000, p. 423, available at https://www.congress.gov/106/crpt/hrpt616/CRPT-106hrpt616.pdf.

scientific benefits that could be gained from long-term cooperative joint research projects and exchange programs."[488] This requirement, contained in the SASC report accompanying its version of the FY 2003 NDAA, was not included in the final enacted bill, though Congress continued to provide funds for various biological weapons proliferation prevention activities in the former Soviet Union.

Nuclear Reactor Core Conversion

Another controversial CTR issue was the project to convert Russia's three plutonium-producing nuclear reactors to less-proliferation risky civilian uses, whereby lower-grade fuel would be used to provide power to local communities. This was seen as a way to end Russia's production of plutonium. However, rather than convert the reactors, as DoD had originally intended, Russia decided it would be preferable and less costly to shut them down entirely — as long as an alternate means of power generation could be found.

The proposed solution was to build several fossil fuel plants that would provide energy to local communities. DoD supported this approach as a nonproliferation objective and agreed to provide funding for it since the project would result in the permanent shuttering of Russia's remaining plutonium-producing reactors. However, skeptical members on the HASC argued that building fossil fuel energy plants to provide electricity and power to Russian communities was not an appropriate function of the Department of Defense. This particular project was seen

---

[488] *Report of the Senate Committee on Armed Services on S. 2514, the National Defense Authorization Act for Fiscal Year 2003*, 15 May 2002, p. 401, available at https://www.congress.gov/107/crpt/srpt151/CRPT-107srpt151.pdf.

by some as a form of "mission creep" that went beyond the original intent of the CTR legislation.

In its committee report on the FY 2001 NDAA, the HASC stated:

> Although the committee supports the elimination of Russia's weapons-grade plutonium production and the shutting down of these reactors, the committee does not believe that CTR funds should be used to build fossil fuel plants in Russia. Therefore, if this option is chosen, the committee believes that any U.S. assistance provided for this activity should be funded through other means, external to the Department of Defense. Consequently, the committee recommends a provision... that would prohibit the obligation or expenditure of any CTR funds for the construction of fossil fuel plants in Russia.[489]

In a "Statement of Administration Policy," the Clinton Administration took issue with the HASC position, stating, "The Administration opposes the prohibition on building fossil fuel plants as a means of shutting down the three Russian nuclear reactors that produce weapons grade plutonium. Such a ban prevents what may be the most timely, cost effective, and most effective non-proliferation approach to ending the production of weapons grade plutonium."[490]

---

[489] *Report of the House Committee on Armed Services on H.R. 4205, the Floyd D. Spence National Defense Authorization Act for Fiscal Year 2001,* 12 May 2000, op. cit., p. 427.

[490] Office of Management and Budget, The White House, "Statement of Administration Policy: H.R. 4205 - Floyd D. Spence National Defense Authorization Act for Fiscal Year 2001," 17 May 2000, available at https://www.presidency.ucsb.edu/documents/statement-administration-policy-hr-4205-floyd-d-spence-national-defense-authorization-act.

The SASC was also generally supportive of this effort, though expressing concern that delays in the project due to the change in approach would prevent the department from spending the entire amount requested. Despite the administration's opposition to a funding cutoff and the SASC's overall support for the effort, the final conference outcome in the FY 2001 NDAA prohibited any funds from being spent for this purpose.[491] President Clinton signed the bill into law on October 30, 2000. Funding was subsequently provided by DOE and the last of the three plutonium producing reactors was shut down in April 2010.[492]

Chemical Weapons Destruction

Perhaps the most controversial aspect of the CTR program was an effort to build a chemical weapons destruction facility (CWDF) in the town of Shchuch'ye, Russia. It was generally acknowledged that the Soviet Union possessed the world's largest declared stockpile of chemical weapons—roughly 40,000 tons of nerve agents and blister agents—and that these weapons posed a significant proliferation risk. DoD was supportive of this effort because it would advance U.S. nonproliferation objectives. If successful, it would also assist Russia in meeting its Chemical Weapons Convention elimination obligations, which was considered to be in the U.S. national security interest.

---

[491] Section 1307 of Public Law 106-398, 30 October 2000, available at https://www.congress.gov/106/plaws/publ398/PLAW-106publ398.pdf.

[492] "Countries: Russia," International Panel on Fissile Materials, 12 February 2018, available at http://fissilematerials.org/countries/russia.html.

The HASC repeatedly objected to the planned CWDF in multiple NDAAs. Skeptics on the committee cited numerous concerns, among them:

- The costs to the United States could not be determined because a specific site for the facility had yet to be chosen; however, estimates suggested the price tag could be as high as $800 million;

- Russia's commitment to destroying its legacy stockpile of chemical weapons munitions was questionable, as Russia had only invested a relatively minimal amount of money in chemical weapons elimination due to its economic situation;

- Foreign financing for the project was lacking and the United States would be the only country picking up the tab for the CWDF;

- The Shchuch'ye facility would not be collocated with the sites where Russia stored its chemical weapons, meaning that roads or rail lines would need to be built to transport the weapons from storage to the destruction facility and the costs of doing so would be additive;

- The CWDF would only be able to destroy 14 percent of Russia's overall chemical weapons stockpile and would take at least a decade to do so; to destroy all of Russia's 40,000 tons of chemical munitions would require building at least six similar facilities at tremendous cost;

- The United States and Russia disagreed over what kind of chemical munitions (i.e., air-delivered or artillery-delivered) would be destroyed first; Russia wanted the CWDF to destroy leaky artillery munitions first, but these were considered less threatening to the United States and more of an "environmental cleanup" problem for Russia, which some members did not want to fund with U.S. taxpayer dollars;

- There were reports that Russia was continuing to develop newer generations of chemical weapons, and absorbing the cost of building a destruction facility for older weapons was seen by critics as subsidizing Moscow's ongoing chemical weapons program; and

- There was a general belief that CTR should focus on eliminating those weapons most threatening to the United States (i.e., strategic nuclear weapons) and not those environmentally most threatening to Russia.[493]

The GAO issued several reports detailing concerns with the Shchuch'ye CWDF project. For example, in 1996 it reported:

Concerns regarding the potential high cost of the chemical weapons destruction facility are compounded by uncertainties regarding its impact on the Russian chemical weapons threat. DOD officials consider this threat to be less urgent than the Russian nuclear threat. By itself, the facility would require over a decade to destroy declared chemical weapons stocks at one location. Russia would need to construct six more facilities to meet Chemical Weapons Convention requirements. Other nations' commitments fall short of the billions of dollars that Russia will need to comply with the convention.[494]

---

[493] These concerns are discussed in greater detail in the various HASC reports accompanying the annual NDAAs from 1997 to 2002.

[494] General Accounting Office, "WEAPONS OF MASS DESTRUCTION - Status of the Cooperative Threat Reduction Program," Report

In a 2006 report, the GAO highlighted cost and schedule issues with respect to the CWDF, again raising concerns within Congress that the project was not only hugely expensive but would not fully meet U.S. national security objectives. As the GAO pointed out, "Since 1992, Congress has passed 27 laws addressing the CTR program... [with some] directed at the Shchuch'ye project, including a requirement for a presidential certification that the project is in the U.S. national security interest." GAO also noted that "Congress has conditioned funding for the Shchuch'ye facility on the Secretary of Defense's certification that, among other conditions, Russia has allocated at least $25 million to eliminating its chemical weapons and has developed a practical plan for destroying its chemical weapons stockpile."[495]

In its version of the FY 2000 NDAA, the HASC prohibited any funding for the CWDF. The Clinton Administration criticized this action in a Statement of Administration Policy, declaring: "The Administration opposes language that prohibits the use of Cooperative Threat Reduction (CTR) funds for the construction of a chemical weapons destruction facility. Terminating this project risks preservation of the threat posed by Russia's most modern chemical weapons and lowers Russia's ability to comply with the Chemical Weapons Convention."[496]

GAO/NSIAD-96-222, September 1996, p. 4, available at
https://www.gao.gov/assets/230/223207.pdf.

[495] Government Accountability Office, "COOPERATIVE THREAT REDUCTION - DOD Needs More Reliable Data to Better Estimate the Cost and Schedule of the Shchuch'ye Facility," Report GAO-06-692, May 2006, pp. 6-7, available at
https://www.gao.gov/assets/260/250332.pdf.

[496] Office of Management and Budget, The White House, "Statement of Administration Policy: H.R. 1401 - National Defense Authorization Act for Fiscal Year 2000," 9 June 1999, available at
https://www.presidency.ucsb.edu/documents/statement-

Although the SASC version of the bill recommended fully funding the budget request for CTR, including funding for the CWDF, the final conference outcome and the bill signed by the president stated, "No fiscal year 2000 Cooperative Threat Reduction funds, and no funds appropriated for Cooperative Threat Reduction programs after the date of the enactment of this Act, may be obligated or expended for planning, design, or construction of a chemical weapons destruction facility in Russia."[497]

This funding cutoff continued in the FY 2001 NDAA, which contained a non-binding "Sense of Congress" provision calling on the international community to assist Russia in the elimination of its chemical weapons stockpile based on Russia's commitment to take certain actions itself in this area.[498] The Clinton Administration again objected to the lack of funding for the CWDF, stating, "The nerve agent at this site is in small, modern munitions that are easily transported and mated to delivery systems that exist throughout the world. They are highly desirable weapons for both terrorists and states of concern and they represent a serious proliferation risk. It is vital to U.S. security to assist Russia in eliminating these munitions."[499]

The controversy over this issue resulted in its elevation to the "Big Four" during conference, where the chairman and ranking members of the HASC and SASC engaged in negotiations over the final outcome. Only the most stubborn issues get elevated to the "Big Four," with some of them engendering veto threats by the president as part of

---

administration-policy-hr-1401-national-defense-authorization-act-for-fiscal-year.

[497] Section 1305 of Public Law 106-65, 5 October 1999, available at https://www.congress.gov/106/plaws/publ65/PLAW-106publ65.pdf.

[498] Section 1309 of Public Law 106-398, 30 October 2000, op. cit.

[499] Office of Management and Budget, The White House, "Statement of Administration Policy: H.R. 4205 - Floyd D. Spence National Defense Authorization Act for Fiscal Year 2001," op. cit.

the administration's attempt to shape the conference outcome.

As noted in Chapter One, I was intimately involved in the HASC's oversight efforts on the CTR program, including the controversial CWDF project. After the HASC position on the CWDF funding cutoff was successfully upheld in conference and signed into law as part of the NDAA, I approached the committee's Staff Director, Robert Rangel, to say how pleased I was to have helped the committee and the chairman achieve a permanent funding cutoff for the project. His response to me was deflating. "C'mon Dave," he said, "you should know that nothing in this town is permanent." Indeed, he was right. The prohibition was lifted in the FY 2002 NDAA, with funding allowed to continue, subject to some certifications by the Secretary of Defense.[500]

The Shchuch'ye chemical weapons destruction facility was built and began operation in 2009. Six years and more than $1 billion later, it completed the elimination of more than 5,000 tons of chemical agents and closed in 2015.[501]

Postscript

My personal involvement with the CWDF project touched all three sides of what has been (often derisively) referred to

---

[500] Section 1308 of Public Law 107-107, 28 December 2001, available at https://www.congress.gov/107/plaws/publ107/PLAW-107publ107.pdf.

[501] Philip P. Pan, "Facility to Destroy Chemical Weapons Opens in Russia," *The Washington Post*, 30 May 2009, available at https://www.washingtonpost.com/wp-dyn/content/article/2009/05/29/AR2009052903109.html. Also see Brian A. Howey, "Nunn-Lugar mission ends at Shchuch'ye with nerve gas destroyed," *Howey Politics Indiana*, 21 November 2015, available at https://howeypolitics.com/Content/Default/Lead-Story/Article/Nunn-Lugar-mission-ends-at-Shchuch-ye-with-nerve-gas-destroyed/-3/346/13251.

as the "Iron Triangle" – the relationship between private industry, the Congress, and the executive branch bureaucracy. In the early 1990s, I worked for a defense contractor that bid on the project to build the Shchuch'ye facility. I participated in drafting our company's proposal in both English and Russian. Though the contract was awarded to one of our competitors, the experience provided me with a good understanding of how the private sector supports the implementation of government policy. After becoming a HASC PSM, I helped the committee maneuver through the multitude of complex issues that led to the prohibition on funding the CWDF. When I transitioned to the Pentagon in 2001, the funding cutoff was still in place, but DoD was interested in seeing it repealed.

During a meeting in the Pentagon between senior DoD policy officials and a visiting Russian delegation concerned about the Shchuch'ye project, we shared the Russians' lament over Congress' action, but explained that DoD's hands were tied and that it was clear Congress would not change course without seeing a solid commitment from Russia to address its concerns. It was an odd feeling to participate in that meeting, knowing that I had been heavily involved in helping draft the legislative language that resulted in the funding cutoff I was now opposing as a senior DoD official. I doubt if our Russian visitors were aware of my former role. But I do believe that both the Clinton and Bush Administrations, though opposed to the constraints Congress imposed on the CTR program, found them a useful tool for reinforcing the argument that Russia needed to step up and address Congress' concerns.

There were other controversies surrounding the CTR program as well, including additional chemical weapons elimination issues, concerns over so-called defense conversion projects, and other activities beyond Russia. These also generated a fair share of congressional interest and attention.

Ultimately, I believe the actions the HASC took with respect to the CTR program improved the program, established important oversight benchmarks, encouraged Russia to be more forthcoming with its own contributions to the various CTR projects, and led to a better overall outcome that served both to enhance U.S. nonproliferation objectives and to strengthen congressional oversight of a critical WMD-related national security issue. In talking with former Clinton Administration DoD officials with whom I sparred at the time, I believe they share my view. Over time, the program was managed better and accomplished more than I believe it would have had Congress not agreed to press the issue as robustly as it did. As the HASC noted in 2001, "the oversight provided by Congress since the program's inception has served to improve the overall management of the program and to increase its effectiveness."[502]

As noted previously, the CTR program has expanded in size and scope, with projects implemented in Africa, Asia, and the Middle East. These have included a border security project with Jordan to counter WMD proliferation from Syria; improving biological security and partnership capacity with Kenya and Uganda; and enhancing maritime surveillance capabilities in Southeast Asia. The success of the CTR program spawned other similar nonproliferation

---

[502] *Report of the House Committee on Armed Services on H.R. 2586, the National Defense Authorization Act for Fiscal Year 2002*, 4 September 2001, p. 363, available at
https://books.google.com/books?id=sO7Zj2wGDCsC&pg=PA363&lpg
=PA363&dq=fy+2002+the+oversight+provided+by+Congress+since+th
e+program%27s+inception+has+served+to+improve+the+overall+man
agement+of+the+program&source=bl&ots=5JuZF_i4fn&sig=ACfU3U0c
O3ZmfIWjs3QzzXO_gujfzZKT7w&hl=en&sa=X&ved=2ahUKEwj6mN2
nqonnAhWynOAKHfaODa8Q6AEwAHoECAYQAQ#v=onepage&q=fy
%202002%20the%20oversight%20provided%20by%20Congress%20since
%20the%20program's%20inception%20has%20served%20to%20improv
e%20the%20overall%20management%20of%20the%20program&f=false.

efforts, including the Global Threat Reduction Initiative and the Global Partnership Against the Spread of Weapons of Mass Destruction, and involves other agencies beyond DoD, including the Departments of State, Energy, Agriculture, Homeland Security, and Health and Human Services. Various NGOs are also involved.

The "Nunn-Lugar" CTR example demonstrates that Congress can indeed have a major influence in formulating, developing, or changing U.S. national security policy. It shows how Congress can use the various tools at its disposal to enhance its oversight powers and to gather information that can be used to shape the administration's course of action. By using the "power of the purse" to withhold funds, Congress can force the administration to act or make the price of inaction onerously high. In sum, this case study provides a lesson in how Congress can wield power in national security policy and decision making.

CHAPTER THIRTEEN

THE USE OF EXPORT CONTROLS AND SANCTIONS AS A NONPROLIFERATION TOOL

One of the most complex and confusing national security issues that Congress wrestles with is the subject of export controls. As noted in previous chapters, export controls are intended to ensure that the transfer of military or dual-use items and materials to other parties is properly approved and licensed in accordance with established rules and regulations. This includes the transfer of defense services and information. Keeping sensitive military or military-related systems and technologies out of the hands of bad actors is a challenging but essential task. Various multilateral export control regimes exist to try to harmonize the national export policies of other countries so that illicit transfers are blocked, and legitimate transfers are conducted with full transparency.

During the Cold War, the United States participated in the "Coordinating Committee for Multilateral Export Controls" or CoCOM. CoCOM was established by the Western powers after World War II to prevent sensitive military technologies from being acquired by the Soviet Union and its Warsaw Pact partners. Similar to today's nonproliferation regimes, CoCOM was a voluntary and informal arrangement among like-minded states that lacked enforcement powers.[503] After the end of the Cold War, it was disbanded in 1994.[504]

In 1996, the "Wassenaar Arrangement on Export Controls for Conventional Arms and Dual-Use Goods and Technologies" was established (named for the Dutch town where the agreement was reached). The Wassenaar Arrangement included former Warsaw Pact countries and its technology transfer restrictions were less restrictive than those of CoCOM, its predecessor. Like CoCOM, however, the Wassenaar Arrangement is not a treaty and is not legally binding on its members. Its primary purpose is "to deal with risks to regional and international security and stability related to the spread of conventional weapons and dual-use goods and technologies."[505]

More than 40 countries participate in the Wassenaar Arrangement today, including Russia. Under the arrangement, participating states agree to exchange information on the export of sensitive dual-use goods and technologies and to report on transfers (or the denial of transfers) that take place to countries that are not part of the arrangement. The list of dual-use goods and technologies is grouped into nine categories that include, among others, electronics, computers, sensors, aerospace items, and

---

[503] See Chapter VIII, "Multilateral Export Control Policy: The Coordinating Committee (CoCom)," Office of Technology Assessment, *Technology and East-West Trade* (U.S. Government Printing Office, Washington, D.C., 1979), pp. 153-170, available at https://www.princeton.edu/~ota/disk3/1979/7918/7918.PDF. Also see Major Rand C. Lewis, USA, "COCOM: An International Attempt to Control Technology," *The DISAM Journal*, Fall 1990, pp. 66-73, available at https://apps.dtic.mil/dtic/tr/fulltext/u2/a497085.pdf.

[504] Subsequently, many former Warsaw Pact states became members of NATO, and continuing to impose strict controls on the sale of military technology to allies would have negatively impacted the U.S. ability to interoperate with them in future military contingencies.

[505] "The Wassenaar Arrangement on Export Controls for Conventional Arms and Dual-Use Goods and Technologies," available at https://www.wassenaar.org/about-us/.

special materials. It also includes a "Sensitive List" and "Very Sensitive List" of dual-use items subject to reporting. The exchange of information between participating states of munitions items includes transfers of tanks, artillery, warships, missiles, and small arms.[506]

In the United States, all transfers of export-controlled items must be licensed by the government. Different agencies are responsible for the licensing process, depending on whether the item is considered a dual-use item or a munition. The State Department licenses munitions and the Commerce Department handles the export of dual-use goods and technologies.

Military munitions are controlled on the U.S. Munitions List (USML) and their export is governed by licensing procedures administered by the Department of State's Directorate of Defense Trade Controls (DDTC). USML items are classified into 20 categories, including, among others, ammunition, aircraft, tanks, military electronics, nuclear weapons items, spacecraft systems, submarines, and directed energy weapons. DDTC reviews and processes roughly 38,000 license applications from industry each year.[507]

The 1976 Arms Export Control Act (AECA) gave the president authority to control the export of defense articles and services, an authority that was subsequently delegated to the Secretary of State. The export of defense goods and services on the USML is governed by the International Trafficking in Arms Regulations, or ITAR, which implements the requirements of the AECA.

---

[506] Ibid. A full list of items on the dual-use and munitions list can be found at https://www.wassenaar.org/app/uploads/2019/12/WA-DOC-19-PUB-002-Public-Docs-Vol-II-2019-List-of-DU-Goods-and-Technologies-and-Munitions-List-Dec-19.pdf.

[507] Directorate of Defense Trade Controls, Department of State, "Defense Export Control and Compliance System (DECCS)," available at https://www.pmddtc.state.gov/ddtc_public?id=ddtc_kb_article_page&sys_id=3d57400edbecb7007ede365e7c9619ba.

Dual-use items are recorded on the Commerce Control List (CCL) and their export is governed by licensing procedures administered by the Department of Commerce's Bureau of Industry and Security (BIS). CCL items are grouped into 10 categories (e.g., computers, telecommunications, sensors, lasers, etc.) and five product groups (e.g., material, software, technology, etc.). Exports of dual-use CCL items are governed by the Export Administration Regulations. As discussed in Chapter Ten, the 1979 EAA, which provided the statutory basis for regulating the export of dual-use technologies, expired in 2001. Although Congress made several attempts to reauthorize it, the provisions contained in the EAA have generally been applied through the president's use of the authorities provided in the International Emergency Economic Powers Act. The Export Controls Act of 2018 subsequently repealed the EAA while providing the president with the necessary authority to control exports of dual-use items.[508]

In 2018, BIS reviewed nearly 35,000 license applications, approving almost 86 percent.[509] DoD and other federal entities get a say in reviewing and recommending whether an export should be approved or denied. The process involves the interagency, and disagreements occasionally emerge. Sometimes, the president becomes the ultimate adjudicator in these cases.

---

[508] Ian F. Fergusson and Paul K. Kerr, "The U.S. Export Control System and the Export Control Reform Initiative," Congressional Research Service, CRS Report R41916, 28 January 2020, available at https://www.everycrsreport.com/files/20200128_R41916_32b4056e547 ad4a9c2c0cab47eba25e87a2314bd.pdf.

[509] Bureau of Industry and Security, Department of Commerce, "Statistics of 2018 BIS License Authorization," available at https://www.bis.doc.gov/index.php/documents/technology-evaluation/ote-data-portal/licensing-analysis/2453-2018-statistical-analysis-of-bis-licensing-pdf-1/file.

Occasionally, a license application will be "Returned Without Action" (RWA). This generally means an export request was denied, but the reason for the denial is withheld, so the license request is simply not acted upon and the export may not occur. Industry generally loathes having a license request returned without action, but there may be valid reasons for withholding this information, especially if it involves the potential disclosure of sensitive intelligence information. According to BIS, the number of license requests returned without action in 2018 declined by almost nine percent over the previous year to slightly more than 4,500.[510]

The issue of "deemed exports" is also a complicated area where misunderstandings can easily occur. An export is "deemed" to take place when controlled information is released to a foreign national without having been licensed for release through the formal export control process.[511] Discussions at technical conferences in the United States or abroad where foreign nationals are present—even a casual conversation with a foreign colleague over lunch—could lead to the exposure of controlled information deemed sensitive and a violation of U.S. export controls. For this reason, companies must be vigilant about ensuring their employees are knowledgeable about U.S. export control rules and regulations as the penalties for violations can be severe, involving both large monetary penalties and potential jail time.

---

[510] Ibid.

[511] Bureau of Industry and Security, Department of Commerce, "Deemed Exports," available at
https://www.bis.doc.gov/index.php/policy-guidance/deemed-exports.

Export Control Reform

The export control process has been and remains controversial. There has been an ongoing debate between those who believe export controls are unnecessarily hindering U.S. industry from selling to foreign markets and damaging America's economic competitiveness, and those who argue for stricter controls on the basis of national security concerns (i.e., to prevent sophisticated militarily useful technologies from being acquired by potential adversaries).

The George W. Bush Administration sought to revise and restructure the export control process to improve its efficiency. In 2002, the administration issued an "Export Control Directive" to expedite the licensing by the State Department of USML items, while noting that "the Administration is committed to ensuring that existing measures to prevent the diversion of such items to unauthorized recipients remain strong and effective."[512] Acting Under Secretary of State for Arms Control and International Security John Rood (who would later become my boss in the Pentagon as the Under Secretary of Defense for Policy in the Trump Administration) acknowledged the need to balance national security issues with economic competitiveness, stating that the reforms were intended to ensure "that our export control system for U.S. defense goods and technologies is administered in a timely, transparent and predictable manner that protects sensitive technology and which permits U.S. companies to remain competitive."[513]

---

[512] Department of State Fact Sheet, "President Issues Export Controls Directive to Reform U.S. Defense Trade Policies and Practices," 22 January 2008, available at https://2001-2009.state.gov/r/pa/prs/ps/2008/jan/99562.htm.

[513] Remarks by John C. Rood at the Center for Strategic and International Studies, "Improvements to the Defense Trade Export

The Obama Administration initiated another substantial restructuring of the U.S. export control process that was implemented in several "waves." This "Export Control Reform (ECR) Initiative" resulted from the administration's 2009 review of the export control system. In 2010, then-Secretary of Defense Robert M. Gates announced plans to make major changes to the export control process. These changes were described as the "four singularities."[514]

The four singularities reflected the move toward a single export licensing agency for both munitions and dual-use items (instead of bifurcating responsibility between the State and Commerce Departments); a unified control list (instead of the separate USML and CCL); a single enforcement coordination agency; and a single information technology system that would allow multiple agencies to access the same license application data base and share information seamlessly.

The reform effort was described as a way of "building higher fences around a smaller yard" — an effort to protect the country's "crown jewels" by tightening controls on the most sensitive technologies while loosening restrictions on the less sensitive and more ubiquitous ones.[515] These reforms would allow the United States to improve military interoperability — i.e., the ability of U.S. military forces to operate with allies and coalition partners by easing restrictions on the export of certain types of technologies.

Control System," 26 February 2008, available at https://2001-2009.state.gov/t/isn/rls/rm/105560.htm.

[514] Ian F. Fergusson and Paul K. Kerr, "The U.S. Export Control System and the Export Control Reform Initiative," Congressional Research Service, op. cit., pp. 1-2, 10.

[515] Speech by Robert M. Gates to Business Executives for National Security, April 20, 2010, available at https://archive.defense.gov/Speeches/Speech.aspx?SpeechID=1453.

Some of the Obama Administration's reforms were phased in unilaterally; others required congressional action.[516]

The Trump Administration also advocated for export control reforms in order to improve interoperability with U.S. allies, in accordance with the priorities established in the *National Defense Strategy*. Under Secretary of Defense for Policy John Rood noted, "Partnering with allies and building their capabilities in addition to ours is critical.... A number of informal processes have developed that have ended up imposing rather long delays and making us unpredictable to our allies.... Congress has a legitimate role in that area by the governing law they passed -- the Arms Export Control Act. But we have a shared interest in being predictable and more regular for our friends and allies in how we are able to move through the export control system."[517]

Outside interest groups have also been engaged in calling for additional actions to revise and reform the U.S. export control process. In response to a requirement in the FY 2019 NDAA, the Center for A New American Security (CNAS) recommended greater restrictions on the sale of certain U.S.-origin products to China to "ensure U.S. technology does not enable China's malign behavior."[518] At the same time, CNAS argued that existing legislation

---

[516] Ian F. Fergusson and Paul K. Kerr, "The U.S. Export Control System and the Export Control Reform Initiative," Congressional Research Service, op. cit., p. 11.

[517] Tony Bertuca, "Top DOD policy official wants export control reform to allow greater tech transfer with U.S. allies," *Inside Defense*, 4 December 2019, available at https://insidedefense.com/daily-news/top-dod-policy-official-wants-export-control-reform-allow-greater-tech-transfer-us-allies.

[518] "Rising to the China Challenge – Renewing American Competitiveness in the Indo-Pacific," Center for A New American Security, December 2019, p. 24, available at https://s3.amazonaws.com/files.cnas.org/documents/CNAS-Report-NDAA-final-6.pdf?mtime=20200116130752.

occasionally "complicates or prohibits security assistance" to U.S. partner countries and called on Congress to "consider narrowly amending some of these laws to permit rare exceptions for those cases in which prohibitions on cooperation either harm U.S. national security or ultimately reduce U.S. leverage...." They note that "legislation should permit the executive branch some discretion to pursue limited cooperation on a case-by-case basis."[519]

Congressional Actions

Attempts by Congress to adapt and update the U.S. export control system to contemporary realities have had mixed results. The failed effort to reauthorize the EAA described in Chapter Ten is an illustration of the difficulty Congress faces when important national security policies fall within the jurisdiction of multiple committees with different agendas and priorities. In wrestling with this issue in 2002, the HASC noted the need "to update current law where appropriate so U.S. export controls address the new national security needs of the United States, the economic realities of globalization, and the changed international security environment of the 21st Century..."[520] Some members of Congress criticized the bill reauthorizing the EAA because of provisions that would have strengthened certain controls on advanced technologies, which "could seriously damage the U.S. military and harm national security."[521] They cited a 1999 Defense Science Board report

---

[519] Ibid., p. 36.

[520] *Report of the House Committee on Armed Services on H.R. 2581, Export Administration Act of 2001*, Report 107-297, Part 2, 8 March 2002, p. 7, available at https://www.congress.gov/107/crpt/hrpt297/CRPT-107hrpt297-pt2.pdf.

[521] See Dissenting Views of Reps. Robert Menendez, Earl Blumenaur, and Jeff Flake in *Report of the House Committee on International Relations on H.R. 2581, Export Administration Act of 2001*, Report 107-297, Part 1, 16

that concluded, "If U.S. high-tech exports are restricted in any significant manner, it could well have a stifling effect on the U.S. military's rate of technological advancement."[522] A subsequent effort to renew the EAA that would have toughened procedures for transferring items from the USML to the CCL, the "Export Administration Renewal Act of 2011," sponsored by Rep. Ileana Ros-Lehtinen (R-FL), died in the House Foreign Affairs Committee. Yet, there have been successful congressional efforts as well, including the aforementioned Export Controls Act of 2018.

The "Export Control Reform Act of 2018" (ECRA) and the "Foreign Investment Risk Review Modernization Act of 2018" (FIRRMA) were both incorporated into the FY 2019 NDAA and reflected congressional efforts to impose tighter controls on the export of certain dual-use technologies, especially to countries like China. The FY 2019 NDAA also gave permanent statutory authority to the Export Administration Regulations, in light of the EAA's expiration in 2001. The law also required more emphasis be placed on controlling "emerging" or "foundational" technologies "essential to national security." Though the Congress did not precisely define these terms, it is generally assumed they include technologies like artificial intelligence, machine learning, additive manufacturing (also referred to as "3-D printing"), and robotics.[523]

How to deal with new and emerging technologies remains a contemporary export control challenge. The

---

November 2001, p. 223, available at
https://www.congress.gov/107/crpt/hrpt297/CRPT-107hrpt297-pt1.pdf.

[522] Ibid.

[523] See "The Export Control Reform Act of 2018 and Possible New Controls on Emerging and Foundational Technologies," *International Trade Alert*, Akin Gump Strauss Hauser & Feld LLP, 12 September 2018, available at
https://www.akingump.com/images/content/9/7/v2/97168/International-Trade-Alert-09-12-2018-The-Export-Control-Refo.pdf.

development of hypersonics, artificial intelligence, 5G communications technology, and quantum computing, for example, raise difficult issues for the export control process that ECRA and FIRRMA do not fully address. Some in Congress clearly believe the United States must aggressively challenge competitors like China in these areas while working to strengthen our defense partnerships. Sen. James M. Inhofe (R-OK), Chairman of the SASC, has noted, "We must remove unnecessary barriers to industrial cooperation that degrade our collective competitive edge.... It's in our best interest to ensure our allies can leverage our technological advantages and we can leverage theirs."[524]

The contemporary debate over whether to allow U.S. sales to the Chinese telecommunications company Huawei demonstrates the continuing schism between those who see China as a national security threat and those who believe U.S. manufacturers will be disadvantaged in the expanding global telecommunications marketplace. Senators Marco Rubio (R-FL), Ben Sasse (R-NE), and Tom Cotton (R-AR) have argued, "Huawei is an arm of the Chinese Communist Party and should be treated as such."[525] A number of industry groups, however, have declared that preventing U.S. sales to Huawei "would have serious negative

---

[524] Sen. James Inhofe, "We Must Build the National Security Innovation Base Our Defense Strategy Requires," *DefenseNews*, 2 December 2019, available at
https://www.defensenews.com/outlook/2019/12/02/sasc-chairman-we-must-build-the-national-security-innovation-base-our-defense-strategy-requires/.

[525] Zak Doffman, "Huawei: U.S. Senators Compare Company To KGB As They Question New Pentagon Decision," *Forbes*, 24 January 2020, available at
https://www.forbes.com/sites/zakdoffman/2020/01/24/us-senators-demand-huawei--explanation-from-pentagon-its-like-working-with-the-kgb/#27eae8a9399d.

consequences for U.S. economic leadership and, ultimately, U.S. national security."[526]

This debate has roiled the executive branch as well, with some in the Defense Department and Commerce Department at odds. In general, the complexity of export control issues, the actions of external interest groups, and the shared jurisdictional responsibilities for export issues held by multiple committees of Congress have made this national security issue a difficult one for legislators. In addition, the issue of export controls has blurred the traditional distinction between political parties; Republicans and Democrats have both argued for and against tighter export controls, as national security and economic competitiveness arguments are not mutually exclusive and often cross party lines.

Sanctions

If wrestling with export control issues has been a struggle for Congress, the application of sanctions on export control violators, as well as the passing of sanctions legislation more generally, has been much easier. A "sanction" is a penalty imposed on others for taking an action contrary to law or policy. Congress often defaults to imposing sanctions as a means of punishing other countries or entities for acting against U.S. national security interests. Although Congress can, and often does impose its own sanctions, the president has legal authority—as a result of legislation Congress has passed—also to impose sanctions.

The George W. Bush Administration's 2002 *National Strategy to Combat Weapons of Mass Destruction* declared,

---

[526] Ana Swanson, "Tougher Huawei Restrictions Stall After Defense Department Objects," *The New York Times,* 24 January 2020, available at https://www.nytimes.com/2020/01/24/business/economy/huawei-restrictions.html.

"Sanctions can be a valuable component of our overall strategy against WMD proliferation. At times, however, sanctions have proven inflexible and ineffective. We will develop a comprehensive sanctions policy to better integrate sanctions into our overall strategy and work with Congress to consolidate and modify existing sanctions legislation."[527] More recently, the Trump Administration's *National Strategy for Countering Weapons of Mass Destruction Terrorism*, released in 2018, stated, "…the United States will seek to deter individuals and institutions who are beyond state control from aiding and abetting WMD terrorism, including through 'targeted' sanctions and other means of exposing their activities."[528]

There is significant disagreement over whether sanctions work as a tool of U.S. foreign policy. Some believe they are grossly ineffective and penalize those least able to affect the decision making of other countries. Former President Jimmy Carter argued that economic sanctions are "most often ineffective and can be counterproductive." He advocated for targeted sanctions that focus on "travel, foreign bank accounts and other special privileges of government officials who make decisions, not on destroying the economy that determines the living conditions of oppressed people."[529] The imposition of sanctions against Iraq after its 1990 invasion of Kuwait and

---

[527] The White House, *National Strategy to Combat Weapons of Mass Destruction*, December 2002, op. cit., p. 5.

[528] The White House, *National Strategy for Countering Weapons of Mass Destruction Terrorism*, December 2018, p. 9, available at https://www.whitehouse.gov/wp-content/uploads/2018/12/20181210_National-Strategy-for-Countering-WMD-Terrorism.pdf.

[529] Jimmy Carter, "Cuba, North Korea, and getting sanctions right," *The Washington Post*, 26 December 2014, available at https://www.washingtonpost.com/opinions/jimmy-carter-cuba-north-korea-and-getting-sanctions-right/2014/12/26/c39a55a2-8aed-11e4-9e8d-0c687bc18da4_story.html.

amid concerns over Saddam Hussein's WMD program was seen by some as counterproductive. Several officials of the UN World Food Program in Iraq resigned in protest over the effect sanctions had on the Iraqi civil population.[530] The UN sanctions regime included restrictions on the export of pencils to Iraq because graphite was listed as a dual-use item with military applications.[531]

Others believe sanctions can and do work by changing the cost-benefit calculus of foreign leaders and regimes. The Trump Administration has imposed multiple sanctions on individuals and entities in Russia, Venezuela, Iran, and North Korea as part of its "maximum pressure" campaign. In response to concerns that Iraq may formally request the withdrawal of U.S. troops after a U.S. drone strike killed Iranian General Qassem Soleimani in Baghdad, President Trump stated, "If there's any hostility, that they do anything we think is inappropriate, we are going to put sanctions on Iraq – very big sanctions on Iraq.... It'll make Iranian sanctions look somewhat tame." White House Counselor Kellyanne Conway said President Trump is "a man of action in a town of talk, and sanctions are a preferred tool in a well-stocked diplomatic arsenal."[532]

---

[530] Ewen MacAskill, "Second official quits UN Iraq team," *The Guardian*, 15 February 2000, available at https://www.theguardian.com/world/2000/feb/16/iraq.unitednations.

[531] CNN, "Jordan Collects Pencils in Protest of U.N. Sanctions on Iraq," 20 February 2000, available at http://webcache.googleusercontent.com/search?q=cache:ruUZ1ges5Y MJ:www.cnn.com/TRANSCRIPTS/0002/20/wr.09.html+&cd=1&hl=en &ct=clnk&gl=us. Also see "Jordan activists send banned pencils to Iraq," *The Irish Times*, 31 January 2000, available at https://www.irishtimes.com/news/jordan-activists-send-banned-pencils-to-iraq-1.239656.

[532] Ashley Parker, "Trump uses sanctions as a favorite form of retribution — against friend and foe alike," *The Washington Post*, 9 January 2020, available at https://www.washingtonpost.com/politics/trump-uses-sanctions-as-

Congressional Actions

Nearly two dozen laws currently in force contain sanctions provisions for certain violations of nonproliferation rules. These include the Arms Export Control Act; the International Emergency Economic Powers Act; the Foreign Assistance Act; the Iran Sanctions Act of 1996; the North Korea Threat Reduction Act of 1999; the Trading With the Enemy Act; the Foreign Narcotics Kingpin Designation Act; the Iran, North Korea, and Syria Nonproliferation Act of 2000; and the Countering America's Adversaries Through Sanctions Act (CAATSA). The Department of the Treasury's Office of Foreign Assets Control (OFAC) administers a variety of economic sanctions on more than a dozen countries. Sanctions can be imposed on countries, companies, persons, or entities. Most sanctions legislation allows the president to waive sanctions if it is determined, and Congress is notified, that imposing them would be counter to the national interest.

In the 1970s and 1980s, Congress required the cutoff of foreign assistance to countries engaged in nuclear-related proliferation activities. In 1990, Congress enacted guidelines for the imposition of trade sanctions related to missile proliferation. By the mid-1990s, however, some began to criticize the use of sanctions as too blunt an instrument that penalized civilian populations more than the regimes that were responsible for proliferation activities. Yet, Congress continued to impose sanctions in response to significant proliferation developments, such as the Indian nuclear tests in 1998 and North Korea's withdrawal from the Nuclear Nonproliferation Treaty in 2003 and its nuclear test in 2006. Though some believe targeted sanctions are more effective than general aid

---

a-favorite-form-of-retribution--against-friend-and-foe-alike/2020/01/08/0b9ad6ee-317c-11ea-a053-dc6d944ba776_story.html.

cutoffs (e.g., targeting financial assets or freezing the funds of individuals or entities), others question their utility.[533]

Some have argued that sanctions are a way for Congress to reassert its predominance over the executive branch when it comes to foreign and national security policy. As one analyst has argued:

> Sanctions are a foreign policy tool uniquely entrusted to Congress by the Constitution, which provides that Congress shall "regulate commerce with foreign nations." Unlike the other major levers of U.S. foreign policy — diplomacy and military force, over which the Constitution divides control between Congress and the executive — the president has no inherent power to impose sanctions or to refuse to implement congressionally mandated sanctions. As sanctions continue to grow in importance, becoming the default U.S. policy response to a range of international crises, Congress will enjoy newfound potential to shape U.S. foreign policy in ways that have eluded it for decades.[534]

In 1998, Congress passed the "Iran Missile Proliferation Sanctions Act" requiring that sanctions be imposed on foreign individuals and companies if there is "credible information" indicating that they transferred certain items or provided assistance to help Iran's missile program. President Clinton vetoed the bill, calling its sanctions provisions "indiscriminate" and "inflexible," arguing that

---

[533] Mamta Badkar, "Here's Why Sanctions Don't Work," *Business Insider*, 16 July 2014, available at https://www.businessinsider.com/why-sanctions-wont-work-july-16-2014-7.

[534] Benjamin Alter, "Sanctions Are Congress's Path Back to Foreign Policy Relevance," *Lawfare*, 27 March 2018, available at https://www.lawfareblog.com/sanctions-are-congresss-path-back-foreign-policy-relevance.

the "credible information" standard was "an unworkably low standard of evidence."[535] The "Iran Nonproliferation Act of 2000," which passed unanimously in both the House and Senate, required sanctions on persons and entities that transfer certain goods, services, or technologies to Iran. President Clinton said some of its provisions were duplicative with existing laws, but signed the bill anyway, arguing it "will not harm our efforts to halt international cooperation with Iran's WMD and missile programs."[536]

As a key supplier of nuclear and missile-related technology to countries like Pakistan, China has repeatedly been subject to U.S. sanctions. Both the George H.W. Bush and Clinton Administrations imposed sanctions on China but exercised the waiver provision to allow the export of satellites to China (an issue that became controversial in Congress and which is described in more detail in Chapter Fourteen).[537] The George W. Bush Administration imposed sanctions on Chinese entities numerous times for missile and chemical weapons-related transfers to Pakistan, Iran,

---

[535] Message from the President of the United States Transmitting His Veto of H. R. 2709, the "Iran Missile Proliferation Sanctions Act of 1998," House Document 105-276, 24 June 1998, p. 1, available at https://static.votesmart.org/static/vetotext/50662.pdf.

[536] William J. Clinton, "Statement on Signing the Iran Nonproliferation Act of 2000," 14 March 2000, available at https://books.google.com/books?id=h4FlY1GCxRsC&pg=PA550&lpg=PA550&dq=will+not+harm+our+efforts+to+halt+international+cooperation+with+Iran%E2%80%99s+WMD+and+missile+programs&source=bl&ots=XXi6O7zz_1&sig=ACfU3U3aPPZjRX-XMGr_AkpOlujP12tgKQ&hl=en&sa=X&ved=2ahUKEwib1N-gzZLnAhXJSt8KHd83B3YQ6AEwAXoECAoQAQ#v=onepage&q=will%20not%20harm%20our%20efforts%20to%20halt%20international%20cooperation%20with%20Iran%E2%80%99s%20WMD%20and%20missile%20programs&f=false.

[537] "China: Economic Sanctions," Congressional Research Service, CRS Report R44605, 22 August 2016, p. 9, available at https://www.everycrsreport.com/files/20160822_R44605_160c92226c43bf33f590663dd758fe9b4e0b8caa.pdf.

and other countries. In 2003, sanctions were imposed on the China North Industries Corporation (NORINCO) for contributing to Iran's WMD and missile program (an action that NORINCO called "completely groundless and unjustified").[538] The Obama Administration also imposed sanctions on China multiple times for missile and other proliferation activities.   And in 2017, the Trump Administration sanctioned China, noting that it will "continue to increase pressure on North Korea by targeting those who support the advancement of nuclear and ballistic missile programs." China reacted by calling the sanctions "not helpful."[539]

The "Iran Freedom and Counter-Proliferation Act of 2012" imposed sanctions on Iran's energy, shipping, and shipbuilding sectors and restricted trade in certain materials. The bill was included as part of the FY 2013 NDAA and signed into law. Numerous other sanctions were subsequently imposed on Iran, but these sanctions were not universally supported. A panel of former U.S. officials argued that U.S. sanctions policy may be backfiring, noting that sanctions have "contributed to an increase in repression and corruption within Iran" and "may be sowing the seeds of long-term alienation between the Iranian people and the United States."[540] Years later, Trump Administration officials argued that the latest round

---

[538] "NORINCO Issues Statement on US Sanctions," *Xinhua News Agency*, 5 June 2003, available at
http://www.china.org.cn/english/2003/Jun/66359.htm.

[539] Alex Ward, "The US sanctioned China so it would help with North Korea. China defended Pyongyang instead.," Vox, 23 August 2017, available at
https://www.vox.com/world/2017/8/23/16189170/china-sanctions-north-korea-russia-mnuchin-trump-august-22-2017.

[540] David E. Sanger, "Report Urges White House to Rethink Iran Penalties," *The New York Times*, 17 April 2013, available at
https://www.nytimes.com/2013/04/18/world/middleeast/report-on-iran-urges-obama-to-rethink-sanctions.html?pagewanted=all.

of sanctions imposed on Iran as part of its "maximum pressure" campaign were having their intended effect. In January 2020, Treasury Secretary Steven Mnuchin stated, "I think we have 100 percent confidence and we are consistent in our view that the economic sanctions are working."[541]

In the wake of Russia's annexation of Crimea (never recognized by the United States), the Obama Administration imposed sanctions restricting the transfer of USML items to Russia. The Trump Administration imposed multiple sanctions on Russia in connection with its invasion of Ukraine, support for the Nicolas Maduro regime in Venezuela, various cyberattacks, interference in the 2016 U.S. elections, and the chemical weapons attack on the Skripals in the UK.[542]

Sanctions continue to be heavily relied upon by the executive branch and are generally seen as a useful tool by the Congress, despite continued concern among some that they are useless at best and counterproductive at worst. Moreover, the imposition of sanctions by Congress has not always been viewed favorably by the executive branch, as some believe they tie the president's hands in the exercise of U.S. foreign policy and national security interests. Some also argue that unilateral sanctions imposed by the United States are less effective than multilateral sanctions. As a former CIA and Treasury Department official asserted, "Despite their extensive use [by the Trump Administration] against North Korea, Iran, Russia and Venezuela, sanctions

---

[541] Brian Naylor, "Trump Administration Announces More Economic Sanctions Against Iran," National Public Radio, 10 January 2020, available at https://www.npr.org/2020/01/10/795224662/trump-administration-announces-more-economic-sanctions-against-iran.

[542] For a list of sanctions imposed by the Trump Administration on Russia, see Alina Polyakova and Filippos Letsas, "On the record: The U.S. administration's actions on Russia," The Brookings Institution, 3 June 2019, available at https://www.brookings.edu/blog/order-from-chaos/2018/09/25/on-the-record-the-u-s-administrations-actions-on-russia/.

are not working particularly well to solve any of these national security challenges.... The extensive use of unilateral sanctions in pursuit of unclear or unattainable goals is more likely to diminish the power of sanctions, as other countries develop workarounds that avoid the dollar and the U.S. financial system."[543]

The "Otto Warmbier North Korea Nuclear Sanctions and Enforcement Act of 2019" was included in the FY 2020 NDAA and imposed additional sanctions on North Korea.[544] Named for the American student who died in North Korean captivity, it added to the Trump Administration's "maximum pressure" campaign against Pyongyang. However, the effectiveness of this campaign remains debatable, with some arguing that additional pressure is warranted or that the sanctions regime has been a failure in getting North Korea to abandon its nuclear weapons and missile programs.[545]

The issue of sanctions remains highly controversial. A 2019 GAO report noted the "difficulties in assessing sanctions' effectiveness in meeting broader U.S. policy goals" and concluded, "Sanctions may also have unintended consequences for targeted countries, such as

---

[543] David S. Cohen, "Why Trump's sanctions aren't working," *The Washington Post*, 30 March 2019, available at https://www.washingtonpost.com/opinions/why-trumps-sanctions-arent-working/2019/03/30/9dd6b1b6-525e-11e9-8d28-f5149e5a2fda_story.html?noredirect=on.

[544] See Title LXXI of Public Law 116-92, 20 December 2019, available at https://www.govinfo.gov/content/pkg/BILLS-116s1790enr/pdf/BILLS-116s1790enr.pdf.

[545] See, for example, Christopher J. Watterson, "Maximum Pressure Made Permeable: The Trouble with Washington's North Korea Sanctions," *War on the Rocks*, 24 January 2020, available at https://warontherocks.com/2020/01/maximum-pressure-made-permeable-the-trouble-with-washingtons-north-korea-sanctions/?utm_source=Members&utm_campaign=3c2bd763d7-EMAIL_CAMPAIGN_2020_01_27_03_08&utm_medium=email&utm_te rm=0_e842221dc2-3c2bd763d7-147762833.

negative impacts on human rights or public health."[546] Rep. Ilhan Omar (D-MN), argued that sanctions "rarely achieve their desired goals" and noted, "Questioning and changing the near-automatic reliance on sanctions is fully compatible with advancing our interests and defending national security. It's time to stop relying on the same failed playbook."[547]

A quick search for sanctions bills in the 116th Congress produced 145 results.[548] This suggests that, despite lingering concerns over their effectiveness, Congress still views sanctions as a useful tool of American foreign policy.

---

[546] Government Accountability Office, "ECONOMIC SANCTIONS Agencies Assess Impacts on Targets, and Studies Suggest Several Factors Contribute to Sanctions' Effectiveness," Report GAO-20-145, October 2019, available at
https://www.gao.gov/assets/710/701891.pdf.

[547] Ilhan Omar, "Sanctions are part of a failed foreign policy playbook. Stop relying on them.," *The Washington Post*, 23 October 2019, available at https://www.washingtonpost.com/opinions/ilhan-omar-sanctions-are-part-of-a-failed-foreign-policy-playbook-stop-relying-on-them/2019/10/23/b7cbb1ca-f510-11e9-a285-882a8e386a96_story.html.

[548] See https://www.govtrack.us/congress/bills/subjects/sanctions/6232.

CHAPTER FOURTEEN

CASE STUDIES ON THE EXPORT OF COMMERCIAL SATELLITES AND HIGH-PERFORMANCE COMPUTERS

Two hot-button issues that seized the Republican-controlled Congress' attention in the 1990s and led to significant confrontation with the Clinton Administration involved the export of high-performance computers (so-called "supercomputers") and commercial satellites. These issues roiled the legislative and executive branches for several years and led to the Congress rewriting the rules governing the export of these technologies.

Space... The Final Frontier

In 1996, the Clinton Administration issued an Executive Order shifting the licensing responsibility for commercial satellite exports from the State Department to the Commerce Department. That same year, a Chinese "Long March" rocket carrying a U.S.-built commercial communications satellite crashed after launch. The subsequent investigation of the launch failure discovered that militarily sensitive encryption chips in the satellite were missing. As a result of the investigation, a post-crash report was provided to the Chinese, and the satellite manufacturers, Loral and Hughes, were accused of sharing secret technology with China that could be used to improve the accuracy of its nuclear missiles.[549] Loral was eventually fined $14 million and Hughes agreed to pay $32 million.[550]

Congress spent the next two years holding hearings on the export of sensitive technologies to China and looking for ways to tighten export restrictions. The House National Security Committee and the House International Relations Committee held unusual joint hearings, as the issue fell within the oversight jurisdiction of both committees.

In 1998, the Clinton Administration approved the sale of another Loral satellite to China, stoking additional congressional concerns that business and cost considerations were taking precedence over national security requirements. As part of its oversight effort, Congress established the Select Committee on U.S. National Security and Military/Commercial Concerns with the People's Republic of China. Chaired by Rep. Christopher Cox (R-CA), the bipartisan "Cox Committee" concluded that China "has stolen or otherwise illegally obtained U.S. missile and space technology that improves the [its] military and intelligence capabilities."[551] Specifically, the committee's reported stated, "It is almost certain that the U.S. satellite manufacturers' recommendations led to improvements in [China's] rockets and that the improvements would not have been considered or

---

[549] Roberto Suro and John Mintz, "Bureaucracy, Bungled Report Collide at Loral," *The Washington Post*, 31 May 1998, p. A16, available at https://www.washingtonpost.com/wp-srv/politics/special/campfin/stories/loral053198.htm.

[550] Peter Pae, "Boeing, Hughes to Pay $32 Million for Helping China With Technology," *Los Angeles Times*, 6 March 2003, available at https://www.latimes.com/archives/la-xpm-2003-mar-06-fi-boeing6-story.html.

[551] Report of the Select Committee on U.S. National Security and Military/Commercial Concerns with the People's Republic of China, Report 105-851, 3 January 1999, p. xii, available at https://www.govinfo.gov/content/pkg/GPO-CRPT-105hrpt851/pdf/GPO-CRPT-105hrpt851.pdf.

implemented so soon without the U.S. assistance.... information passed during each of the failure analyses has the potential to benefit [China's] ballistic missile program."[552]

In part as a result of the Cox Committee's investigation, the FY 1999 NDAA overturned the Clinton Administration's Executive Order transferring export license responsibility for commercial satellites to the Commerce Department, placing the licensing function back in the State Department's hands. For the next 14 years, all U.S. commercial satellite exports were treated as though they were munitions, subjecting them to the more rigorous licensing procedures of the Department of State. This was one of the NDAA issues that fell within my purview while serving as a PSM on the HASC.

The U.S. satellite industry argued that U.S. commercial competitiveness was being irreparably damaged and that the stricter controls on U.S. satellite exports would force other countries to go elsewhere for satellite technology, as foreign suppliers imposed fewer restrictions on the export of their satellites. According to a 2012 report by the Aerospace Industries Association (AIA), the tightened U.S. export rules were "overly restrictive" and "draconian." AIA argued that U.S. export constraints "contributed to the loss of U.S. commercial satellite market share and fostered the competitiveness and capabilities of U.S. competitors abroad."[553] AIA noted, "We estimate that U.S. manufacturers lost $21 billion in satellite revenue from 1999 to 2009, costing about 9,000 direct jobs annually" and

---

[552] Ibid., pp. xv-xvi.

[553] Aerospace Industries Association, *Competing for Space - Satellite Export Policy and U.S. National Security*, January 2012, available at https://www.aia-aerospace.org/report/competing-for-space-satellite-export-policy-and-u-s-national-security/.

concluded, "Simply put, we have legislated away our nation's dominance in space."[554]

This issue played out in Congress with congressional supporters of the NDAA action arguing that the United States needed to strengthen its efforts to keep sophisticated militarily relevant technologies out of the hands of adversaries, and congressional opponents arguing that the foreign availability of increasingly ubiquitous satellite technology would damage U.S. industrial competitiveness. Ultimately, almost a decade and a half later, economic competitiveness arguments carried the day. In the FY 2013 NDAA, the Congress repealed the requirement that commercial satellites be licensed as munitions and gave the president authority to determine licensing requirements, with certain caveats.[555]

In its export control reform effort, the Obama Administration proposed a new category for export licenses called "Strategic Trade Authorization" or STA. Licensing requirements for items in this category would be eased for export to 36 specific allied countries. In 2012, the Obama Administration issued a joint DoD-State Department report on revising U.S. satellite export controls. The report called revising the FY 1999 NDAA restrictions a "national security imperative," noting that commercial satellites are "the sole USML items for which the President does not have the legal authority to appropriately adjust the controls to ensure they meet current and anticipated U.S. national security requirements and to ensure they do not unintentionally harm the U.S. satellite industry and its supplier base." The

---

[554] Ibid. Also see the statement by AIA President & CEO Marion C. Blakey, "AIA Welcomes Congressional Action on Satellite Export Control Reform," 18 May 2012, available at https://www.prnewswire.com/news-releases/aia-welcomes-congressional-action-on-satellite-export-control-reform-152076355.html.

[555] Section 1261 of Public Law 112-239, 2 January 2013, available at https://www.congress.gov/112/plaws/publ239/PLAW-112publ239.pdf.

report proposed a number of recommendations to modify the law, declaring, "The Administration is committed to continue to work with Congress to enact legislation to ensure that U.S. export controls meet our current and anticipated national security requirements."[556] The Obama Administration also moved commercial communications satellites back to the Commerce Control List in 2017 in response to market conditions and industry concerns over the more restrictive export requirements of the ITAR.[557]

Interestingly, the debate over satellite export controls was not strictly partisan. Strong pro-national security Republicans were pitted against equally strong pro-business Republicans. In addition, the congressional debate on this issue demonstrated the impact outside groups like AIA could have in providing information to members of Congress to support their preferred outcome.

Supercomputers

As part of the Clinton Administration's effort to revise U.S. export control policies after the end of the Cold War, restrictions on the export of high-performance computers ("supercomputers") to Russia and China were eased in 1995. The administration established four "tiers" of computer export controls — U.S. allies were included in "Tier 1" and potentially hostile countries like North Korea and Iran were grouped in "Tier 4." Countries thought to pose relatively minor proliferation risks were placed in

---

[556] The White House, "FACT SHEET: Release of National Security Report on Revising U.S. Export Controls on Satellites," 18 April 2012, available at https://obamawhitehouse.archives.gov/the-press-office/2012/04/18/fact-sheet-release-national-security-report-revising-us-export-controls-.

[557] Ian F. Fergusson and Paul K. Kerr, "The U.S. Export Control System and the Export Control Reform Initiative," Congressional Research Service, op. cit., p. 19.

"Tier 2." Russia and China were placed in "Tier 3," which allowed high-performance computers to be exported in certain cases without going through a rigorous licensing process.

In 1997, the Russian Ministry of Atomic Energy (MINATOM) announced that it had received five U.S. supercomputers made by IBM and Silicon Graphics for use in maintaining the safety and reliability of Russia's nuclear arsenal. At the time, a supercomputer's capability was measured in "MTOPS" or Millions of Theoretical Operations Per Second. In 1997, a laptop computer with an Intel Pentium processor was rated at 200 MTOPS; the machines acquired by Russia were rated at up to 10,000 MTOPS. The announcement by Russian Minister of Atomic Energy Viktor Mikhailov shocked many in Congress and the administration. Mikhailov stated that the supercomputers were up to 10 times more powerful than anything Russia had previously acquired and would be used at Russia's nuclear weapons laboratories.[558] Mikhailov's revelations led Congress to conduct hearings, where it was revealed that the United States had exported more than 1,400 supercomputers between January 1996 and March 1997, including 47 to China and 10 to Russia.[559]

The rapidly increasing computational speed and power of computers has long been recognized as posing difficult

---

[558] Michael R. Gordon, "Russia Atom Aides Buy I.B.M. Supercomputer Despite U.S. Curbs," *The New York Times*, 25 February 1997, available at https://www.nytimes.com/1997/02/25/world/russia-atom-aides-buy-ibm-supercomputer-despite-us-curbs.html. Also see testimony of Gary Milhollin before the House Committee on National Security Subcommittee on Military Procurement, 15 April 1997, available at https://www.wisconsinproject.org/selling-us-supercomputers/.

[559] Testimony of William Reinsch, Under Secretary of Commerce for Export Administration, before the House National Security Committee, 13 November 1997, available at http://commdocs.house.gov/committees/security/has317000.000/has 317000_1.HTM.

issues for U.S. export control policy. Computers are said to follow "Moore's Law," which postulates that computing speed doubles every 18 months. In fact, today's smartphones have more computational power than the supercomputers of only a few decades ago. While I was a HASC staffer, I recall discussions over how to address the Japanese export of Sony PlayStation 2s, as the computer chips in them had more computing power than some of the most powerful computers at the time. In essence, taking a PlayStation 2 on a trip overseas could mean running afoul of U.S. export control laws, subjecting the offender to harsh penalties. In fact, Japan's Ministry of International Trade and Industry, recognizing that the powerful graphics chip in the PlayStation 2 could be used by bad actors for nefarious purposes, like improving the guidance systems on missiles, imposed a limitation on how many of the toys an individual could take out of Japan.[560]

The revelation of China's acquisition of U.S. supercomputers also was investigated by the Cox Commission, which concluded that China "has been using HPCs [high-performance computers] for nuclear weapons applications" and noted that the computers obtained from the United States "represent a major increase in [China's] computing power."[561]

Concern over the end use of these computers led Congress in the FY 1998 NDAA to require licensing of supercomputers in excess of 2,000 MTOPS to Tier 3

---

[560] Tony Smith, "PlayStation 2 exports to be restricted – again," *The Register*, 17 April 2000, available at https://www.theregister.co.uk/2000/04/17/playstation_2_exports/. Also see "Sony's High-Tech Playstation2 Will Require Military Export License," Associated Press, 17 April 2000, available at https://www.latimes.com/archives/la-xpm-2000-apr-17-fi-20482-story.html.

[561] Report of the Select Committee on U.S. National Security and Military/Commercial Concerns with the People's Republic of China, Report 105-851, 3 January 1999, op. cit., p. 99.

countries. Congress also mandated a report on all such shipments and establishment of a post-shipment verification regime to verify the end user and end use. In addition, Congress directed the GAO to investigate the issue. In its report, the GAO concluded that the Clinton Administration's decision to relax exports of high-performance computers was based on a Stanford University study that "lacked empirical evidence or analysis," relying on the assertions of the computer industry rather than actual sales data.[562]

The computer industry raised economic competitiveness arguments similar to those of the satellite industry. Indeed, various studies suggested that MTOPS was no longer an adequate measure of computing capability, and the MTOPS threshold for licensing computer sales was repeatedly adjusted upward. In a subsequent study, the GAO cited the views of computer experts who argued that MTOPS "is an outdated and invalid means for determining whether individual high performance computers should be licensed for export" and concluded, "The current export control system for high performance computers, which focuses on controlling individual machines, is ineffective because it cannot prevent countries of concern from linking or clustering many lower performance uncontrolled computers to collectively perform at higher levels than current export controls allow."[563]

In 2000, the Clinton Administration decided to allow the export of supercomputers with processing speeds up to

---

[562] General Accounting Office, "EXPORT CONTROLS - Information on the Decision to Revise High Performance Computer Controls," Report GAO/NSIAD-98-196, September 1998, p. 4, available at https://www.gao.gov/assets/230/226287.pdf.

[563] General Accounting Office, "EXPORT CONTROLS - System for Controlling Exports of High Performance Computing Is Ineffective," Report GAO-01-10, December 2000, p. 5, available at https://www.gao.gov/assets/240/231030.pdf.

28,000 MTOPS to Tier 3 countries. In January 2001, the administration again adjusted the threshold, revising it upward for the sixth time since 1993, from 28,000 to 85,000 MTOPS.[564] The following year, it was revised upward yet again to 190,000 MTOPs "to reflect the widespread availability of [high-performance] computers."[565] This argument was challenged by the GAO, which argued that the administration's "prediction that computers capable of performing at the new threshold will be widely available through foreign and domestic companies by early 2002 has not materialized."[566] In 2006, President Bush announced a revised standard for measuring computational speed, "Weighted TeraFLOPS."[567]

The continued upward revision of the standard for controlling the export of high-performance computers was a reflection of rapid advancements in technology but was not universally condoned. Some nonproliferation experts were concerned over the implications for the proliferation

---

[564] Alex Wagner, "Clinton Revises Computer Export Control Regulations," *Arms Control Today*, March 2001, available at https://www.armscontrol.org/print/808.

[565] See Department of Commerce, Bureau of Export Administration, "Implementation of the Wassenaar Arrangement List of Dual-Use Items Revisions: Computers; and Revisions to License Exception CTP," published in the *Federal Register*, Vol. 67, 8 March 2002, pp. 10611-10617, available at https://www.govinfo.gov/content/pkg/FR-2002-03-08/pdf/FR-2002-03-08.pdf.

[566] General Accounting Office, "EXPORT CONTROLS – More Thorough Analysis Needed to Justify Changes in High Performance Computer Controls," Report GAO-02-892, August 2002, p. 3, available at https://www.gao.gov/assets/240/235322.pdf.

[567] Text of a letter from the president to the Chairmen of the House and Senate Committees on Armed Services, Chairman of the House Committee on International Relations, and Chairman of the Senate Committee on Banking, Housing, and Urban Affairs released February 3, 2006, available at https://www.bis.doc.gov/index.php/all-articles/16-policy-guidance/product-guidance/263-archive-of-hpc-news-items.

of WMD to countries of concern.   As Gary Milhollin, Director of the Wisconsin Project on Nuclear Arms Control, argued:

> In effect, America is competing against itself. Ironically, it is trying to base its security on advanced technology, while at the same time hawking that technology to the rest of the world. It simply won't work. With the revolution in military affairs, the modern battlefield is electronic, and computing power now decides the outcome of wars. In future conflicts, do Americans really want American soldiers to face powerful American computers in the hands of the enemy? That is the real question posed by export controls. The answer should be no.[568]

Today's supercomputers are faster and more capable than ever.   In 2013, China reportedly developed a supercomputer (the "Tianhe-2") that for the first time exceeded U.S. models in performance capability at nearly 34 "petaFLOPS."[569]   In an effort to reclaim the lead, the Department of Energy announced the following year that it would install two IBM supercomputers at Lawrence Livermore National Laboratory and Oak Ridge National Laboratory capable of carrying out calculations five-to-seven times faster than the most advanced generation of U.S. supercomputers in use at the time.[570]

---

[568] Gary Milhollin, "Clinton's Super Computer Push," *The Wall Street Journal*, 19 September 2000, available at
https://www.wsj.com/articles/SB969312250292290668.
[569] See "China's Tianhe-2 Supercomputer Takes No. 1 Ranking on 41st TOP500 List," 17 June 2013, available at
https://www.top500.org/news/lists/2013/06/press-release/.
[570] Department of Energy, "Fact Sheet: Collaboration of Oak Ridge, Argonne, and Livermore (CORAL)," 17 December 2014, available at

Proliferation Implications

The case studies above not only illustrate the occasional tug-of-war between the president and the Congress on critical nonproliferation issues; they also highlight the role that external actors can play in influencing important policy decisions. In addition, they underscore the relationship between economic security and national security, which, as noted earlier, does not always break cleanly along partisan political lines.

Keeping technologies that can be used by potential adversaries for WMD-related purposes out of the hands of bad actors is a matter of continuous interest on Capitol Hill. As these two case studies demonstrate, technology is advancing at an incredible rate and more and more foreign actors are acquiring the capabilities necessary to use technology in nefarious ways. While controlling the spread of rapidly evolving technology is increasingly challenging, this is one area where greater collaboration between the executive and legislative branches of government could be immensely productive in ensuring U.S. national security throughout the 21st century.

---

https://www.energy.gov/sites/prod/files/2014/12/f19/CORAL%20F act%20Sheet__FINAL%20AS%20ISSUED_UPDATED.pdf.

CHAPTER FIFTEEN

CONCLUSION

By now it should be readily apparent to the reader that the Congress can wield enormous power when it comes to crafting or changing U.S. national security policy. Using the numerous tools at its disposal, Congress can work its will either in support of executive branch priorities or in opposition to them.

Many factors come into play in determining when and how Congress exercises its authorities on national security matters. From personal beliefs and political party loyalties to external pressures and electoral considerations, members seek to balance their views of what is in the national security interest with the desires of their constituents. By requiring various executive branch reports, Congress can obtain information that allows it to conduct its oversight responsibilities more effectively. Through the use of the GAO, Congress can investigate issues it believes need greater attention and, in so doing, can challenge administration policies. By creating executive branch positions, it can focus the administration's actions on areas that Congress believes require greater prioritization. And by exercising its "power of the purse," Congress can approve, restrict, condition, or deny funding for national security initiatives. In short, by legislating actions, it can shape and mold national security policy to its liking.

There are those who will argue that Congress has ceded too much of its authority and power to the executive branch. Others believe that the Congress meddles too much in areas that are wholly and properly within the purview of executive branch prerogatives. Examples of both positions can be found within the pages of this book.

Readers may wonder why I have refrained from opining on whether our lawgivers exercise too much or too little power in the area of national security decision making. This is an issue that remains hotly contested and the subject of extensive debate. My time on Capitol Hill hardly makes me qualified to render a definitive judgment here. I prefer to leave such arguments to the lawyers, historians, and constitutional scholars who have studied the issue more intently, though I recognize consensus on this point is likely to be as elusive as my winning the Powerball lottery.

My intent in writing this book was to give the reader, in easily digestible terms, a clearer understanding of how Congress works, what motivates congressional behavior, and how the legislative branch has struggled with the executive branch since the founding of our nation for "the privilege of directing American foreign policy." This struggle will continue, as the Founding Fathers intended. There are, of course, many other examples that can be cited in these pages to illustrate the congressional-executive dynamic. But the cases included here should be sufficient for the reader to gain a hearty appreciation for the interaction. My ultimate goal has been to inform and educate so that interested American citizens as well as students and national security practitioners can gain a better understanding of, and appreciation for, how their elected representatives conduct the important affairs of state. I also believe that working on Capitol Hill, though it can be enormously challenging, is not only worth the experience but provides a valuable public service to the country and its citizenry.

I am under no illusion that knowing how Congress works (or sometime doesn't) will move the needle on Congress' public approval rating, which still hovers at near historic lows. But if the information contained in this book is even minimally successful in helping explain the reasons behind certain actions Congress takes then I will consider it to have been a success.

There are numerous other works written by scholars that explain in much greater detail the mechanics by which Congress carries out its constitutional authorities. Some are referenced in these pages. Other more recent publications worth noting are *Congress and Its Members* by Roger H. Davidson, Walter J. Oleszek, Frances E. Lee, and Eric Schickler (2020); *Congressional Procedures and the Policy Process* (Eleventh Edition, 2019) by Walter J. Oleszek, Mark J. Oleszek, Elizabeth Rybicki, and Bill Heniff Jr.; and *Inside Congress – A Guide for Navigating the Politics of the House and Senate Floors* by Trevor Corning, Reema Dodin, and Kyle Nevins (2017). It is my hope that this book—which augments some of the historical and procedural information contained elsewhere with recollections and anecdotes based on my personal experiences as a Hill staffer—will contribute in a positive way to a greater understanding of the unique characteristics and authorities that the Founding Fathers entrusted to Congress, and how those authorities are executed in furtherance of U.S. national security interests.

Of course, history will be the ultimate arbiter of Ben Franklin's observation that the new government of the United States would be a Republic "if you can keep it." This task falls to the policy makers charged with doing so and the American people. Whether they succeed or fail depends on whether they continue to appreciate the wisdom of the Founders in creating a system of government that was intended to make governing difficult.

As Teddy Roosevelt once said, "Nothing in the world is worth having or worth doing unless it means effort, pain, difficulty." In my view, preserving our constitutional form of government is worth doing, despite the effort it requires and the difficulty it causes. Americans are certainly up to the challenge and the "American experiment" is certainly worth preserving. I hope that those reading this book will agree.

Index

ABOUT THE AUTHOR

David J. Trachtenberg is Vice President of the National Institute for Public Policy, a nonprofit research center in Fairfax, Virginia. He was confirmed by the U.S. Senate on October 17, 2017 as Deputy Under Secretary of Defense for Policy and served in this capacity until his retirement from government service in July 2019. Until January 2018, he also served as the Acting Under Secretary of Defense for Policy, the principal civilian adviser to the Secretary of Defense on defense policy matters. He was also the senior Department of Defense civilian official responsible for DoD policy on civilian casualties resulting from military operations.

Prior to his confirmation, Mr. Trachtenberg was President and CEO of Shortwaver Consulting, LLC. Earlier, he was a Vice President at CACI and Senior Vice President for Homeland Security at National Security Research, Inc.

Prior to joining NSR, Mr. Trachtenberg was Principal Deputy Assistant Secretary of Defense for International Security Policy and Acting Deputy Assistant Secretary of Defense for Forces Policy.

From 1995-2001, Mr. Trachtenberg was a Professional Staff Member with the House Committee on Armed Services (HASC) in Washington, D.C, serving as head of the committee's policy staff and staff lead for the HASC Special Oversight Panel on Terrorism.

Mr. Trachtenberg is a two-time recipient of the Department of Defense Medal for Distinguished Public Service. He holds an A.B. in International Relations from the University of Southern California and a M.S. degree in Foreign Service from Georgetown University. He currently teaches graduate seminars in nuclear deterrence and strategy and the role of Congress in national security policy at the Fairfax, Virginia campus of Missouri State University's Defense and Strategic Studies Program.

CPSIA information can be obtained
at www.ICGtesting.com
Printed in the USA
BVHW031254200822
645085BV00011B/187